New Labour and Thatcherism

Also by Richard Heffernan

DEFEAT FROM THE JAWS OF VICTORY: Inside Kinnock's Labour Party (*with Mike Marqusee*)

THE LABOUR PARTY: A Centenary History (*editor with Brian Brivati*)

New Labour and Thatcherism

Political Change in Britain

Richard Heffernan
Lecturer in Government and Politics
The Open University
Milton Keynes

First published in hardcover 2000

First published in paperback 2001 by PALGRAVE
Houndmills, Basingstoke, Hampshire RG21 6XS and
175 Fifth Avenue, New York, N. Y. 10010
Companies and representatives throughout the world

PALGRAVE is the new global academic imprint of
St. Martin's Press LLC Scholarly and Reference Division and
Palgrave Publishers Ltd (formerly Macmillan Press Ltd).

ISBN 0–333–73897–7 hardback (*outside North America*)
ISBN 0–312–22973–9 hardback (*in North America*)
ISBN 0–333–94940–4 paperback (*worldwide*)

This book is printed on paper suitable for recycling and
made from fully managed and sustained forest sources.

A catalogue record for this book is available
from the British Library.

The Library of Congress has cataloged the hardcover edition as follows:
Heffernan, Richard.
    New labour and Thatcherism : political change in Britain /
    Richard Heffernan.
        p. cm.
    Includes bibliographical references and index.
    ISBN 0–312–22973–9
        1. Labour Party (Great Britain) 2. Great Britain—Politics
    and government—1979–1997. 3. Great Britain—Politics
    and government—1997– I. Title.
    JN1129.L3? H393 1999
    324.24107—dc21
                                    99–046780

Printed and bound by Antony Rowe Ltd, Eastbourne

Contents

Preface to the Paperback Edition

In May 1997, Tony Blair's modernised New Labour made electoral hay thanks to an electorate weary of a jaded, discredited Conservative Party, and returned to government in a landslide in terms of Commons seats won, if not actual votes cast. Debates about whether Labour won that election or the Conservatives lost it can be left to historians and psephologists, but, while it is too soon to fully judge the government's policy record, one thing which critics and supporters of New Labour alike agree on is that it very much differs from Old Labour. The party's remaking was a slow, incremental process, one enacted over a ten to fifteen year period, and the years between the 1983 and 1992 elections are as important as the much remarked post-1994 'Blairite reformation'. However we judge Tony Blair's ability at reforming his party, it is important not to ascribe all of the changes in the contemporary Labour Party to his one agency, nor just to the efforts of a collection of like minded supporters within the party he came to lead.

This book argues that neither Blair's election as leader in July 1994 nor his arrival as Prime Minister in May 1997 qualify for the title of 'year zero' in Labour politics. The emergence of New Labour was the product of organisational and programmatic reforms which built on foundations slowly and painfully constructed by his predecessors, most notably Neil Kinnock and his associates, some of whom – Peter Mandelson leaps instantaneously to mind – in time worked closely with Blair. In addition, no internal party project is ever isolated from what happens in the wider political world. As this book also seeks to demonstrate, the remaking of Labour was actually prompted by far reaching changes external to the party, most notably the political success of the Thatcher and Major governments, specifically their accomplishment in rooting existing neo-liberalism ever deeper within Britain's political and economic system.

Twentieth-century British politics have been characterised by the duality of collectivism and individualism, and of statism and anti-statism. First, the rise of the former, and second, its eclipse by the resurgence of the latter. This movement, illustrated by the rise and decline of public doctrines, finds expression in ideological politics. The gradual, if hesitant, post-1880 rise of a more collectivist politics was typified by the rise of Labour in the first two-thirds of the twentieth century. Reform minded Conservatism aside, Labour was the political movement to articulate, pursue, and occasionally enact, social democratic aspirations in the 1940s, 1960s and 1970s. It advanced a reformist agenda informed by statist economics and welfare politics, programmatic reforms in which liberals such as Keynes and Beveridge were enlisted. The then twin engines of Labour policy, progressive taxation and increasing public expenditure, reflected a state managed collectivist paradigm of the post-1940 era, when it was accepted that curbing market forces through government intervention was the means by which Labour governments would pursue social justice reforms. To this end, Labour ministers declared in favour of the task of manipulating, controlling, directing and taming the market through the apparatus of the social democratic, loosely corporatist state. However, in today's deregulated, liberalised, increasingly internationalised economic marketplace, the idea that government or the state should discharge such an economic role has been emphatically rejected by Labour policy makers. Once commonly held by all parties, collectivist Keynesian and Beveridgian policies are now deemed part of the problem; no longer an adequate solution to the problems of a market economy which should not be over-regulated, over-governed, over-taxed or over-managed. Rather than manage, focus, restrict, or restrain the market in the traditional social democratic manner, Labour now seeks to empower, free and liberalise it in an economic interest by championing wealth creation, promoting business and encouraging entrepreneurship.

Today, New Labour clearly rejects traditional social democratic means (as well as a great number of its ends) and so rules out high rates of progressive taxation and increased levels of social expenditure. Egalitarianism and a redistributive politics, both key tenants of revisionist social democracy (not to mention radical alternatives to its left), no longer count at all. The revised politics of New Labour is an illustration of a neo-liberal paradigm that characterises the contemporary socio-economic policy agenda. What Thomas Friedman calls in his over exuberant tale of globalisation, *The Lexus and the Olive Tree*, the 'golden straight jacket', the willingness of government to maintain zero inflation and price stability, produce a balanced budget, remove restrictions on foreign investment, deregulate capital markets, cut corporation taxes, downsize the state bureaucracy, privatise state owned industries, and prioritise private sector consumption, are all policies reflecting the fact that policy makers are now to some extent influenced by a post-collectivist neo-liberalism. Of course, the neo-liberal imprint on all liberal democracies is more a product of perceived economic reality, political necessity and ideological choice, rather than an automatic, unthinking response to such a phenomenon like 'globalisation'.

This book argues that to understand the Labour government today requires us to explain what the party Labour had become by 1997, and to appreciate the formative influences that encouraged its remaking in the 1980s and 1990s. The 'actually existing Third Way', the policy followed by the Blair government as opposed to the normative recommendations urged upon it, was, therefore, established before Labour entered government in 1997. It is not a simultaneous rejection of social democratic collectivism and neo-liberalism, but a resounding rejection of the first and a reformist variant of the second. The ideology of New Labour is not a reinvention of, nor a return to traditional social democracy. While avoiding the crude assertion that the Blair government is simply Thatcherite, this book contends that in terms of a spatial model of ideological comparison, Tony Blair stands far closer to Margaret Thatcher than he does, say, to a social democratic revisionist such as Tony Crosland. This may be because Blair's politics reflect the demands of his time. Indeed, were Crosland an active politician today, he too may be well to the political right of his previous political stance. Over time, dominant political agendas change, ideological stances alter and, as office-seeking political parties come to terms with a transformed status quo, the policy prescriptions politicians advance may change also.

Labour now works within a policy terrain bequeathed it by the Thatcher and Major governments. If, as suggested by the April 1999 Blair–Schröder document 'The Third Way/Die Neue Mitte', politicians 'approach issues without ideological preconceptions and... search for practical solutions to their problems through honest well-constructed and pragmatic policies', they inevitably find themselves initially obliged to adapt (rather than simply adopt) the status quo in some form. All politicians have 'ideological preconceptions'. These are both inherited and acquired and, as previously mentioned, they certainly change over time, sometimes marginally, other times dramatically. Political parties may seek to manage and reform a status quo, but they begin by working within it; they inherit before they choose. The principal questions, therefore, suggest themselves: how do reform agendas reform the status quo?; how does a contemporary agenda become the status quo?; why (rather than how) do parties change their programmatic stance or abandon an ideological tradition? As defined in this book, the phenomenon of Thatcherism, the domestic transmission belt for a internationalised neo-liberalism, explains why the Blair government is decidedly more 'modern' and neo-liberal than 'traditional' and social democratic.

Rather than change automatically, the world is changed by a variety of agencies, among them political actors in government armed with an ideas based, radical reform agenda, and possessing the opportunity to pursue it when the existing agenda is perceived to be outdated and worn out. Such opportunities arise rarely, but when they do the potential for far reaching political change is considerable. This book argues that the period after 1975 was such an occasion, and that the Thatcher-led Conservative Party was to play a crucial role in the remaking of the British political agenda. To this end, to fully understand contemporary politics at the beginning of the twenty-first century, we need to reassess the politics of the 1970s, 1980s and early 1990s, particularly as set against those of the post-1945 era. Slowly and painfully, from the mid-1970s onwards, building on pre-existing intellectual foundations, New Right politics, when enacted into policy, reconstructed the political middle ground. They did so to such an extent that neo-liberal diagnoses and prescriptions came to bound the policy horizon, reflecting the cognitive maps of a dominant ideology which eventually became the paradigm for politicians, administrators and commentators alike and the starting point for Labour's own reform agenda. The politics of New Labour clearly illustrate that Labour finally settled for reworking rather than replacing the Thatcherite markings gouged on the palimpsest of British politics.

RICHARD HEFFERNAN

Preface and Acknowledgments

'The Labour Party stands accused and convicted of wanting to interfere with the free operation of free market forces. I plead guilty and ask for innumerable other offences – past and future – to be taken into account.' (Roy Hattersley, Labour Party Deputy Leader, October 1985).

'Old Labour thought the role of government was to interfere with the market. New Labour believes the task of government is to make the market more dynamic, to provide people and business with the means of success.' (Tony Blair, Labour Party Leader, April 1996).

'Economics are the method; the objective is to change the heart and soul.' (Margaret Thatcher, 1993).

Labour's May 1997 election victory was widely credited to the party's re-invention of itself as a new, improved version of the older (not so) grand old party. Its return from the electoral wilderness saw the party form its first government in eighteen years, its victory at the polls sweet recompense for four straight defeats during the long dog-days of opposition from 1979. Having been frequently written off during the electoral and political ascendancy of the Thatcher-led Conservatives, Labour not only once more found itself back in government but had secured its largest ever Parliamentary majority. In terms of seats won (65 per cent of the House of Commons on 44 per cent of the vote), its 1997 success surpassed the poll of 1945. Labour's often predicted demise had clearly been grossly over-exaggerated.

Today, demonstrably no longer the party it was in 1983, or even for that matter 1970, Labour has replaced the statist, leftist appeal of the 1983 manifesto (the so-called 'longest suicide note in history') with a policy stance significantly to the political right of past Labour practice. Its stance in government was trailed well in advance of the 1997 election, its political stall so firmly set in opposition that only a political innocent will have been surprised by the approach the government has adopted in office. The policy stance of 'New' as compared to 'Old' Labour is foremost an acknowledgement that the familiar landscape of British public policy has been fundamentally reformed in recent years.

The changing Labour Party reflects the extensive political changes enacted in the eighteen years from 1979.

This book questions the claim that 'New' Labour came to office to represent a 'third way', one distinct from old traditions and beyond the old taxonomies of 'left' and 'right'. Much contemporary debate on this supposed 'third way' too often blurs the necessary distinction between a normative project offering recommendations as to what the Labour government should do and an analysis of what the Labour government actually is doing. Constructing a 'wish list' of what the government should do is not the same as explaining what it is doing. This book therefore seeks to explain 'New' Labour. It challenges the notion that Labour has merely updated and modernised itself, by 'applying traditional values in a modern setting'. It argues that in rejecting the collectivist politics of its past practice, Labour has moved away from traditional social democratic politics. Tony Blair's government owes more to a neoliberal appreciation of the world than to any social democratic perspective.

Labour now accepts that previously dominant statist patterns of government intervention requiring the exercise of direct controls over the market have receded. The mixed economy, government demand management, full employment and the welfare state, the four pillars of postwar policy, have been called into question by the 'political revolution' of the 1980s. Where Labour had previously presupposed that the role of the state was to directly regulate the market in a social interest, it now conceives its role as being to empower the market in an economic interest and (when possible) in a social interest. Its contemporary stance reflects the neo-liberal belief that the notion of a interventionist state imposing collective political decisions upon the system of economic market exchange is outmoded and irrelevant.

While located in a wider context than UK politics, contemporary Labour practice is essentially cast in the 'shadow' of Thatcherism, that much misunderstood and grossly misnamed political construct enacted by the Thatcher and Major-led governments from 1979 to 1997. This book defines Thatcherism as a political and economic project rooted in the ideology of the New Right. While subject to the interplay of opportunity and circumstance, chance and fortune, the Thatcher and Major governments did pursue and largely enact a coherent political agenda. As an *agent* of political change, Thatcherism presided over a dramatic shift in favour of right-reformist neo-liberal politics at the expense of left-reformist social democratic politics. The much remarked transformation of the Labour Party since 1983 is positive proof of this.

The book will explore Thatcherism and its impact on the Labour Party in order to develop an understanding of how and why political change comes about. Labour's leadership had long claimed that the party could be successful only if it dramatically repositioned itself by moving with the times and embracing fundamental shifts in contemporary politics and society. As promoted by Thatcherism, Conservative neo-liberalism provided the formative experience of the Blair-led politicians who rose to prominence during its years of dominance. It helped shape the political–economic–ideological environment within which Labour now exists. Because parties are a product of such environments, party change is often a reflection of the wider political changes which affect them. Labour modernisation therefore reflects a process described as 'catch-up' party competition. This notion is prompted by an understanding that Labour's engagement with Thatcherism is best explored through the process of Labour–Conservative party competition as it was acted out across five electoral cycles. The Thatcher-led Conservatives successfully helped map out a dominant political agenda, one altering the environment(s) within which Labour is located. Where they led, Labour has eventually followed. Here, inter-party competition between an electorally successful Thatcher government and an unsuccessful Labour opposition was the catalyst of the remaking of Labour. 'New' Labour demonstrates how the phenomenon of party change is acutely related to wider political change.

As a result, the book suggests a definition of consensus politics as a development of a series of contestable political beliefs translated over time into a set of assumptions common to all parties. These assumptions find expression in an implicit 'agreement' acknowledging a prevailing political orthodoxy. Within an ideological space stretching from left to right, consensus politics finds expression in a political middle ground around which all major political parties locate. The political consequences of Thatcherism lie in the fact that contemporary UK party politics are now enacted within a set of parameters enclosing a space on the centre-right of politics within which Labour and the Conservatives now locate. Modernisation is therefore a metaphor for Labour's accommodation with Thatcherism. This is not to say there are no distinctions in policy outlook nor of inherent difference in political values between the Labour government and its Conservative predecessors. Rather, it is that as an agency of change Thatcherism's significant contribution to far-reaching political change realised in public policy has helped recast mainstream ideological politics. It has thereby influenced the prevailing political agenda to which

Labour as an office-seeking (and policy-seeking) political agent has to work.

Labour's governing agenda begins with the status quo bequeathed by Thatcherism because its policy and programme is cast within a pre-existing political, economic and ideological paradigm, one fashioned as a result of the worldwide resurgence of market liberalism into which Thatcherism tapped. More often than not governing practice exemplifies continuity rather than discontinuity. Of course (for reasons explored in this book), there are exceptions to this rule: the Thatcher decade is one such exception. While New Labour is strongly informed by Thatcherite neo-liberalism, its politics are not always entirely reducible to it, as is demonstrated by its position on constitutional reform and the European Union. Although the impact of Thatcherism explains from where Labour has come, it is the political practices that Thatcherism helped establish that influences where Labour is going. While acknowledging the primary role of the market in the production, distribution and exchange of social goods, Labour need not necessarily follow the laizzez-faire social Darwinist philosophy some have evidenced in the Thatcherite project. None the less, the New Labour government begins where its Thatcher and Major-led predecessors led: it, just as much as them, is part of the continuing shift away from statist informed collectivism toward market-rooted individualism. This book is about Thatcherism and its contribution to the party Labour had become on its return to government in 1997 after eighteen years in opposition. Understanding what happened in 1975–1997 tells us something about what is happening now. This is why the changes engineered by Thatcherism and the subsequent changes provoked in the Labour Party are best understood as a process unfolding over time. To this end the book uses them to exemplify and develop a concept of political change and a theory of consensus politics.

Acknowledgements

This research was funded by the Economic and Social Research Council and I am immensely grateful for their sponsorship. The Government Department at the London School of Economics proved an extremely stimulating place in which to work. Numerous debts were incurred during the writing of this study that will be hard to repay. I am naturally in the debt of a great many writers and commentators who have previously quarried this great subject; the bibliography is an indication of the extent of what I owe. In particular, a great many friends and colleagues offered various advice and insights: thanks are due to them all. Alan Beattie provided steadfast and reliable support and was willing to offer suggestions and telling criticisms in helpful measure. Andrew Gamble and John Barnes read a version of the book and also gave sound and helpful advice. Thanks are particularly due to Patrick Dunleavy for innumerable kindnesses and generous assistance.

Special mention should also go to Brian Brivati, Mark Doyle, Andy Chadwick, Andrew Gardener, Andy Hindmoor, Oliver James and James Stanyer. As ever, the Rt Hon Tony Benn MP was extremely helpful not least in making available the Benn archive. Thanks to Keith Povey for getting the manuscript into shape. Finally, especial thanks are due to Helen Barry for her invaluable friendship and support without which this work (and everything else) would have proved impossible. Naturally, no one bears any responsibility for the arguments that follow. All inadequacies are mine alone.

RICHARD HEFFERNAN

1
Exploring Political Change

Since 1975 the reform agenda in British politics has been dominated by the politics of market liberalism. Policy has been recast in as close a neo-liberal guise as has proved politically possible and/or administratively practicable. As a result, government is no longer expected to radically reform economic relations. Limited moves toward egalitarianism have been abandoned and moderate attempts to redistribute income and wealth (in cash or in kind) are no longer considered to be acceptable objectives. Both Labour and the Conservatives rule out high rates of progressive taxation and support policy instruments such as market-isation, deregulation, neo-classical economics, lower borrowing and (when possible) less public spending, reform of the welfare state to encourage individual self-reliance and reduce dependency, and the introduction of new public management techniques. The privatisation of state-owned industries and utilities demonstrates the withdrawal of the state from direct control over a great deal of economic activity.

These shifts mark the passage of the New Right from vilified hetero-doxy to predominant orthodoxy, a shift that has taken place within a political generation. Across political parties, traditional models of col-lectivism and state provision are now commonly presented as political goals which restricted freedom, limited opportunity, fostered depen-dence and damaged the national interest. Today, a broadly defined neo-liberal ideological disposition informs the political ideas which form part of a belief system eventually translated into public policy. Contemporary politics is structured around an altered discourse, one that reflects a different set of practical priorities and a new conception of the purpose of government and the role of the state: while a great many normative principles remain intact the method of realising them has altered. The politics of 1999 were dramatically different from those of

1

1979. Over time, a series of contestable political beliefs have become translated into a set of assumptions common to some extent to all political elites. Neo-liberal political attitudes have pervaded the body politic, colonising intellectual territory inch by inch, suggesting that individual choices exercised within a system of economic market exchange are preferable to collective political decision-making enacted through an interventionist state.[1] As a result, institutions and actors of the centre-left which were past advocates of reformist social democracy (what is known in the US as 'reform liberalism'[2]) display an altered perception of the world and their political role within it.

While the political concerns of the 1970s were very largely those of the 1950s, the political agenda of the 1990s is remarkably different from that of the 1970s. Within the UK, this is very much a consequence of the neo-liberal politics associated with the phenomenon of Thatcherism. Thatcherism helped fashion an altered politics, one which reflected changes in the ideological terrain upon which political activity took place. Contrary to the widespread fears of right-wing commentators expressed in the 1970s, it is the political right and not the political left which has succeeded in capturing much of the political agenda of the 1970s, 1980s and 1990s. From the perspective of the mid-1990s the idea expressed in the first publication of the Thatcherite pace-setter of the 1970s, the Centre for Policy Studies, that 'socialist ideas and other varieties of collectivist, centralist or statist philosophies have come to dominate political thought... Socialist assumptions in economics, social policy, and education have gained general bipartisan acceptance with only minor modifications',[3] now appears a ludicrous suggestion. Today, Labour's election victory of May 1997 notwithstanding, this and similar assumptions have been completely turned on their head. The vocabulary of political and social debate has been so captured by the right that it is the left – indeed traditionalist centre-left social democracy – that finds itself consigned to the political sidelines.

The 1980s were dominated by the Thatcher-led Conservative governments. While debates on contemporary politics are rightly influenced by the series of policies, political style and ideological outlook popularised as Thatcherism, the term itself is both facile and unhelpful. We are apparently stuck with it rather in the same mistaken way Keynesianism is used to describe the economic practices of successive post-war governments. As with the terminology of most branches of social enquiry we are obliged to use pre-invented language devised by other people at other times for purposes other than our own. Like it or not, the phrase is here to stay. While the phrase should offer nothing more than

a useful shorthand to discuss the policy and programme of the governments led by Margaret Thatcher, the notion of Thatcherism is extremely
helpful in analysing contemporary politics. It is best understood as an
ideological phenomenon, one that is rooted in the ideas of the New
Right but also informed by electoral and economic dimensions. Above
all else, Thatcherism is an on-going project through which political
actors had some success in applying policy as a practical tool in the
pursuit of identifiable ends.

The record of actually existing Thatcherism (even when narrowly
defined as what the Thatcher and Major governments did in office)
demonstrates that politicians can advocate a governing philosophy,
sponsor ideas, and thereby have some success in advancing an ideological disposition through policy innovation. The crisis the Thatcher
government claimed to address was one of ineffective governance, a
product of the failed post-war institutional and political framework it
inherited and which past Conservative governments had attempted to
administer. Contemporary political change can be explored in light of
the social, political, and electoral consequences of Thatcherism and the
far-reaching changes it promoted at all levels of British society. Over
time, British politics has come to reflect an emerging Thatcherite (or
post-Thatcher) settlement. Given that history is often made in circumstances not of actors' own choosing, useful explanations of contemporary political change in the UK may well be uncovered in the political
process as it developed through the electoral cycles of 1974–9, 1979–83,
1983–7, 1987–92, 1992–7 and post-1997.

Political circumstances change as different political ideas come into
vogue or else fall out of fashion. The world moves on, and with it parties
change, variously 'responding' to obligations to modernise their appeal
or redefine their role. Maurice Duverger's claim that a party is dominant
when 'it is identified with a epoch; when its doctrines, ideas, methods,
its style so to speak, coincide with the epoch'[4] has to an extent found
illustration not in the Conservative election victories of the 1980s but in
the altered politics of the 1990s. Even so, it was not the Conservative
Party itself which became dominant but the political ideas it espoused.
That Labour now acknowledges the purchase Thatcherite ideas have on
contemporary politics is demonstrated by any number of empirical case
studies, among them privatisation, economic and fiscal policy, defence
policy and trade union law. The remaking of the Labour Party was
enacted against the backdrop of the neo-liberal agenda that 'actually
existing' Thatcherism strove to enact in office. It is therefore a consequence of the political changes wrought by that phenomenon.

Hence, the task facing any exploration of current political events requires engaging with the process and dynamics of political change as enacted in the politics of the 1980s and 1990s.

The history of political economy is characterised by the duality of collectivism and individualism, a process of trend and cycle illustrated by the rise and decline of public doctrines expressed as ideological politics.[5] In a grand historical sweep Milton Friedman has classified the period since 1800 as the Age of Adam Smith, the Age of Maynard Keynes and the Age of Hayek.[6] The twentieth century has witnessed the polarity of collectivism and individualism, a process typified by the rise of a semi-collectivist social democracy common to all parties in the 1950s and 1960s, one informed by statist welfare politics and Keynesian economics and which was ultimately reconfigured by the revival of market liberalism. Here, the process of political change within British politics can be broadly classified into the pre-social democratic Keynesian era lasting up to 1940; the social democratic Keynesian era lasting up to 1975; and the neo-liberal post-social democratic era after 1975. Of course, the present is made within the past; the moment of political change is not easily identifiable and no simple or clear break may be discernible.

Despite its association with parties of the left, actually existing social democracy was never simply 'the key set of key organising principles and axiomatic propositions that drive the programmatic vision of social-ist parties and is invoked by socialist politicians to propose solutions for concrete policy problems in the economic, social or cultural realm'.[7] As a movement of the left it can be defined as 'a hybrid political tradition composed of socialism and liberalism common to social democratic parties'[8] but it was also a governing philosophy, one which was adopted by mainstream parties of left and right in the immediate post-war era:

> [R]evisionist social democracy had come to terms with reformed liberal capitalism. A compromise had been reached in which a market economy was made responsive to certain social ends – general affluence and economic security, full employment, individual fulfil-ment within an open society... Old political battlefields were de-serted as Conservative and Christian Democratic parties came to accept the terms of the compromise. There was, in short, a con-vergence between the parties of Right and Left.[9]

Social democracy is defined as 'an attempt to humanize capitalism. The productive advantages of capitalism are to be retained, but some of its human costs eliminated.' While a number of political issues and perspectives divided Labour and Conservatives in the post-war period they had a shared perspective on the objectives of government. As David Miller suggests: 'First, economic management techniques are to be used to smooth out business cycles and to maintain full employment, which in turn will increase the bargaining power of workers *vis-à-vis* their employers. Second, the tax system is to be used to correct the excessive inequalities of income and wealth that an unreformed capitalist economy throws up. Third, a politically funded welfare state is to serve to eliminate poverty, provide for those with special needs, and contribute further to the reduction of inequality.'[10]

While political developments post-1940 witnessed the gradual 'emergence of a progressive centre, distinct from the political left or right',[11] today much has changed. In understanding the process of change typified by the eclipse of social democracy and the rise of neo-liberalism the moment(s) of transition from one to the other must be located and the dynamics of change identified. Contemporary affairs are not usually marked by shifting tides of attention and public opinion. If dramatic policy change is an occasional occurrence, what role do political parties play as an agent of policy transformation? How and why did Thatcherism succeed in advancing a reform agenda? Political change is naturally dependent upon events and circumstances; not all reform agendas succeed. Here, the successes of Thatcherism (matched against its many failures) were due to the opportunities it received. Its reform agendas drew sustenance from the failure of the existing pre-Thatcherite political agenda and the worn-out policy mechanisms previously used to address social, economic and political problems. For new political ideas to flourish, older, existing ideas must be discredited or otherwise deemed to have failed. The supposed crisis of the 'corporatist state' in the 1970s found expression in the work of a number of political scientists who characterised it variously as the outcome of 'adversary politics', 'legitimation crisis', 'government overload' and 'the fiscal crisis of the state'.

After 1974, the resurgence of interest in neo-liberalism in the UK was wholly confined to Conservative circles. This owed much to the realisation that Keynesian social democracy was failing to deliver its promises. Rising inflation, stagnant economic growth, unprofitability, loss-leading public enterprise, and union power manifested in increased militancy, all encouraged the Conservative charge (one echoed widely in the United States) that Britain had become the sick man of Europe plagued by the 'British diseases' of social discontent and de-industrialisation.

The limitations of both the Heath Conservative government and the Wilson and Callaghan-led Labour governments contrasted sharply with the claims of the Thatcher-led opposition that it had the cure for the country's ills. The OPEC oil shock of 1973–4 and the global recession it engendered joined with continuing economic and political difficulties as symbolised by the IMF crisis of 1976 and the 'Winter of Discontent' of 1978–9.

By 1979, it was widely believed that social democracy had entered a profound ideological crisis. The application of Keynesian management to achieve economic growth, price stability and full employment was throughly discredited and had now to be abandoned. Government policies aimed at redistributing economic surpluses through fiscal policy, welfare programmes and social insurance were widely criticised for the contribution they made to the governing crisis of the state. Assailed from a resurgent left and right from within and without the Labour Party, the collapse of the post-war settlement in the face of the re-emergence of a serious and sustained economic crisis granted Thatcherism its chance and opportunity.

After the mid-1970s social democratic practices found themselves increasingly on the defensive. Many social democratic parties lost their virtually monopolistic positions as the sole guardians of their respective countries' reform spaces in the wake of the resurgent New Right. This situation therefore generated an interest in alternative ideas, and the theory of monetarist economics was a pace-setter, spreading like wildfire, leading policy-makers to increasingly accept that full employment had to be abandoned to wage war on inflation.[12] From 1979, the idea of a resurgent market liberalism was gradually enacted into public policy as the New Right entered the governmental citadel. In the realm of economic, industrial and social policy huge changes were brought about under Thatcherism. Only in the case of foreign affairs and defence (with the possible exception of the occasional tilt away from a European ideal) did policy remained entirely in keeping with the pre-1979 status quo.

Understanding political change

Political change can be classified into three particular types: non-change (remains the same); serial adaptation (an increasing rate of change); and dramatic transformation (major and significant change). Dramatic change is both rare and exceptional; ditto non-change. The rate, type and extent of change are all variable factors. Describing and explaining what political change is requires us to understand how it comes about. Understanding political change is often as difficult as describing the proverbial elephant; we all know what it is but find it hard to either describe or analyse it. Political change can be classified into four inter-related forms:

1 social;
2 economic;
3 political-electoral; and
4 political-ideological.

Political ideas matter to political change. Empirical analysis of electoral change tends often to dominate studies of political change. Voting behaviour, party competition, election campaigning and demographic or social change are often the principal focus of attention. In our obsession with the electoral cycle, political scientists often show less interest in the ebb and flow of political ideas within and without the electoral process. While a continuing interest in the 'consumer side of politics', defined as what the electorate does and why it does it, is necessary, additional emphasis should be placed on the 'producer side', focusing on what motivates parties to act; understanding why they do what they do is as important as uncovering the motivations which explain what electors do and why: 'Political scientists should...give heed to the "supply" side of democratic politics: to the alternatives that the parties present to the voters and to the innovations and the other actions of government that are important in themselves and that voters respond to.'[13]

The development of political opinion at the level of elite or mass can illuminate political change. The particular form of change analysed in this book considers changes in the political-ideological context within which political activity is conducted. Put simply: political-ideological change is most usually reflected in a new status-quo which influences the suppositions that underpin policy formation. In this respect significant political change can illustrate a change in the *Zeitgeist* (itself an indefinable concept to all but the political philosopher). Ideas are more significant in political life than they are often given credit for: they come of age, fall out of fashion, are championed or otherwise dropped. Political change can therefore be mapped out by changing ideas, a change marked by the fall and rise of fashion when ideas determine the direction of state policy, when the dominant discourse is drawn from the political ideas in circulation. Anthony King rightly suggests that 'at least two, and probably all three, of the three great policy discontinuities in the Britain of the twentieth century cannot be understood without an understanding of the movement of ideas that helped to give rise to them and subsequently shaped them'.[14]

Ideas naturally determine, shape and change political attitudes, values, and opinions. Anthony Seldon argues that the interplay of ideas, individuals, circumstances and interests provides four possible causes for policy change. Utilising Galbraith's notion of a prevailing 'conventional wisdom', he suggests that 'the preponderance of one idea or another at any given point in time conditions the entire way in which judgements are made by policy elites'.[15] When political change is most easily demonstrated by policy departure, then the ideas which underpin policy formation (or more significantly the political attitudes, values and opinions that find expression in policy) are very important. Political change finds expression in the 'policy goals; policy means; policy outcomes; political style; the presentation of policy to the electorate; and even the range of policies excluded from the political agenda'[16] that characterise the form government takes. Change is often explained by the rise of new ideas that come to demonstrate their economic, political and administrative viability: here ideas once promoted can be an engine of change. A study of the course and causes of political change should consider the prevailing conditions that encourage an alteration in the role and purpose of government encompassing what it does; why it does things; and how it does them.

If distinctive political ideas are capable of determining the set of policies presented in the form of public or administrative choices, then the dominant political discourse forms a series of normative recommendations, constructing a broadly informed belief system that has far-reaching social implications when realised as public policy. Rather than an abstract conception, changing ideological prescriptions affect the political–economic–social context within which government operates. This structures what political actors and governmental institutions actually do by impacting upon the outputs of the state. Of course, a pragmatic response to social and economic pressures may serve to modify the impact that a political ideology might have. Equally, the reception that an ideological project meets with is an important factor. As argued above, for one agenda to succeed, others have to fail; for change to prosper, the status quo has to be discredited. The failure of Keynesianism paved the way for the resurgence of market liberalism in the same way as the limitations of individualism and the emergence of a mass polity previously prepared the way for the rise of social democratic collectivism.

While dependent upon interests, actors, institutions and circumstantial context, political change is a reflection of the rise of new ideas and practices that political and economic elites come to accept as necessary, inevitable and, in certain cases, unchallengeable. Distinctive political ideas must demonstrate their economic, political and administrative viability before they can have far-reaching implications when realised as public policy. It is therefore important to explore how and why particular ideological dispositions are eventually translated into public policy. Dominant ideas do not simply arise but are sponsored, transmitted and, when necessary, popularised. They have different impacts at specific times and win distinct audiences, be it at the level of the elite or the mass.

Mapping out the process of political change lies at the heart of an analysis of the historical shift in political life, one in which political change is evidenced. Peter Hall poses two related questions: Why is any one set of ideas influential at any one time and place? How do new ideas acquire influence over policy making?[17] While a natural feature of social life, the actual form political change takes is not inevitable. Attitudes are not fixed or given, they are shaped and remade by the interplay of both structure and agency; by a variety of social factors and political actors. Exploring, understanding, and mapping out political change requires an explanation of (1) what changes came about; (2) when they came about; (3) how they came about; and (4) what consequences they have had.

The idea of a 'paradigm-shift' was developed by Thomas Kuhn who distinguished between set structured forms of scientific enquiry which utilised different frameworks of both analysis and understanding. These distinctive forms of activity established patterns of behaviour and defined what scientists did. Thus distinctive paradigms (for example Aristotelian and Newtonian physics) structured all forms of scientific enquiry. These established patterns of analysis took the form of 'normal science' as standardised and routine activity working within an established framework; scientists continued to work in this framework and followed the unwritten 'rules' and 'regulations' set out by the discipline within which they worked.[18]

Kuhn counterposed 'normal science' with 'revolutionary science', a form of scientific enquiry established when anomalies generated within 'normal science' create a crisis in the existing paradigm (and so create a change in the scientific perception of a number of scientists) which is resolved by a process of change from the old to a new paradigm (paradigm-shift). Once established the new paradigm becomes the basis for

contemporary scientific enquiry characterised by the collective acceptance of the ideas and attitudes upon which it is based. Scientists return
to normal science within that new paradigm.[19] Shifting paradigms
involve an alteration in the dominant ideology which finds expression
in the activities of political institutions and political and administrative
actors. Here, dominant ideas are applied to practical politics to define
problems and offer ways to resolve them. Over time, given success, they
can forge a new or revamped political structure, an altered ideological
discourse as it is realised in a different policy agenda. Only when translated into practical politics does ideology have a significant impact upon
political affairs.

Paradigms are born, they reach maturity and then pass, succeeded by
a new paradigm as the framework shaped by its predecessor loses its
utility. A political paradigm is a structure in itself – a set of accepted
practices which inform the content and purpose of policy and the
context within which it is developed by defining what is seen as desirable and possible. Political change progresses at different speeds at different times – 'normal' rather than 'revolutionary' science is the norm.
The process of paradigm-shift typified by the transition from a social
democratic ideological discourse to one informed by neo-liberalism is
one of gradual disengagement from the practices of the past combined
with their partial retention in some form. Here, a social democratic
polity can be seen to have been neo-liberalised; not all past policies
have been abandoned in the wake of Thatcherism, as the persistence
of the Beveridgian welfare state testifies.

From this perspective, the past can be more than prologue. Where its
legacy is refashioned as a result of a newly dominant elite discourse, it
may continue to exert an influence over what the state does and, as
crucially, the expectations civil society has of it. Nevertheless, the past
being changed is itself a process of 'modernisation' as new ideas enter
(or are otherwise injected into) the policy universe.

Actors, agency, structure: factors behind political change

Political change is in constant development, a process at some times
sharp and dramatic, at others gradual and imperceptible. It is not something that springs fully formed in a period typified by an election date
such as 1979 or 1945. As a modification (be it dramatic or modest) of the
status quo, it can be closely related to the rise of new (or, as likely,
updated or repackaged) political ideas. Such new ideas may capture the
imagination of key elements of the electorate and, more significantly,

political and administrative elites. Dominant political ideas extend across party political boundaries and do not necessarily recognise political or institutional affiliations. Did not Hayek dedicate *The Road to Serfdom* to 'socialists of all parties' in recognition of the dominance of social democratic attitudes proposing collectivist control of the economy?

In terms of a spatial model of ideological discourse, the political environment has been changed over the past twenty years. Characterised by alterations in the suppositions governing policy formation, political change can be both a response and an impetus to an altered policy universe. It is illustrated by alterations in the attitudes regarding the form that public policy takes and the ends it serves. In historical terms the transition from one paradigm to another is a constant process, one that is fluid and often indeterminate. As a moment(s) of transition from one paradigm to another, the dynamics of political change underpinning the fall of social democracy and the rise of neo-liberalism must be identified. Of course, identifying these moment(s) is one thing, understanding the process of transition is quite another.

Subsequent chapters do not attempt to explain political change by offering a holistic, all-encompassing model conclusively demonstrating how change is brought about. Where sociological determinists assume that political agendas are the product of historical forces, political change is also the result of non-structural socio-economic–political factors. The short-lived electoral and long-term political success enjoyed by the Conservative Party after 1979 was not simply the automatic product of an historical or social situation. Political parties can make their own history even as they are made by the influence of other factors. Given that the 1980s and 1990s witnessed the widespread acceptance of a series of neo-liberal prescriptions, this period begs the question: how exactly did a political agenda informed by a neo-liberal critique of social democracy become the universal orthodoxy it is today? Determinist explanations of political change too often ignore the impact of contingency factors. Structures matter but so too do other factors; modernity is a concept fashioned by the interplay of actors and ideas against the background of events and circumstances.

In the *General Theory*, Keynes famously suggested that the world is ruled by ideas.[20] However, dominant ideas, rather than simply arising, have different impacts at specific times; they either fail or succeed in winning distinct audiences at the level of the political elite and/or the mass; by themselves they are not enough. Keynes was therefore wrong about the power of ideas. They require champions in the form of engaged and active and, most importantly, successful political actors. The 'time' of an idea does not merely 'come'. Its success or failure is dependent upon its interaction with social–political–economic interests and institutions as mediated by the opportunities or restraints offered by contemporary circumstances. As 'consequential actors', politicians can matter because they are involved in 'formulating, advocating and selecting courses of action (i.e. policy options) that are intended to resolve the delimitated substantive problems in question'.[21] Voice and visibility are terribly important in distinguishing who influences what and how. Governments count because they provide direction and momentum, impetus and initiation. The Thatcher-led Conservatives seized the chance to pursue their ideologically motivated reform agenda and had the opportunity to do. As Bob Jessop *et al.* rightly conclude, 'Thatcherism is neither a natural necessity nor a wilful contingency. It is a complex, contradictory, unstable, inchoate, and provisional product of social forces seeking to make their own history – but doing so in circumstances they have not chosen, cannot fully understand, and cannot hope to master.'[22]

While actors, institutions, interests and circumstantial context all contribute to the success or otherwise of ideas, the general political environment is important. In real life, political actors make history or, should this be too grandiose a concept, influence events under circumstances not of their own choosing. All actors are affected by their environment even if they seek to reorder and shape it. Swimmers can swim with a tide but may also choose to swim against it with varying degrees of success. Alternatively, they may well decide not to swim at all: political actors make choices. Within any policy domain actors within institutions do not wholly determine things; nor are they wholly determined by things. Collective political actors are not insignificant. Their influence over policy decisions varies over time with the intensity of their own efforts and those of other participants. The primary sources of political change are not always socio-economic in origin; structural factors cannot and should not be discounted. Subject to both structure and contingent factors (among them opportunities and resources), actors within institutions do count.

Through the agency of Thatcherism the Conservative Party found politicians with strong persuasive powers, clear ideas, a gradually emergent agenda and, as important, the opportunities to pursue the reform agenda (in part if not in whole) they came to identify. It is not the case that structural factors would have led any party to follow the same path as that of the Thatcher government in the 1980s. That government was not simply a cypher of social, economic and political structures. Labour in office would not have enacted the same programme. Of course, because the global socio-economic forces that saw a general reaction against statism the world over was at the same time a reaction against social democratic tradition, it provided an incentive to the Thatcherite reform agenda. The initial political choices made by Thatcherite actors were invariably just that: choices. The policy avenues they explored in the 1979 and 1983 Parliaments were not pre-ordained or given but were in many cases attempts to reorder the status quo Thatcherism did not like and pledged itself to change.

Naturally, the politics of Thatcherism should be placed in its international context. The spread of neo-liberalism in the latter part of the twentieth century is comparable to the advance of Keynesianism in the 1940s and 1950s or the rise of free trade in the late nineteenth century. While the Thatcher and Major governments blazed the trail for the New Right in the UK, its political agenda was neither totally unique nor distinct. Thatcherite reforms found an echo in (among others) the policy of the Reagan administration in the US, the French governments of Mitterrand and Chirac, and the Hawke governments in Australia. Deregulation, privatisation and neo-classical economics were part of a worldwide phenomenon in the latter part of the 1980s. That said, it is too often suggested that Thatcherism was a reaction to political events over which it had no control; that these events determined its policy agenda, rather than this policy agenda influenced or otherwise helped shape events. Yet, while subject to a great many constraints and limitations (the global economy; the weakening of national economies; the interaction of market and non-market institutions; the political and social demands of a sovereign electorate) Thatcherism did seek to kick against the many barriers it faced: sometimes it was successful, elsewhere it failed spectacularly. At different times and in different contexts Thatcherism both determined events and was determined by them.

If political change is ultimately realised in public policy it does not happen as if by magic. The behaviour of political actors is neither random nor is it wholly rational and calculating. Rarely do actors develop strategy to determinedly pursue an agenda; contingency and incrementalism are important. So too are structural factors, but the role of actors and their ideas within institutions should not be ignored. As Peter Hall argues, 'Structural accounts can tell us a great deal about the constraint facing policy makers, but policy making is about creation as well as constraint.'[23] None the less, the ability of political actors to engineer significant political change is necessarily subject to certain limitations. The structural and contextual constraints brought to bear on the reform agendas of political actors located with institutions are twofold:

1 *economic*: domestic fiscal constraints; the globalised economy; international capital markets; international institutions.
2 *political*: electoral demands; electoral outcomes; governmental and administrative structures; institutional policy agendas.

These two factors are examples of environmental conditions that affect what political actors can and cannot do. Economic and political imperatives such as the global economy; international factors; the prevailing political culture; the tide of domestic opinion; uncontrollable circumstances and the impact of events, all impact upon political actors and to some extent constrain its policy agenda. Although he is a critic of the idea that Thatcherism was an exceptional phenomenon, David Marsh's argument that governments are composed of 'calculating subjects, operating on a strategic terrain, much of which is not made up of their own choosing, who can change and negotiate the constraints with which they are faced but only in a limited and partially successful way'[24] indicates a limited freedom of manoeuvre enjoyed by political actors. A determinist view all too often assumes that agents are always and everywhere wholly constrained. This is not so. Too often structures are seen to restrain rather than enable political actions. Together with state–society relations, exogenous circumstances, and the state of political discourse, the orientation of the governing party can be an instrumental factor in the promotion of change. Hence, actors within institutions matter.

   The autonomy of political actors is in large part determined as structural conditions permit. Even if a structured context defines a range of social actions, political actors can initiate change provided the actor is an intentional agent located in a favourable social context. The Thatcher government was working within a number of national and international constraints. None the less, dependent upon the relationship between structural and contingent factors, ideas, interests, actors and institutions all together influence political outcomes.[25] Thus, dominant political ideas can restrain political actors by virtue of being the prevailing orthodoxy, the ideological paradigm within which political attitudes are forged. Political agenda can also influence political change and, once change has taken place, non-change. The relationship of ideas to policies finds expression in this notion of the political agenda, itself an abstract and imprecise, if common, concept. While it should be properly defined before it can be widely applied, the notion of a political agenda, when shorn of pluralist preconceptions, can usefully illuminate political change as well as stability between periods of change. In certain times in particular circumstances, a wider political tide can be swelled by an alteration in the prevailing climate of opinion. Dramatic change is exceptional but a paradigmatic shift in the policy universe is possible.

Hard definitions of what constitutes the political agenda are rarely forthcoming. 'Agenda setting', 'agenda building' and 'agenda managing' are vague and unsubstantial concepts. The existing political science literature on political agenda setting is weak and undeveloped. For the most part it is somewhat out of date, United States-based and cast in a hyper-pluralist universe, heavily skewed in favour of such notions as bottom-up policy development.[26] Defining the agenda as the dominant set of ideas governing the selection of policy options this framework of analysis suggests that: (1) a dominant political agenda exists which overshadows subordinate, less influential agendas; (2) a series of political ideas have made a significant contribution to this form of political change; and (3) this dominant political agenda can advance a set of political actors who have been able to either determine elite (not necessarily popular) political opinion or ride the tide of changing opinion and so influence the set of ideological predispositions that inform policy choice.

Above all else, the political agenda both reflects and reinforces the prevailing set of ideas, attitudes and values within political discourse; it underpins the paradigm within which contemporary politics is conducted. The relative success of Thatcherism in helping to engineer a shift in the political landscape of the UK finds reflection in a reordered political agenda; one which lies at the heart of the political change from a social-democratic-inspired political world view to one which owes more to neo-liberalism. This reordered political agenda provides almost a mock theory of governance, one which guides what governments (and, as importantly, prospective governments) can and should do and what they consider themselves able to do. Political change, be it gradual or dramatic, is ultimately realised as the transition from one paradigm to another. A dominant political agenda is structured around a series of contestable political beliefs that have over time become translated into a set of assumptions, an implicit 'agreement' on the role of public administration, one existing as a 'framework', which acknowledges a prevailing political orthodoxy.

For reasons explored in later chapters, a dominant political agenda structures a political consensus. Defined as a set of assumptions providing the framework within which policy emerges, a consensus encourages political actors to broadly accept or actively endorse a series of policy options they regard as given, unchangeable and therefore acceptable. Of course, a theory of consensus politics is not reducible to an 'agreement of opinion'; consensus does not take the form of deliberate bipartisanship. Rather than taking the form of complete and total agreement between parties across political issues, an adversary style of politics continues in any period of consensus; only the form of disagreement changes as key assumptions are held in common. Given the adversarial nature of party competition within the British political system, adversarial politics will usually prosper. Naturally, all parties continue to seek electoral preferment. With regard to office-seeking, they continue to disagree and often do so violently. The notion of consensus applied here does not simply reflect a policy coincidence: it implies a broad association on general principles which inform the policy decisions parties take in government.

Of course, irrespective of the solidity of any consensus, the ideology of the public sphere is not wholly reducible to the paradigm which the dominant agenda reflects. Subordinate agendas continue to attract attention at the same time as they are overshadowed by the dominant discourse; 'Hayek's ideas' were in circulation during the 'time of Keynes' even though they were not articulated at the level of the state and did not form part of the dominant political agenda. The circulation of political ideas involves both winning and losing arguments; stronger and weaker proposals; dominant and subordinate agendas. Political change involves newer ideas supplanting older ones. Thatcherism colonised what intellectual territory it won slowly and steadily inch by inch. Its opponents – both within and without the Conservative Party – did not vacate the field easily or willingly. None the less, just as social democratic collectivism altered the politics of post-war Britain, Thatcherism clearly influenced the course of the 1980s and 1990s. The period 1982–8 were the years its political agenda advanced in spite of the ever present (and at times very real) danger of electoral unpopularity. Contemporary politics is all the more different as a result.

2
Beyond the Thatcher Decade: The Politics of 'New' Labour

As is often quoted, toward the end of the 1979 election campaign, the then Labour Prime Minister, Jim Callaghan, all but resigned to impending defeat, remarked to his then adviser Bernard Donoughue: 'You know there are times, perhaps once every thirty years, there is a sea change in politics. It then does not matter what you say or do. There is a shift in what the public wants and what it approves of. I suspect there is now such a sea change – and it is for Mrs Thatcher.'[1] This much over-used and therefore somewhat well-worn quotation effectively makes a point: the advent of Thatcherite politics after 1979 did see a political sea-change, one heralded before 1979 as well as after. As a dominant force in British politics Thatcherism did make a significant contribution to changes in the ideological assumptions that inform policy choice.[2]

Everyone, it often appeared, spent the 1980s talking about the 'Thatcher Decade' and the 'Thatcher Experiment', Thatcher-this and Thatcher-that, all the time referring to Thatcherism as a 'catch-all' construct to which all sorts of outcomes, real and imagined, positive and negative, could be attributed. Of course, Thatcherism, a specific form of Conservatism differing from its post-war predecessors, is not reducible to the particular imprint of Margaret Thatcher. Her enforced withdrawal from the political scene in November 1990 did not result in the collapse of the project to which Thatcherism subscribed. While she failed to go 'on and on and on' in her ambition to remain Prime Minister indefinitely, the creed to which commentators lent her name continued to do so.

Described by Keith Middlemas as a 'portmanteau word',[3] Thatcherism has many meanings and can be used in a variety of ways. It can be seen as: (1) a short hard description of what the Thatcher-led Conservative governments did at any one time; (2) a popular political movement; (3) a policy style; (4) a form of political leadership; or else, the definition employed here and examined at length in the next two chapters, (5) an ideological project, a vehicle which advanced a post-social democratic neo-liberal political agenda. According to one determined supporter, Shirley Letwin, Thatcherism is a 'form of practical politics devoted to achieving certain concrete results'.[4] Whatever the limitations of her own claims for the phenomenon (the idea it is a moral crusade concerned with restoring 'vigorous virtues' to all levels of the British polity), Letwin is right to argue that it is not in itself a theory. Indeed, given that the politics of Thatcherism reflects a particular political semi-doctrine within specific historical circumstances of itself, it cannot be considered an ideology. It is not an 'ism' in the sense of the term as it should be used in political discourse.[5]

There is little point endlessly revisiting the circumstances following Thatcher's accession to the Conservative leadership in January 1975 nor ceaselessly replaying the descriptive record of her time in Number 10 Downing Street. In situating an explanation of Thatcherism at a series of interconnected levels, the methodological approach selected to interrogate the phenomenon may take three forms: (1) description; (2) definition; and (3) an assessment of impact. An heuristic approach would require all three approaches to be undertaken simultaneously. To define Thatcherism seriously requires us to describe it. Similarly, it cannot be defined without first having been empirically described; particularly in the form of detailed policy case studies. Thatcherism can only be understood (and its consequences mapped out) by an analysis of the impact it has had at the level of political ideas and at public policy. More particularly, it can be judged by its consequences for British politics.

Theories of political change usually focus on the idea of social, economic and electoral transformations and their impact upon the assumptions and opinions that guide and inform the actions of political actors and administrators as policy-makers (and would-be policy-makers) is necessarily a reflection of these factors. But, as suggested earlier, it is also a consequence of a change in the form of those dominant political ideas that come to structure what government does and which find form in public policy and in political attitudes. Mapping out the process of political change provokes an analysis of the shift in British politics, one in which the concerns of contemporary politics differ markedly from earlier concerns. This is what makes the phenomenon of New Labour so fundamentally interesting.

As with the social democratic attitudes that characterised post-war politics, the depth of the Thatcherite imprint on contemporary politics is very deep, one that has altered the form politics takes. Thatcherism is decidedly not yet a matter of interest only to political historians or contemporary biographers. It is far from being a relic of the 1980s ready to be consigned to the museum together with yuppies, power dressing, the filofax and the rubik cube. Although Thatcher herself has all but left the political scene, her sporadic interventions mostly fuelled by dissatisfaction with her Conservative political successors, the neo-liberal agenda bequeathed by her governments remains a live and viable political force. The politics of the present can only be understood by reference to the immediate and long-term past. Put simply: To understand contemporary politics we need to know from where today's political actors have come and what they now stand for.

Labour's first Prime Minister in eighteen years, Tony Blair, makes much of the claim that his government is committed to 'moving beyond the solutions of the old left and the new right'.[6] In 1996, he declared that Labour would fail 'if it sees its task as dismantling Thatcherism. We can't just switch the clock back to where we were.'[7] Yet, while claiming to reject much of the agenda of New Right conservatives, Blair's Labour government willingly peers at the world in economic terms through neo-liberal lenses. These structure its appreciation of political and economic 'realities' and influence the constructive vision ministers offer. The politics of the New Right, enacted into policy over a twenty-year cycle, now bound the policy horizon, reflecting the cognitive maps fashioned by a newly dominant neo-liberal paradigm. They form the new status quo, one embracing the dominant ideas underpinning policy selection from which all reform agendas begin. In common with other sets of political actors in comparable countries, the Thatcher and Major governments led the way in the UK in the recasting of the political agenda.

The making of 'New' Labour is a result of the party's experiences in the political environment of the 1980s and 1990s. Shirley Letwin commented in 1992 on how '[o]ld socialists [have] learnt to chant in praise of a "social market economy"', a phenomenon born of the fact that 'the battle between socialism and free enterprise was over. And the line between the parties...became blurred. As a result, for the immediate future, whichever party is in power, the major changes made by Thatcherism are not likely to be reversed.'[8] Richard Cockett has characterised contemporary politics as reflecting 'the economic liberal agenda that the Conservative party espoused during the 1980s...[This was] duly adopted by the Labour Party in the wake of their 1987 defeat, out of a recognition that a party proposing the old economic solutions of Key-nesian public spending and nationalisation (as Labour had done in 1983 and 1987) could no longer appeal to a broad mass of the newly affluent electorate.'[9]

Although the election victory of May 1997 saw the end of a Conser-vative political domination of electoral politics which had lasted some twenty-odd years, the politics of 'New' Labour is itself positive proof of the ideological transformations Thatcherism wrought in British politics. The forward march of the New Right has prompted Labour to alter its programmatic stance, electoral strategy and stated political objectives. Unrecognisable as the party which fought the 1983 general election, the word a 'shift' is too subtle to describe what has happened to Labour since 1983; 're-invention' nearer the mark but 'transformation' perhaps more accurate. This change is both deep and fundamental. It was not an elaborate charade imposed on a reluctant party by the Kinnock and Blair leaderships. While attempts at programmatic renewal were opposed by an increasingly ineffective left minority, they won the active support of others. Throughout, the re-fashioning of Labour required the support of the Parliamentary Party: it depended upon the endorsement of trade union leaders, and last and, in this case, certainly least, the acquiescence of a dramatically changing party membership.

Labour's transformation was encouraged by the belief that 'The great ideological contest of the twentieth century has been settled. Free mar-ket capitalism has won; state planning and communism, of which social-market capitalism is alleged to be a subset, has lost.'[10] The 1980s and 1990s saw social democrats and socialists alike on the defensive: 'The old faith in Keynesian instruments of economic management is in decline. States no longer commit themselves to full employment; they do not believe it to be possible. Instead they crave price stability and the approval of the global bond markets for their fiscal rectitude.'[11] Labour now accepts that traditional social democracy is a thing of the past, acknowledging its replacement by a new orthodoxy informed by neo-liberalism where inflation is the greatest economic evil, government borrowing unwise, progressive taxation a proven electoral millstone and an expanded public sector an impossible fantasy. Reconciled to privatisation, committed to Tory trade union legislation and extraordi-narily supportive of the 'enterprise society', the party is no longer willing to contest many changes of the Thatcher years. Labour has undergone an extraordinary transformation, a fundamental shift engineered during the dog-days of opposition and the repeated electoral setbacks of the

1980s and 1990s. As were the Thatcher and Major governments before it, Labour in government is committed to guaranteeing monetary and fiscal stability and embracing the interests of the business community and promoting flexible labour markets.

Labour modernisers claim a 'New' Labour Party had been constructed out of the ashes of that defeated in 1983 and 1987. Labour was united, disciplined, moderate, and modern. The socialist left had been marginalised and former policy liabilities, including unilateralism, nationalisation and central economic planning had been jettisoned; not merely corporatism but even co-operation with a revitalised trade union movement was no longer on Labour's policy agenda. Slowly, piecemeal, almost imperceptibly, and certainly dramatically, Labour moved painfully away from the political ground previously staked out. Defining his party as having stripped 'outdated ideology' from its values, Tony Blair has explicitly set out the principles of the Labour Party he has led since 1994. 'To become a serious party of government Labour required a quantum leap'; it had to 'reconstruct [its] ideology and organisation', marking 'the long march back from the dark days of the early 1980s when, frankly, [Labour] was unelectable.'[12] While a number of differences remain between Labour and Conservatives (definitions of the 'good society', a commitment to modernisation, constitutional reform, attitudes to Europe), Blair disavows any intention to 'switch the clock back to the 1970s',[13] a view which in itself illustrates Labour's willingness to gradually and painfully re-evaluate its own political appeal and govern in line with an ideological map inherited from previous governments.

Initially, left, right and centre of the Labour Party fought the Thatcherite agenda tooth and nail; Denis Healey on the right detested Thatcherism just as much as did Tony Benn on the left. The 1980s were a period of hand-to-hand combat, a long war fought with a great many battles and fierce skirmishes. Here, Thatcherism simultaneously presented a reform agenda and attempted to discredit alternative perspectives; it ran against the past and disclaimed alternative futures. Labour's exclusion from office between 1979 and 1997 severely questioned its vote-seeking capabilities and, for some, damned its opposition to Thatcherism. Each repeated election defeat was taken as proof not only of electoral decline but of the party's ideological crisis. Having first repackaged and then reformed its policy product in 1987 and 1992, Labour's continuing failures encouraged the belief that the party was itself at fault. The initial preconception favoured by the leadership after 1983, that out-of-date Labour was out of touch with the aspirations of the electorate, was ultimately reinforced by the conviction that the party was out of step with the 'political spirit' abroad throughout the land. The conclusion increasingly drawn was that Labour could not expect to win unless and until it changed its image by drastically modernising its appeal.[14]

Subsequent chapters map out the ideological realignment charac-terised by this reconfiguration of Labour and Conservatives around a post-Thatcherite political agenda. Such is the breathtaking extent of Labour's transformation that any number of examples of its policy shifts can demonstrate this phenomenon. One may suffice for the moment. In October 1985, Roy Hattersley told the Labour Conference at Bourne-mouth that 'The Labour Party stands accused and convicted of wanting to interfere with the free operation of free market forces. I plead guilty and ask for innumerable other offences – past and future – to be taken into account.'[15] Some ten years later, Tony Blair as Labour leader was to sharply distance himself from such an approach. In a speech to the British Chamber of Commerce in May 1995 he declared that 'Old Labour thought the role of government was to interfere with the market. New Labour believes the task of government is to make the market more dynamic, to provide people and business with the means of success.'[16] These two speech extracts demonstrate the fundamental difference between so-called 'Old' and 'New' Labour, a difference which is not one of Labour's left and right (Benn and Callaghan in 1980, or, in an earlier incarnation, Bevan and Gaitskell before 1958) but between two essential mainstream figures of the Labour right in different periods, Hattersley in 1985 and Blair in 1995.

Will Hutton's book, *The State We're In*, became an unlikely best-seller in 1995–6. In it he lambasted British capitalism and argued the need for the state to reassert its role in managing the economy. He developed the concept of 'stakeholding', involving a reconstruction of both state and economy based upon an expansionist economic policy within a broad quasi-Keynesian framework. For many, stakeholding offered Labour the big idea it needed. In a number of speeches delivered during a tour of the Far East in January 1996, Blair seized upon the phrase but not the idea as it had been developed by Hutton. While elements on the Blairite centre-left supported Hutton's arguments, elements far closer to Blair did not. Encouraged by his economic advisor, Derek Scott, a past Labour defector to the SDP, Blair opposed the idea as too radical and too associated with 'Old' rather than 'New' Labour. Privately dismayed by the suggestion that stakeholding meant that corporate firms had responsibilities for and obligations to trade unionists and consumers, Blair's antipathy to Hutton's agenda was an open secret. Having inadvertently raised the issue through his use of the word (rather than the concept), Blair quickly dropped the word; with regard to the Blair agenda, stakeholding as an idea got no further than the starting block.[17]

Compared to Labour's total hostility to all things Thatcherite for most of the 1980s the extent of Labour's transformation cannot be under-estimated. In his first speech to the House of Commons as Thatcher's Industry Secretary, Keith Joseph spoke of 'six poisons' which had long polluted the UK economy and brought about economic decline: exces-sive government spending; high direct taxation; egalitarianism; exces-sive nationalisation; a politicised trade union movement associated with Luddism; and an anti-enterprise culture were all evils to be driven out.[18] These 'six poisons' are now widely considered undesirable by political parties seriously competing for government office, none more so than the Labour Party. In the same speech Joseph poured scorn on the outgoing Callaghan administration and claimed that 'Labour's answer to our problems is still more of the same poisons. Its answer is more egalitarianism, more state spending, more direct taxes, more power to the unions and more discouragement to the entrepreneur.'[19] Although similar charges are no doubt regularly made from Conservative benches in the House of Commons, no independent commentator would accept that such a description of the contemporary Labour Party has any basis in reality.

As leader, Blair made clear his commitment to the enterprise society fashioned in the 1980s and made no secret of his determination to both win the endorsement of businessmen and to forge a partnership with business:[20] 'The deal is this: we leave intact the main changes of the 1980s in industrial relations and enterprise. And now, together, we address a new agenda for the twenty-first century: education, welfare reform, infrastructure, and leadership in Europe.'[21] In pursuing this 'accord' with business, Labour's unwillingness to closely associate with trade union rights was almost worn as a badge of courage. In a piece written for the *Daily Mail* in March 1997, Blair argued: 'Even after the changes the Labour Party is proposing in this area, Britain will remain with the most restrictive trade union laws anywhere in the western world.'[22] Blair made clear that Labour would encourage rather than limit flexible labour markets: 'Our proposals for change, including the minimum wage, would amount to less labour market regulation than in the US.'[23]

Such is Tony Blair's willingness to closely associate himself with busi-ness interests as part of his preparedness to embrace Thatcherite politics, New Labour has reached out well to the right of the Old Labour constituency. This has won Blair the warm private praise of Margaret Thatcher who has declared the country 'safe in his hands'. By way of a January 1997 remark to Peter Stothard, editor of *The Times*, she suggested that 'he won't let Britain down'.[24] When the story entered the public realm during the general election campaign Thatcher's office refused to either confirm or deny it, preferring to make no comment. In May 1996, Thatcher had gone on record in the *Sunday Times* as saying that Blair was 'probably the most formidable' Labour leader of modern times: 'I see a lot of socialism behind [Labour's] front bench, but not in Mr Blair. I think he has genuinely moved.'[25] Other more recent private comments from the Thatcher camp are said to be even more supportive. Blair's economic conservative credo of 'sound money' and 'fiscal prudence' as part of his support for the idea of 'government helping business succeed' has won him the most unexpected of friends (among them Rupert Murdoch and, as tellingly, the Adam Smith Institute). At the 1997 general election, Labour secured considerable endorsements from the world of business. While the Chairman of British Petroleum, David Simon, was given a peerage and appointed a Minister of State for Competitiveness in Europe at the DTI, the ranks of unofficial advisors were swelled by a number of individuals drawn from the corporate world, among them Peter Davies of Prudential Insurance, Martin Taylor of Barclays Bank, Bob Ayling of British Airways, Dennis Stevenson of Pearson, and even Alan Sugar of Amstrad, long a self-confessed admirer of Margaret Thatcher.

Several commentators, Adam Przeworski foremost among them, have suggested that social democratic parties of the left such as Labour find it hard to win office given the willingness of workers to reject radical socialism. When they do enter government they are then obliged to moderate their policies in acknowledgment of the structural constraints imposed by capitalism.[26] Although this 'structural constraints' thesis is challenged by (among others) Esping-Anderson,[27] the argument demonstrates the moderation of the social democratic reform project as historically practised; at the heart of this project is the centrality of gradual, cumulative reforms as opposed to wholesale, dramatic transformation. But as a 'moderate', 'reformist' as opposed to 'radical' or 'revolutionary' social democratic party, Labour has been previously willing to negotiate, modify, or otherwise seek to overcome the structural constraints that capitalism brings to bear upon it. Certainly, it has declared a willingness to do so in opposition, even if it has not always done so in government. Labour's contemporary rapprochement with a dominant neo-liberal agenda well to the right of its traditional stance is an indica-

tion not of the historic limitations of social democracy, but of the extent
to which the policy and ideology of the party has changed over a fifteen-
year period. It demonstrates the ultimate success of the New Right in
winning the battle of ideas since the 1970s.
Thatcherism may be defined as an agency of change if not the agent
itself. Richard Rose suggests that parties often cannot make a difference:
'Much of a party's record in office will be stamped upon it by forces
beyond its control. British parties are not the primary forces shaping the
destiny of British society; it is shaped by something stronger than parties.'[28] Yet, if a dominant political agenda can influence the policy
formulation process, political actors can play a significant role in determining this agenda. Thatcherite actors helped construct a new political
agenda through the course of the 1980s: firstly, through problem identification; secondly, through policy formation in the form of remedial
suggestion; and thirdly, as the outcome achieved as policy implementation. The dominant political agenda will structure political discourse
and so influence elite attitudes on policy selection and the issues and
values that underpin the selection of policy in the form of a programmatic appeal. Rather than being predetermined, political actors can
reflect, reinforce and, to some extent, determine these defining political
and ideological environments.

By themselves social and economic structural factors have not wholly
created the Thatcherite agenda. Economic and political imperatives are
not of themselves uncontrollable circumstances which totally constrain
political actors. While the rise of neo-liberalism in the context of the UK
is not entirely due to the Thatcher government it still owes much to the
agency of Thatcherism. Accounting for recent political change requires
Thatcherism to be explained, its impact assessed and, as significantly, its
consequences evaluated. Understanding the nature of political change
in the UK prompts a multi-pronged approach:

1 Defining Thatcherism as a coherent project.
2 Measuring the success of Thatcherism.
3 Evaluating the consequences of Thatcherism.

The paradigmatic shift over which actually existing Thatcherism has
presided has to be both described and explained. Andrew Gamble suggests that 'A major shift in policy becomes permanent when the opposition parties adopt it as their own.'[29] In exploring political change (and
charting the provenance of New Labour) it is instructive to discuss the
statecraft of the Conservative government under Margaret Thatcher and
to compare it with the changing approach of Labour in opposition

under Jim Callaghan, Michael Foot, Neil Kinnock, John Smith and Tony Blair. Present-day party politics are concerned with working inside the structures of the Thatcher settlement. Today, in socio-economic terms, the Thatcherite political agenda is now a significant constraint affecting what present-day political actors can do. This promotes an additional objective:

4 Mapping out the provenance of 'New' Labour.

In her memoirs published in 1993 Margaret Thatcher described the outcome of the 1983 election as a having been a watershed in British politics: it was 'the single most devastating defeat ever inflicted upon democratic socialism in Britain. After being defeated on a manifesto that was the most candid statement of socialist aims ever in this century, the Left could never again credibly claim popular appeal for their programme of massive nationalisation, hugely increased public spending, greater trade union power and unilateral nuclear disarmament.'[30] This view was widely (if somewhat hopefully) shared among fellow Conservatives at the time. In the latter part of the 1980s, it became common currency. It was, in short, an observation elevated to the status of political fact, one eagerly championed by first Neil Kinnock and then by his eventual successor, Tony Blair, and his circle of Labour modernisers.

The roots of the transformation of the Labour Party lie in contemporary politics: New Labour is not best explained as an updating of socialism in the face of modernity but nor is it simple Tory clothes-stealing, a necessary or unnecessary concession to political enemies solely in the interest of securing an electoral victory. However, the politics of the contemporary Labour Party exemplify the Thatcherite reform agenda and the ability of the Thatcher and (to a lesser extent) the Major government to help recast the political agenda upon which current economic, political, and ideological debates take place. All too often, where the Thatcher and Major-led Conservatives have led, Labour under Kinnock, Smith and Blair have gradually followed. Any consideration of Conservative statecraft and Labour strategy after 1979 has therefore to pursue the rather larger questions of explaining the consequences of the fact that Labour lost four consecutive elections at the same time as it explores how and why the Conservative Party won.

Political change is neither commonplace nor rare, indeed it is very much a fact of life; its pace and significance is however a defining factor. Dramatic change in particular is the exception rather than the rule. As

Christopher Hood argues, 'it is easy to identify turning points in retrospect, but harder to explain exactly why they took place when they did or what caused the reversal.'[31] Much of the literature on Thatcherism 'confines itself to establishing that it represents a change in the tide without providing an explanation of why the change took place.'[32] Or even how and with what consequences. In contributing to the debate surrounding the remaking of the Labour Party, Martin J. Smith usefully (if somewhat artificially) distinguishes a 'modernisation thesis' from 'accommodationist explanations'.[33] Accommodationist explanations, later described as the 'politics of catch-up', strongly suggest that Labour has followed where Thatcher and Major (and the electorate) have led it.[34] Today, Labour and the Conservatives as principal competitors for public office largely share the very same political agenda. While continuing to disagree sharply in their pursuit of office as well as on the broader objectives to which policy is directed (competing definitions of the 'good society' discernible at the rhetorical level), both parties have none the less aligned themselves on the same ideological territory characterised by a shared acceptance of the reworked boundaries of the public–private sector and a belief in the primacy of the private over the public in the management of the economy.[35]

Understanding the present through the prism of the past enables past events to be analysed as staging posts constructing the political present. What past political actors have done all too often determines what present-day actors can do. As a chronological account of provocations and counter-provocations, reactions and structured responses to previous happenings, political change is almost a chain reaction. Political positions are struck in response to those previously taken by other political actors. Because political actors work within a set of established practices and assumptions, political changes can engender a new status quo. This is why Labour's current political stance reflects the Thatcherite political agenda. It is a form of accommodation to the prevailing orthodoxy. The party finds itself in a political environment determined by the experiences of the 1980s and the 1990s, a period shaped by Thatcherite success. Labour counselled itself to embrace and work within the mood, aspirations and culture of Britain as it had become in the Thatcherite 1980s and the post-Thatcher 1990s. Instead of endlessly harking back to long-forgotten days of 1945 and 1979, the case put by Labour modernisers was both simple and stark; Labour should (indeed must) respond to social and political trends. Hence, Labour under Blair does not intend to challenge the ascendancy of neo-liberal economics. As a result, the cognitive maps established over the past twenty years which determine the political, economic, and ideological assumptions governing policy formation are to be retained. A new political consensus has been arrived at: from this perspective, Tony Blair to date has been more a weather-cock than a signpost.

3
The Politics of Thatcherism

Thatcherism is best explored in terms of its causes, chronology and, ultimately, its consequences. The first steps in the evaluation of the Thatcherite project are: What was it and what did it seek to do? In assessing the impact that it has had, its achievements (matched against those it set itself) must be measured. Andrew Gamble argues that Thatcherism can be variously defined as 'a set of intellectual doctrines, as a popular political movement, as a style of leadership, as a bloc of interests and as a programme of policy'.[1] His view (which has set the yardstick against which all discussions of this issue follow) is that Thatcherism had three overriding objectives: 'To restore the political fortunes of the Conservative Party, to revive market liberalism as the dominant public philosophy and to create the conditions for a free economy by limiting the scope of the state while restoring its authority to act.'[2] Its project was to centre the free market at the heart of economic activity.

While the Thatcherite project was constrained by the politics of the Conservative Party it was none the less informed by a New Right appreciation of political realities: in the variety of its forms the New Right marries neo-liberalism (the individual; freedom of choice; laissez-faire; minimal government) with neo-conservatism (strong government; social authoritarianism; hierarchy and discipline; the nation). The two key principles of economic liberalism are (1) the central role of the free market in the production, distribution and exchange of goods and services; (2) limiting the interventionist role of the state in the economy. Eager to use 'the market-driven decision-making process to shape the way interests are represented and public choices made',[3] it offered an economic policy informed by neo-liberalism which counterposed the interventionist state with a light touch regulatory state; this is the tradition within which Thatcherism is located, one reflecting an agenda which was itself a shift away from modern (post-war) Conservatism.

Much of the literature conceives of Thatcherism as 'not so much an identifiable political outlook, [but] as a bundle of attributes, held together by time and place'.[4] David Marsh and Rod Rhodes suggest 'five broad dimensions' across which Thatcherism may be evaluated: an economic dimension; an electoral dimension; an ideological dimension; a policy style dimension; and a policy agenda dimension.[5] Thatcherism, often narrowly defined in terms of a leadership style, is all too often a discussion of what 'Thatcher did next', where chronological description is offered in place of a deeper analysis. Its nature is such that studies of Thatcherism can offer all things to all people ranging from an analysis of Thatcher's personality and leadership style to a discussion of questions of political economy.

Evaluations of Thatcherism, partisan and non-partisan, critical and positive, usually take two interrelated forms: firstly, descriptive accounts of the course followed by the Thatcher and Major governments; secondly, analytical explanations which use a national and/or international perspective to define what Thatcherism actually is or what is was. These pose the general questions of how and why it was (or is not) different from other forms of politics. Although the question of whether Thatcherism was a good or a bad thing can be put to one side, competing definitions and perspectives litter the swollen academic literature. In offering a number of either partial or exclusive explanations which singularly or severally encompass a variety of factors, commentators tend to favour one set of explanatory variables over others. Among others, David Marsh (separately and with R.A.W. Rhodes) has questioned the preponderance of 'uni-dimensional explanations' and rightly argues for an inclusive, multi-theoretical explanation of Thatcherism, one that does not concentrate exclusively upon one explanatory variable at the expense of others.[6] Of course, as Marsh suggests by his appeal for a 'multi-dimensional analysis', all factors as they relate to one another play some explanatory role.

Thatcherism as phenomenon

As a specific phenomenon, Thatcherism is best explained by reference to its ideological, economic and political aspects, although, as Peter Taylor observes, '[It] is fundamentally a set of political actions. They are, no doubt, responses to economic circumstances and their collective motives may be designated in ideological terms, but at the heart of

Thatcherism is an attempt to restructure political relations.'[7] The present author accepts the premise, argued by a number of friends and foes alike, that the impact of the Thatcher-led Conservative governments has altered the form of British politics. Thatcherism had a strategic purpose, one determined by its conception of how the political world was and how it should be. More specifically, it advanced prescriptions as to what form the political world should take.

In contrast, it is often suggested that the Thatcher government was far less ideological and much more pragmatic than is often suggested. See, for example, Peter Riddell's suggestion that 'For all but the most passionate adherents to Mrs Thatcher's cause, the shifts that occurred were more a response to changed circumstances and changed times rather than any dramatic reversal of policy.'[8] What are the 'changed circumstances' and 'changed times' to which Riddell refers? How can the political, economic and social changes brought about in the twenty-odd years since 1979 be explained? How did they come about? If times and circumstances change, how exactly do they do so? Tony Blair's numerous references to 'the changes of the 1980s' led *Times* columnist Matthew Parris to suggest that Blair talks 'about the reforms of the 1980s as though "the Eighties", rather than a group of Conservative women and men, had enacted these reforms'.[9] Too often commentators fall into this cosy trap (and others) of mistaking the reforms enacted by political actors and public administrators for the inevitable and anonymous forward march of modernity: 'history' doesn't just happen, it is made.

Several authors, chief among them Riddell and, to a lesser extent, R.A.W. Rhodes and David Marsh, do question the view that the Thatcher government made strategic political decisions which reflected a consistent or coherent world view. Rhodes and Marsh's survey of the Thatcherite policy agenda suggests to them three tentative conclusions: 'First, that there is no constant set of Thatcherite policies. Second, the relative priority accorded to particular policies did not remain the same over the decade. Third, it cannot be assumed that consistent policies were pursued. Both priority and consistence remain matters for investigation, not assumption.'[10] Marsh's suggestion that it is wrong to insist that Thatcherism had a 'developed, coherent programme which was evolved in opposition and carried out in government'[11] lies at the heart of his (and others') objection to the idea that Thatcherism is an 'exceptional' (his phrase) phenomenon. His suggestion that the absence of such a programme invalidates the case that Thatcherism was a coherent project is profoundly mistaken: contra Marsh, no theory of Thatcherite exceptionalism seriously argues, in his own depiction of the thesis, that 'It is easy with hindsight to characterise Conservative...policy as a developed, coherent programme which was evolved in opposition and carried out in government. Hindsight is a dangerous tool of analysis.'[12]

For Marsh and Rhodes, too many writers overestimate the Thatcher effect, and they observe that 'it was only in the field of housing that [the Thatcher] government achieved its policy and political aims. In the other three areas of fundamental change – industrial relations, privatisation and local government – a great deal changed in terms of legislation but much less changed in terms of outcomes.'[13] Yet this goes much too far in underestimating both the overall consistency of approach and the outcomes which resulted. Obviously, no 'developed, coherent programme' existed in opposition before 1979. Which influential authors argue that one existed? Clearly, the emergent Thatcherites had definitive aspirations in a number of policy fields; their task was to identify, however incoherently, certain objectives both before and especially after 1979 and to devise realisable methods to secure those objectives. With regard to, say, privatisation, by learning through doing the government gradually enacted a programme, one which first addressed the margins of the public sector before proceeding to divest the state of key industries and services at the heart of the state-owned economy. It is hard to conclude that the privatisation of state concerns such as British Telecom, British Gas, water, electricity, rail and coal meant that little changed in the outcome of public policy.[14]

David Marsh is also too quick to argue that the Thatcher governments were less (even non) ideologically orientated than is commonly supposed. His position is that it is commonly and erroneously suggested that the Thatcher government adopted 'a step-by-step approach, that it consciously pursued a strategy in which each development in a policy area built on the last as if to complete a jigsaw in which the picture being gradually completed was based upon New Right ideology...this is a mistaken analysis; looking back credits the strategy with a coherence which it did not possess at the outset'.[15] While identifying an important facet of Thatcherism – its incremental pursuit of a conscious set of objectives – this view offers a flawed interpretation of the Thatcherite phenomenon. As Marsh *et al.* suggest, the government was indeed 'constrained by economic problems' and did always respond to them with 'one very wide-open eye on political (and particularly electoral) advantage',[16] but this does not mean that the government did not also seek opportunities to achieve its ideological and political reform agenda. Its New Right ideological disposition served as a compass rather than a road map. It aimed in government to gradually seek out ways and means to secure a number of designated ends.

Commentators can scour the historical record to identify the motivations and core political beliefs that underpinned the activities of the Thatcher government. Here, ideology (broadly defined as a neo-liberal disposition) often provided a key to what ministers did and why they did it, because it provided the initiative for policy formation. Of course, ideological considerations can be tempered by the pragmatic dictates of electoral and political considerations. Tactical political judgements were very important in terms of ministers discovering what they could and could not do. Interpreting constraints in order to attempt to negotiate obstacles requires the strategic use of ideology. Rather than being a free agent, the government was required to respond to political events at the same time that it sought to shape those events; it was determined by events as it sought to determine them. With regard to practical politics, an ideological perspective influenced how the government defined problems and sought to resolve them.

That said, while it is impossible to endorse the 'extreme' perspective that Thatcherism was *ad hoc*, incremental, ill-thought-out and pragmatic, the alternative 'extreme' interpretation, that it was the product of a detailed agenda for radical change designed in opposition and executed in power, is just as invalid. In his misguided haste to question the second school of thought, Marsh (together with Rhodes) too easily aligns himself with the first. Moreover, in his depiction of the alternative case (which he describes as the 'exceptionalist' thesis), he constructs a straw man, one easy to knock down in order to strengthen his own perspective. With Rhodes, Marsh also argues that Thatcherism is characterised by an 'implementation gap', one that demonstrates 'the Thatcherite revolution is more a product of rhetoric than of the reality of policy impact',[17] but Colin Hay righty counterposes this with the idea of a 'strategy gap', one which distinguishes the difference between what a government would like to see happen and what does in fact happen.[18]

As Shirley Letwin would have it: 'Whether right or wrong, lovable or objectionable, Thatcherism has offered a coherent political attitude; it has provided a coherent set of responses to things as they are, or were seen to be, in Britain at the end of the twentieth century. And it has translated these responses into action in a coherent and distinctive manner.'[19] A political project is very different from a political programme; in specifying objective and method, the careful commentator should distinguish one from the other. While a distinction can be made

between those accounts which (1) describe Thatcherism as both pragmatic and reactive and emphasise strategy, leadership and statecraft,
and those which (2) suggest it was fiercely ideological and political,[20]
this polarity is both false and misleading. For reasons explored later,
despite excursions into short- and long-term electoralist statecraft,
Thatcherism was prepared to pursue an ideological–political–economic
project. When necessary, it did so by the most pragmatic of means. It
had a direction and an identifiable set of objectives: 'While pragmatic
calculations have informed the [Thatcherites'] choice between policy
options, most of these options have themselves belonged to a neo-
liberal framework.... To quibble about whether they are simply pragmatic extensions of extant policy or "genuine" versions of neo-liberalism is to miss the point.'[21]

Thus, Thatcherism was advanced by political actors prepared to
attempt to use their executive governance of the state to bring about
fundamental political change. In a number of policy areas they were
remarkably successful where the direction of policy change was framed
by an ideologically informed world view. Even if at times inchoate and
disorganised, the overall strategy of the government was not random
nor necessarily inconsistent; all projects are often as reactive as they are
proactive. Although policy can be determined by a series of piecemeal
reforms shaped by a number of factors, the genesis of the reforms of the
Thatcher government was not just the simple pursuit of a series of
pragmatic measures. Although pragmatism or incrementalism in policy
development should not be ruled out, the overall picture created by a
range of specific initiatives and outcomes demonstrate that Thatcherism
is best described as a general political project. It dealt in broad brush
strokes; the identifiable political beliefs which underlay policy development were as much a core set of convictions as a set of ideas derived
from philosophical reflection. A variety of policy instruments served
wider political ends.

Did the Thatcher government choose to restrict trade union activity
by chance? On a whim? Or for a political purpose? In opposition before
1979, the Tory Shadow Cabinet was divided on the question of how far
trade union reform should go: Thatcher, Joseph, Howe and others were
all in favour and commissioned the 'Stepping Stones' report into possible controls from John Hoskins and Norman Strauss in 1978. The
Employment spokesperson, the 'wet' Jim Prior, was among those hostile. In government Thatcherite ministers considered trade unions to be
an important part of the wider political problem with which they had to
deal. Thatcher damned the 1980 Employment Act and Prior was

dismissed from Employment in September 1981. His successors, assisted by the impact that mass unemployment had on trade union power, incrementally legislated away the voluntarist rights unions had hitherto enjoyed. Corporatism was to be consigned to the pages of history.

Although David Marsh argues that Simon Auerbach's work on Thatcher's trade union legislation reflects his own analysis, Auerbach's suggestion that trade union legislation was the product of 'a distinctive combination of policy, politics, pragmatism and philosophy'[22] demonstrates the impact that Thatcherite ministers had on policy outcomes. The central objective of the Thatcher government was to curb trade union activity: '[while] pragmatic and political factors . . . served to shape the particular contents of the legislation at each stage, the influence of the government's essential philosophical outlook was nonetheless pervasive at the broadest level, and in more insidious ways. The broad thrust of almost all the changes was in the direction of removing, restricting or regulating the rights of trade unions and employees.'[23] Ministers sought to reach their destination were it to prove possible to do so.

An aspiration informed by a ideologically informed world view need not require a detailed initial programme or blueprint. An ideological compass led the Thatcher governments to identify objectives. They then had to design the method of achieving them. The reforms enacted by Thatcherism in office reflected a consistent desire to recast both state and society. As Will Hutton suggests: 'Unlike any of her post-war predecessors [Thatcher's] objective was not to make unions "responsible" or to find some way of transforming collective bargaining so that better trade-offs could be achieved between inflation, growth and unemployment. Rather she wanted to abolish collective bargaining all together, along with all its baggage – Keynesian economics, industrial policy, state intervention, incomes policy and even aspects of the welfare state. She would proceed cautiously, recognising that every attempt to attack trade unions in the twentieth century had been beaten back – but her direction from the beginning was unmistakable.'[24] That Thatcherism was a project is reflected in its desire to recast reality in keeping with its world view. As Colin Hay rightly argues: 'Thatcherism was an inherently strategic project which sought to construct a new set of dominant ideologies and "common sense" assumptions. . . . The values of compromise, consensus, equality and welfarism were to be replaced by a combination of those of consumer capitalism, enterprise culture and initiative, tradition, moral fortitude and decency. In Thatcher's own words, 'economics are the method: the object is to change the soul'.[25]

There are, of course, 'many Thatcherisms' in the popular imagination and the phenomenon can be considered at a number of levels for any number of purposes. It is therefore mistaken to think that the institutional and political changes initiated by the Thatcher government were only loosely connected with a general strategy: ideological, political and electoral factors must be incorporated into any rounded analysis of Thatcherism. Also, the social and economic environment in which it was located should not be overlooked. Thatcherism was always a heterogenous phenomenon, one marked by disagreement over pace and direction. This is illustrated by the distinction between neo-conservatism and neo-liberalism within Thatcherism and by the presence of both 'radical' and 'moderate' perspectives. Running from left to right the neo-liberal spectrum also encompasses the dramatic and the mundane in policy terms. Thatcherism included arguments for consolidation or advance. Other political issues, the question of Europe being the most obvious, also cut right across issues of economic policy and were occasions for instability within the Thatcherite camp.

Other criticisms of his analysis of Thatcherism aside, David Marsh does rightly question the use of hindsight in studying Thatcherite policy.[26] The tendency to 'read history backwards' should certainly be avoided but should not be mistaken for an informed retrospective judgement rooted in empirical evidence. The error Marsh falls into is not to see Thatcherism as a process, one in which over time its political attitudes and prejudices find reflection in policy development. Thatcherism was closer to a 'novel, coherent, consistent and successful, ideology-inspired strategy'[27] than it was an *ad hoc*, ill-thought-out and pragmatic set of policy initiatives.

Electoral considerations and ideological goals were not incompatible either; they influenced one another. In fact, the skill of the Thatcher government lay in fitting its ideological project to the demands imposed by electoral imperatives. Qualifying their assertion that Thatcherism was a coherent and radical strategy, Bob Jessop *et al.* suggest that '[I]t would be quite wrong to underestimate the pragmatism of Thatcher's strategy simply because she proclaims herself a conviction politician and appears to be ideologically motivated.'[28] Of course the very reverse also applies. One should not underestimate the ideological nature of the Thatcherite strategy simply because the government often adopted pragmatic measures. Such measures were often a reflection of its preparedness to cut its political cloth to electoral requirements. As explored below, the radical commitments of the Thatcherite project were frequently constrained by political and electoral necessity which often (but not always) encouraged pragmatism on the part of government ministers. As Simon Auerbach argues with regard to trade union policy, 'The forces which consistently weighed in to restrain, modify, or simply reject the New Right agenda, were the products of the political acumen and pragmatism which is liable to be exhibited by any party which has obtained power, and has every intention of keeping it.'[29]

Thatcherism was a means to facilitate political change by initiating policy departures. It is best conceived as a project which used certain practical tools in its pursuit of identifiable ends. This definition links the programmatic activity of the Thatcher-led Conservative Party with the strategies it variously employed to secure the ideological, political and economic ends it identified. Bob Jessop *et al.* usefully define strategy as being 'a complex and continuing process which involves: selecting and ordering objectives; deciding on a pattern and sequence of actions deemed appropriate to attaining these objectives; monitoring performance and progress; and adjusting tactics and objectives as strategic interaction proceeds'.[30] Thus, Thatcherism is thereby distinguished, in Shirley Letwin's helpful phrase, by 'direction, movement and purpose'.[31] It did have a strategic purpose, a project determined by a conception of how the political world was and why it took that form. More specifically, it advanced prescriptions as to what form that world should take. The wider initial question 'What is Thatcherism?' therefore requires both deep and broad analysis. Five dimensions immediately suggest themselves: (1) Where did it come from? (2) How did it emerge? (3) What did it intend to do? (4) Did it succeed? and (5) What consequences has it had?

Understanding Thatcherism: leadership, limitations and constraints

In her speech to the 1980 Conservative Conference, Thatcher declared that 'the task on which the government is engaged [is] to change the national attitude of mind'. Hyperbole aside, it is clear that this is how Thatcher wished to define the purpose of her government. While office gifted her a fortress and her beliefs a political compass, the ideas she clung to were evaluative prescriptions proceeding from normative principles. In terms of political personality, Thatcher was driven by a mix of prejudices – in the dictionary definition – and her beliefs were presented in the form of core convictions. Simon Jenkins considers her an 'intellectual jackdaw', a politician who 'picked up the shiniest stones from the separate strands of English liberalism and conservatism, and carried them back to her nest'.[32]

While she enjoyed the certainty born of conviction, the personal role of Margaret Thatcher is all too easily overstated. The ranks of the Thatcherite movement were swelled by all types; for every general there were a great many foot soldiers. In many ways Thatcher was a figurehead who led from the front. She was cautious as well as bold, someone who had often to be persuaded of the efficacy of a course of action before it would be adopted. The centrality of the Prime Minister in the British system of government and her own powers and dispositions meant she was the key agenda-setter in government. Yet, because the 'Thatcher' part of Thatcherism is so overstated, the 'Thatcherite' part needs re-emphasis. Always cautious, Thatcher had often to be encouraged, cajoled and, occasionally, pushed by colleagues and advisers into adopting a particular course of action and dissuaded from other forms of action.

Leadership is important to Thatcherism but analysis based only on the personality and style of Mrs Thatcher is at best misleading. The close and constant association of Thatcher with Thatcherism all too often obscures the reality of the phenomenon. Accounts which stress Thatcher's personality and style are frankly boring and hagiographical; abusive studies are equally irrelevant. The question 'what happened?' rather than 'who is to blame or who gets the credit?' is far more interesting. Whether she is considered to be nice or nasty, studies of the personality of Margaret Thatcher (when it is unrelated to the process and conduct of government policy and the power of the Prime Minister) are mostly unhelpful. As a leader ('personal, autocratic and radical'[33]) Margaret Thatcher was important but she was not all-important. She should be detached from her 'ism' not to suggest an unexceptionalist thesis but to emphasise the broader role Thatcherites played in the Thatcherism project. As individuals who (broadly) shared (or for career reasons felt obliged to share) a Thatcherite perspective, other political actors played their part in the work of the Thatcher and (as crucially) the Major governments. The role of sometime-paid-up Thatcherites such as Nigel Lawson, Geoffrey Howe, Norman Tebbit, Nicholas Ridley *et al.* (even ex-Heathites such as Douglas Hurd, Kenneth Baker and Chris Patten) is central to any understanding of the record of the government.

In the early years of her premiership Thatcher was often simultaneously leader and follower. Two significant examples of Thatcher as follower may suffice. Although she was personally blamed for the Community Charge/Poll Tax of 1986–90, the conception and enactment of the policy owed much to ministers and officials at the Department of

Environment: Patrick Jenkin's initial eagerness to please; William Waldegrave and Ken Baker's desire to devise the policy; the various attempts of Michael Howard, Michael Portillo and Chris Patten to enact it. The Health Service reforms of 1988–91 were conducted by a special Cabinet Committee under Thatcher's chairmanship but eagerly pursued by three Secretaries of State for Health: John Moore (with little success) in 1987–8, Ken Clarke 1988–90 and William Waldegrave 1990–2. A great many reforms which bore Thatcher's imprimatur were more often than not the collective effort of the government. For example, despite her ever present distaste for British Rail (when Thatcher lunched with British Rail executives 'she treated them... as second-class citizens: "If any of you were any good you would be in private industry" '[34]), John Major was far more 'radical' on the question of rail privatisation.[35]

In short, New Right politics and the emergent neo-liberal agenda are as important as leading personalities in explaining what the Thatcher and Major governments did. New Right ideas were in wide circulation and Thatcherism greatly benefited from New Right cheerleaders such as political think-tanks such as the Institute of Economic Affairs and the Adam Smith Institute.[36] Although it proved adept at the exercise of power, Thatcherism was never always able to get its own way in government. For most of her time as Prime Minister Margaret Thatcher would temper her conviction where it threatened her grip on power. She appeared to lose sight of this distinction toward the end of her reign, when Europe, local government finance, and the management of the economy stand out as policy areas where the Thatcher Cabinet demonstrated spectacular errors of judgement. Similar errors and political divisions were to bedevil the Major government for much of the 1992 Parliament.

Because Thatcherism is not an entirely unique phenomenon, care should be taken not to overstate the coherence of Thatcherite policy or to underestimate the inevitable policy continuity in many areas. Inheritance in public policy is important: as Richard Rose suggests, 'policy makers are heirs before they are choosers'.[37] Conservative governments came up against a great many limitations and constraints. The constraints of electoral politics, the internal politics of the government, and the administrative practicality of proposed reforms all impacted upon what the government could do. Together these factors acted as a series of 'filtering mechanisms' that served to limit the ambitions of the Thatcher and Major governments. In travelling from A to B Thatcherites had no initial road map; all they initially knew was that they did not like A and were prepared to use the powers office conferred to reform this status quo. Of course aspiration is different from achievement. The role of uncertainty in policy innovation must be emphasised, as should the difficulty of moving from one set of doctrines (the known) to another (the unknown).

As an ideological project Thatcherism was variously constrained by (1) the dictates of political statecraft; (2) the obligations arising from electoral imperatives; (3) the demands of administrative realities; and (4) public policy agendas inherited from previous administrations. All successful politicians temper ideology with realism; the extent to which they accept the need to carefully negotiate obstacles rather than needlessly confront them is not so much a sign of weakness or irresolution as a source of strength denoting a sense of purpose. Such realism should not be mistaken for opportunism or vacillation; nor should it be seen to necessarily weaken an ideological perspective. In his memoirs, Nigel Lawson, Chancellor of the Exchequer 1983–9, complains of Thatcher's often stated reluctance to countenance radical solutions to policy difficulties.[38] Her caution (and that of Lawson elsewhere) was born of the belief that politics, the art of the possible, often requires temporary compromise or tactical retreat should the politician recognise that their reach exceed their grasp. The good politician (an ideologue with a sense of purpose; not merely the pragmatist) will simply seek a suitable and reliable method to secure their objective by ensuring that both reach and grasp are married together.

Generally, Hugo Young characterised Thatcher as displaying 'insecurity co-existing with ever more blatant certitude'.[39] While government caution was often due to the unwillingness of ministers to pursue unpopular reform, the most striking example of failure as a result of external constraints was the inability of the Thatcher and Major governments to cut public expenditure in real terms: this objective was set out in the 1979 Conservative manifesto and became a longstanding watchword of economic policy. Public spending comprised 43 per cent of GDP in 1979; 39 per cent in 1990; 42 per cent in 1991; 43 per cent in 1992; and 44.5 per cent in 1994. While altering the nature of the state's income (and the direction of expenditure), Thatcher and her successor, John Major, did not curb overall the state's level of spending. Why was public expenditure not reduced? Due to electoral reasons both Thatcher and Major had to accept the framework of spending commitments inherited from previous governments: health, education, defence and welfare all made significant (and unavoidable) demands of the public purse; these could be damped down, on occasion be restricted, but they could not be dramatically cut.

Reform notwithstanding, demand-led welfare spending such as health and social security kept generating increasing public expenditure. In other policy areas other examples of prudence abound: the settlement of the mining dispute in April 1981; the abandonment of the proposed sale of Rover to Ford and General Motors in March 1986; the cancellation of the sale of water in the 1983 Parliament; the compromise over the sale of British Gas in 1985–6; the abandonment of the Poll Tax after November 1990; divisions over ERM, 1985–92, and exchange rate policy generally; privatisation of the Post Office in 1993. The government's reaction to the leak of the Central Policy Review Staff (CPRS) report into 'Public Expenditure in the Longer Term' in September 1982 is another example of caution: this Cabinet paper proposed dramatic cuts in public expenditure in a privatised NHS, higher education, and social security. Here, ministers (not just of the 'wet' variety) were, in Hugo Young's words, painfully aware that 'the need to do something severe about public spending ranked rather less prominently than the need not to frighten the natives any more than they were frightened already'.[40] Facing the judgement of the electorate in the upcoming election (it was to prove only nine months away), the Thatcher Cabinet backtracked, claiming the CPRS paper was only a discussion document and 'reaffirming its commitment to, broadly speaking, the general pattern of expenditure and government responsibility'.[41]

In addition to the pursuit of a ideological-economic project, electoral politics were also very significant. One element of Thatcherism identified by Andrew Gamble is the objective of rebuilding 'the political dominance of the Conservatives...by assembling a large enough coalition of voters and interest groups'.[42] Throughout their period of office the Thatcher-led Conservatives set out their stall as a self-conscious party of government. In 1979, the Conservatives had lost four out of the last five general elections contested and been in office for only three and a half of the preceding fifteen years since 1964, a shocking record for a party which had enjoyed unparallelled electoral success during what some commentators now call the 'Conservative Century'. Thus, Thatcher's objective to restore her party's electoral fortunes looked assured in the wake of the election victories of 1979, 1983, 1987 and 1992 even if her party's grasp on power was torn loose in the Labour landslide of May 1997; no party can govern for ever, all political careers (individual or collective) eventually end in failure. During the 1980s, having won office the Thatcher and Major-led Conservatives were determined to keep it; this end was another key principle of a government which saw successful office-seeking as the necessary prelude to a policy-seeking strategy. Of course, post-1992 the electoral luck of the Major government ran out as Thatcherite Conservatism was seen to have run out of steam.

Thatcherism saw public opinion as (1) a guide to what was possible; (2) an influence on what they should do; and (3) an obstacle to be negotiated (and certainly to be respected). The notion of 'statecraft', defined as the demonstrated ability to competently manage the affairs of state in matters of 'high politics', gives an insight into the impact that political and electoral factors could have upon the Thatcher government. The three dimensions of statecraft identified by Jim Bulpitt involve: (1) a set of governing objectives; (2) a governing code as defined by a series of coherent ideas underpinning strategy and influencing policy objectives of government; and (3) a set of organising principles to attract and maintain popular support and facilitate state management.[43] Statecraft (particularly the need to maintain popular support and facilitate state management) can be interpreted as a constraint, one that requires governments to pursue whatever convictions they might have by pragmatic measures. It involves state or policy management in the interests of gaining or maintaining office or also in successfully negotiating administrative obstacles in the way of policy innovation. Although Bulpitt considers that 'statecraft' granted Thatcherite Conservatives the key to Whitehall, his narrow conception of 'statecraft' does not detract from the idea of an ideologically informed Thatcherite project: Although ideology may be tempered by circumstance, 'statecraft' (defined in the broader sense as the art of government) need not eschew ideology. Clearly, office was the only game in town, the initial means to the end sought, and, as such, terribly important to the Thatcherite project; without office nothing was possible. Although fear of losing was a common preoccupation, the Thatcher government was not concerned only with 'governing', but with the objectives to which 'government' was directed.

While successfully securing re-election in 1983, 1987 and 1992 both the Thatcher and Major governments experienced significant downturns in popularity between general elections in 1979–92. (Indeed, between 1992 and 1997 the Major administration did not know what electoral popularity was.) These periods, 1980–2, 1985–6, and 1989–90 (matched by significant upturns in 1982–4 and 1986–9), had a significant effect on governments which, while prepared to 'lead' public opinion in the effort to reshape electoral behaviour, acknowledged the need to accommodate electoral opinion. The need to make strategic choices in the face of political and electoral pressures amid the dictates of ideological commitments is an extremely important feature of the Thatcherite phenomenon. While prepared to temper its project in the face of electoral necessities, the Thatcher government was not prepared to make unnecessary concessions to electoral opinion; whenever possible the government and not electors (or the opposition) set the political (and hence, electoral) agenda. Here, where the government sought to lead public (and also elite) opinion from the front it did so in an attempt to forestall the effects of electoral (or other political) constraints. Thus, an alternative conception of 'statecraft' (as applied to Bulpitt's conception of it) need not necessarily limit the political or ideological project of government, merely require actors to be more circumspect about how they go about realising their objectives (or, more appropriately, attempting to achieve their various aims). Obviously, the objective of the office-seeking politician is to attract and maintain popular support; for the Thatcher government, office as a means to an end and not only an end in itself was terribly important.

One example of this may suffice. In early 1983, a Tory landslide was likely but could not be taken for granted. While there were few takers for a Labour government, thoughts of a hung Parliament were far from uncommon. Fear of losing an election made the government (none more so than Thatcher) insecure, all too aware that their project would pay the price of failure. It is hard to escape the conclusion that the Thatcher Cabinet prepared for re-election in the early spring of 1983 quietly confident that enough had been done to secure victory but convinced that discretion remained the better part of valour as far as the 1983 Manifesto was concerned. One true Thatcherite, Nicholas Ridley, variously Secretary of State for Transport, Environment and Trade and Industry in 1983–90, suggested that innate caution led the government to adopt a excessively 'thin' manifesto in 1983 and that 'the 1983 to 1987 Parliament has often been described as a wasted opportunity; that was the time when a serious effort to effect reform should have been made'.[44] In retrospect, Ridley's observations suggest that a fear of electoral defeat in 1981–3 led to the adoption of a cautious and careful approach. For many paid-up Thatcherites the middle period of the Thatcher government was wasted as a result. For Ridley the immediate post-1983 period was 'the window of opportunity which alas [Thatcher] missed'.[45] Thatcher herself was to retrospectively endorse this view. Emboldened by success she ensured that the 1987 Manifesto was far more radical than its predecessors.

The Thatcherite project was also constrained by the internal politics of the Conservative Party. Thatcher famously divided her party into critics and supporters, left and right, and originally 'wets' and 'dries'. The Parliamentary Party was subdivided into leaders and followers, the loyal and the disloyal; those categorised as 'One of Us' were among the most favoured. For the old Heathite Conservative establishment, Margaret Thatcher was most definitely not 'one of them'. She always saw the Cabinet simultaneously as resource and obstacle and, despite her many successes in government, never felt completely at home with a number of colleagues she considered at various times unreliable or otherwise unsound. Cabinet divisions are a fact of political life. In 1979, Thatcher was obliged to appoint a number of 'wets' to her Cabinet: Gilmour, Prior, Whitelaw (who became a loyalist), Walker, Pym and, until the Cabinet re-shuffle of September 1981 (and that fashioned after 1983), she was obliged to act cautiously given the weight of Cabinet opinion. In 1981, Thatcher dispatched a number of 'wet' Tory 'grandees' and took a significant step toward securing the ascendancy of the Thatcherites within the governing circle (if not the Cabinet as a whole).[46]

A cumulatively increasing willingness of Conservative ministers (and would-be want-to-be ministers) to adopt a Thatcherite policy line saw the growing impact of a Thatcherite perspective within governing circles (a process which over time affected the attitudes of the civil service). This did not simply involve Thatcher's control over her government and the decisions of her ministers. Although never sure of the reliability of her political base in government,[47] Thatcher's broad political outlook did succeed in setting the agenda for aspiring Conservative MPs eager to climb the greasy pole. Centrist Tory MPs such as Ken Clarke and Douglas Hurd were obliged to make themselves more or less at home within her Cabinet and their careers prospered. Placing the issue of Europe and Britain's membership of the European Exchange Rate Mechanism (ERM) to one side, Cabinet disagreements (or, rather, vocal disaffections) after the purge of the oppositional 'wets' in 1981 were more likely to concern the process of government rather than the direction of policy; certainly during the 1983 Parliament. None the less, as time went on Thatcher was also to disagree with past friends in addition to implacable foes. She fell out with both Nigel Lawson and Geoffrey Howe, erstwhile allies at the Treasury despite the fact that (the issue of the ERM notwithstanding) they had been fully-paid-up 'true believers' for most of their time in government. Even with a Thatcherite ascendancy more firmly established, the need to placate internal opposition (as well as external critics) was often recognised. The dangers of not doing so were obvious: it was a rule of thumb Thatcher allowed herself to lose sight of toward the end of her premiership.[48]

If aspiration is the first step in policy development, subsequent steps involve attempts at dealing (whenever possible) with limitations and constraints. As a result, Thatcherite politics and its attendant policies were both created by political actors and shaped by a process of development; they were constructed over time and through experience. The advances and retreats of the Thatcher-led government were all part of political life, the lot of any set of political actors however determined they may be to secure their objectives. No political strategy registers an overall 100 per cent success rate. Thus, although Thatcherite actors were greatly influenced both by ideological proclivities and political and electoral judgements, each factor impacted upon the other (and where administrative practicality was another variable factor that impacted upon the policy record of the government).

'Aspiration' must be distinguished from the record of achievement determined by success or failure. Total or partial failure does not invalidate 'desire'. In regard to statecraft, the argument relating to electoral and political constraints can be reversed; an ideological proclivity itself acts as a different type of constraint obliging actors to pursue a particular course of action. Here, an ideological project impacts upon the political actor's perception of political considerations. The interaction of the actor's dominant ideological proclivity and the political considerations they are obliged to take into account can be demonstrated with regard to a five-stage model of policy development:

1 Attitude
2 Intention
3 Chosen Policy Method
4 Designated Objective
5 Policy Outcome.

Here, Attitude; Intention; Designated Objective can be influenced both by a dominant ideological proclivity and by political considerations. Policy Outcome indirectly impacts upon the dominant ideological proclivity but also upon political considerations which in turn acts upon Attitude; Intention; Chosen Policy Method; and Designated Objective either favourably or unfavourably, dependent upon its relative success or failure. Intention is the initial spur to policy formation. If it is overtly influenced by a dominant ideological proclivity then the effect of political or administrative considerations is weakened or else may deter the actor's desire to secure the first. An opportunity has always to be seized and action taken. Policy development within the Thatcher administration was often characterised by a willingness on the part of government to exploit opportunities.

Assuming a distinction can be drawn between policy design and implementation, aspiration (identifying the objective of policy) precedes design (or any other form of choice) and so affects the perception of the problem; the possible solutions advanced; the solution that is formulated; the policy designed; the policy enacted and implemented; and, finally, the assessment of both the impact and consequences of policy. Exigent facts (foremost among them political, economic and administrative considerations) then determine what government can actually do. Peter Clarke contends that leadership is dependent upon its ability to set the agenda, to devise means and mobilise political support to reach its designated ends.[49] 'This is the way to look at the world...this is what we should be doing by means of a four-stage process (1) asking questions; (2) identifying problems; (3) proposing solutions; and, when possible, (4) enacting policy.'

As David Marsh rightly suggests, New Right ideology was a tool of Thatcherism rather than its blueprint.[50] Both internal and external constraints can limit and deter the ideological project, but New Right ideology was (in different ways) as important a tool to both Thatcher and Major as a pipe to a plumber or a stethoscope to a cardiac specialist; unable to do without it they came to see it as irreplaceable. There are a number of occasions where the Thatcher and Major governments found themselves unable to make progress in areas they would like (curbing the level of public expenditure or remaking the welfare state), where external constraints limited (or otherwise deterred) the ideological project but an ideological proclivity was ever present. The politics of Thatcherism was thus simultaneously an attempt to secure a series of goals as it was an effort to overcome difficulties and renegotiate obstacles. Thus, while New Right ideology may not have been a blueprint it was a guidebook; it informed rather than instructed, persuaded rather than determined. In short, it suggested policy options rather than preordained them. Together, electoral–political considerations and ideological outlook provided the twin influences that set the course for the Thatcherite project. More often than not, given the relative success of Thatcherite actors in generating the necessary level of consent within both civil society and the state for what they were doing, ideology proved itself the compass by which they set their sail: policy departures, in turn promoting political change, resulted.

4
Explaining Thatcherism: Project and Process

The impact of Thatcherism has been profound. While the electoral hegemony sought by the Conservative Party was temporary (if not illusory), the Thatcher and Major governments did preside over a dramatic shift in public policy, one clearly evidenced in the shift toward marketisation in the reform of public services; the adoption of new public management techniques; the pursuit of privatisation and deregulation; the reduction of direct taxation; and the establishment of a more centralised system of governments. The Thatcher and Major governments skilfully married political, economic and ideological objectives, a skill which so dramatically deserted the Major-led Conservatives in their public fall from grace after September 1992. None the less, this was an illustration of its willingness to pursue a coherent series of projects against the backdrop of the many political and administrative obstacles it found in its path. Foremost among such projects was the eagerness of key ministers to advance the neo-liberal agenda with which Thatcherism became so associated.

Of course, the significance of the neo-liberal disposition evidenced by Thatcherism has to be qualified. The UK economy and polity have not been wholly altered in line with the neo-liberal agenda evidenced by, say, Hayek; rather it has been 'neo- liberalised'. The status quo inherited by Thatcherism has been in part merely reformed; policy continuity continues to prevail amid significant changes. Thatcherism did not begin with a blank canvas nor was it a revolutionary project. The momentum of the Thatcherite project clearly began to tail off after 1990, so demonstrating the limits to its advance. Social democratic attitudes were reformed rather than abolished outright. Yet Thatcherism was working with the grain not only of domestic developments but also of international trends. The shift in economic policy away from social democratic practices and towards tighter financial and public spending restraint, the move away from public enterprise, corporatist state structures and higher tax regimes began in the mid-1970s. In North America, Australasia, and Europe, similar problems have been diagnosed and now-familiar solutions to questions of social provision and industrial policy offered. The spread of privatisation, deregulation and a move toward laissez-faire has been common.

Although the global spread of neo-liberal politics has had a significant impact upon British politics, the Thatcherite agenda has played a significant part in the development of this general phenomenon: the Thatcher government was a significant agenda-setter. In 1979, it could not be said that Thatcherism was a radical blueprint or a set dogma. No such thing existed. Equally, nor was it just a vague idea propagated by political actors eager to retain office and ever watchful of electoral trends. The common argument that 'radical' reform began only in the third term of the Thatcher government is misleading. The major legislative changes in a remarkable number of fields, including health, education, local government finance, privatisation and deregulation, tax cuts and Whitehall reform, built upon foundations gradually established in the first two terms. Emboldened by its political successes the government sought to press home the advantage that electoral opportunity had granted.

The framework of third-term policy was for the most part established in the 1979 and 1983 Parliament. Post-1987 initiatives were often cast in the pre-1987 period. To take only two examples, the government was convinced of the case for a Poll Tax by November 1985, and privatisation was the product of a rolling programme established in principle in 1982–4 (and following on from the initiatives undertaken in 1979–82). As Thatcher herself claims: 'After a long struggle *during my first term*, from 1979 to 1983, like-minded ministers and I had largely converted the Cabinet, the Conservative Party and opinion in the worlds of finance, business and even the media to a more restrictive view of what the state's role in the economy should be' (my emphasis).[1]

Categorising Thatcherism as a political process

Under Thatcher, individual policy initiatives did exhibit symptoms of crisis management and may well have been the product of an interplay of opportunity and circumstance, chance and fortune. But, given that over time Thatcherite actors pursued an agenda based on a normative world view and sought fundamental and lasting political change,

Thatcherism is best understood not just as a political project but as one enacted as a process over time. There are a number of difficulties in periodising Thatcherism. It is inevitably an arbitrary process; what is looked for is often easily found yet an analytical chronology can be attempted and it is clear that neither the neo-liberal agenda of the New Right nor Thatcherism itself was invented in 1979.[2]

Neo-liberal ideas re-emerged from under the shadow of social democracy in the 1970s and, eagerly championed by political actors in government after 1979, grew exponentially throughout the 1980s. Significant staging posts included: Keith Joseph's turn to the right after 1974; Thatcher's replacement of Heath as Conservative leader in January 1975; Thatcher's period as Leader of the Opposition 1975–9; the Conservative election victory of May 1979; the 1981 Budget; the dismissal of the 'wets' in September 1981; the Falklands War, June 1982; re-election in the June 1983 election; the adoption of the Next Move Forward programme in October 1986; re-election in the June 1987 election; Thatcher's removal from office in November 1990 and John Major's elevation to the premiership; 'Thatcherism without Thatcher'; and victory in the 1992 election. Equally, Thatcherism may be periodised by the electoral cycle; the 1979, 1983, 1987, 1992 Parliaments.

In terms of policy change Thatcherism 'found its way in office'. The perspective that from 1975 onward 'Mrs Thatcher worked out a detailed agenda for radical change which was to break the mould of British politics after her accession to power in 1979'[3] is a gross overstatement. As a process which forged an ongoing (and developing) project, the enactment of Thatcherite policy was incremental in character. Thatcher herself declared in March 1986: 'We're only just beginning. We've barely got past the stage of excavation . . . ' (hence her need to 'go on and on and on and on' in office).[4] But, while unsuccessful in many of its grandiose schemes, Thatcherism did make significant advances, not by means of a step-by-step approach but by change enacted over time (through four Parliaments), from initial aspiration through identified, workable means (and a number of cul-de-sacs and policy disasters) which were deployed in the hope of securing certain objectives; some battles were won, others were lost.[5]

Thatcherism was made flesh by the mid-1980s by the enactment of a political programme of reform against the background of wider political, economic and social forces. It owed much to the perseverance of determined political leaders and the forbearance of a sufficient percentage of the electorate willing to grant the Thatcher and Major-led Conservatives entry to the corridors of Whitehall. Thatcherism did not begin on the day Thatcher entered Downing Street nor did it end on the day she left. The phenomenon emerged over time in opposition before 1979 and in government after 1979. As much as it was influenced by external factors beyond its control, Thatcherism also made itself. It developed and grew in office through a process of evolution. As a staged process significant signposts and staging posts stand out defined as events, trends, issues; milestones rather than rigid demarcation lines or fixed boundaries. Periodisation illuminates process and can help clarify our understanding of Thatcherism. Thatcherism was not merely succoured but strengthened by its own repeated electoral successes pre-1992 (in the same way as the Labour Party was weakened by its own failures). With each election Thatcherism took root further within the political culture of the UK. Essentially, the election of May 1979 may be read as an opportunity which of itself was not a turning point. It granted political actors the chance to pursue an agenda of political and economic reform; of course, what happened after 1979 is all the more important.[6]

Paul Addison's analogy of the road to 1945 in his exploration of the impact of the Churchill Coalition upon the 1945–51 Labour government is instructive here.[7] It is through an examination not simply of the road to 1979 but the road from 1979 that explanations of the emergence of Thatcherism as a political project can be sought. The electoral events of 1979, 1983, 1987 and 1992 and, in time, those of 1997 have played a significant part in the construction of the modern discourse to characterise contemporary politics. So too did the political events of 1979–85, 1985–8, 1988–92, 1992–7. Modernity is constructed. It does not simply happen nor just arise: it is made. If electoral cycles serve as staging posts in this process, 1979 is by itself a false benchmark; the elections of 1983, 1987 and 1992 are just as significant staging posts marking the process of departure from the pre-1979 status quo.

One attempt at periodisation is offered by Bob Jessop *et al.* who detail a series of stages in the Thatcherite project: (1) social movement, a reaction to the politics of the 1970s and as much a repudiation of the experiences of the Heath Government of 1970–4 as the record of the Wilson and Callaghan administrations of 1974–9; (2) policy departure during 1979–82; (3) consolidation in government during 1983–6; (4) radical Thatcherism, in evidence from 1986.[8] Here, Jessop *et al.* attempt to deconstruct the process by which the Thatcherite project took root in British politics. Colin Hay's recent extension of this periodisation argues that Radical Thatcherism (involving the restructuring of state, economy and civil society) was followed by a further stage entitled the Exhaustion of Radical Thatcherism (characterised by the crisis of the Thatcher and Major governments but not necessarily of Thatcherism).[9] The period suggested both by Jessop *et al.* and Hay as 'Radical Thatcherism' and 'the exhaustion of Radical Thatcherism' draws attention to dramatic post-1986 policy initiatives (symbolised by the Community Charge/Poll Tax and key reforms of social institutions and the administrative system) but offers the erroneous presupposition that Thatcherism was not radical in its earlier phases.

Characterised by a process of evolution, Thatcherism is best adjudged in terms of 'stages' rather than 'periods'. As Jessop *et al.* suggest: 'the most appropriate concepts and tools of analysis for understanding Thatcherism have changed as Thatcherism has changed'.[10] As a process, Thatcherism certainly involves an amount of serial disengagement with past practice but continuity is also a feature of the phenomenon.

Using election cycles as a benchmark, three distinctive stages in the emergence, rise and consolidation of a Thatcherite agenda suggest themselves in contrast to the typology offered by Jessop *et al.*:

1 Emergence: the rise of Thatcherism, 1966–79
2 Enactment: the pursuit of Thatcherism, 1979–90
3 Consolidation: the gradual establishment of a post-social democratic neo-liberal agenda, 1990 onward.

The chronology offered by Jessop fails to demonstrate the significance that the 1983 and 1987 general elections had for 'actually existing' Thatcherism and subsequently for the politics of the succeeding decade. Cumulative electoral outcomes do matter; winning office provides the opportunity for successful policy-seeking.

Given that a project can be pursued by strategic methods, the actions of the Thatcher and Major governments were neither entirely coherent nor incoherent: because, as Joel Wolfe suggests, '[t]he Thatcherite reform process grew deeper and wider over time',[11] it should be considered a long-term political project in continuous process. As it evolved (a key term), the specific form taken at various times may have appeared cautious if not contradictory. Although not always coherent, the Thatcher project was remarkably consistent, a linear process which utilised a variety of means to attempt to reorientate state, economy and polity in response to the crisis of the 1970s and (more particularly) in line with its chosen political beliefs and the ideological course these mapped out. In its search for a workable programme the government found itself pushing at a series of doors in the pursuit of a method.

An analogy of a man finding his way down a dark corridor in search of an exit may cast light on the Thatcherism-as-process thesis. Here, the unsighted man knows he wants to traverse the corridor (enacting the passage from A to B) and sets about doing so by feeling his way or groping about as he makes his passage. In the case of the Thatcherite government attempting to find its way in similar fashion, commentators such as Peter Riddell and, to a far lesser extent, David Marsh too often mistake their groping for a method to be nothing other than pragmatic manoeuvring. But the government knew where it would like to end up. As we will see in the next chapter, the politics of privatisation reflect this process as both a political issue and a matter of policy. Its origins and chronology may be considered with regard to the overall project of the Thatcher government. In exploring the emergence and course of the policy a number of metaphors may be mixed: the political agenda was set; the ball was rolling; and momentum was established.[12]

The politics of Thatcherism clearly reflect the ideological commitment the government sought to pursue over time. Collectively, ministers (many of whom were 'here today, gone tomorrow') had no easy or ready-made solutions to the problems they faced: they had to learn how to formulate and implement policy in the light of circumstances. Thatcher's ministers were often as event-driven as project-based. But when ministers found themselves obliged to respond to events their response was more likely to be a reflection of the ideological and political project their government had come to be identified with. Their ability to enact a policy which could secure the ends they sought was constrained by the circumstances they faced and the opportunities they were gifted.[13] Opportunity and chance were significant bedfellows of the Thatcherite project.

Thatcherite policy was at times *ad hoc* and the government may have cut its cloth to suit the electoral occasion but it rarely lost sight of the ultimate political goals it had identified as being its primary objectives (even if it was unable to meet all of them). Whereas institutional continuity is often the result of inertia, turning the government juggernaut is often easier said than done. Policy development requires preparation and usually takes time. The Thatcher administration was not working on a blank canvas. The job had to be assessed, existing workings effaced, the set-up made, the canvas primed, materials prepared and measurements taken. To get to point B the government had first to deal with being at point A, all the time aware that its primary function was to reach point B and not be content with point A: it takes time for the ship of state to turn. Firefighting is as much a feature of modern government as is refurbishment. Policy selection is as often reactive as it is proactive, an attempt to either seize the initiative or respond to events. Policy can be designed to prevent an unfavourable outcome as it can be to secure a favourable objective.

Explaining Thatcherism: objectives and consequences

Margaret Thatcher was initially interested in office not necessarily for its own sake, but for the powers it conferred and the opportunities it granted. In 1979, in imploring electors to not allow the Conservatives to 'pull everything up by the roots', Jim Callaghan conjured up a lurid image of a radical and extremist Conservative government prepared to reinvent Britain by turning the clock back to the 1930s. This last throw of the dice was an attempt by Callaghan to present himself as leader of a conservative, incremental, 'steady as she goes' party. In sharp contrast, Thatcher ran for office firmly against the status quo. Implicit within the somewhat cautious 1979 Tory election manifesto was the recognition of the necessity to make a break with existing practice, and this approach was strengthened in 1983 and 1987: while strongly disavowing any claims of extremism, Margaret Thatcher led a party which did indeed threaten, if it were at all possible, to make attempts to 'pull certain things up by the roots' in order to expiate the politics that ultimately found representational form not simply in the politics of Jim Callaghan but, more particularly, the Labour Party he led and the state over which he presided.

Thatcher claimed that Britain had to cope with a poisonous legacy of socialism which manifested itself in nationalisation, trade union power and a deeply rooted anti-enterprise culture. She pledged herself in office to rooting it out. The Thatcher government reflected a belief that post-war politics lay at the heart of Britain's problems; it had engendered the cumulative political and economic crisis and proved that corporatist state interventionism and semi-collectivist practices needed to be swept away. In 1975, Thatcher had questioned the 'progressive consensus'[14] that she believed had been shared to varying degrees both by members of all political parties and by commentators more generally. For her, this consensus had determined the course of post-war British politics and at its centre lay the belief that the state should be active on many fronts in curbing the autonomy of the free market by the use of public expenditure, progressive taxation and centrally financed public services.[15] Only eight months into her leadership, Thatcher argued that the expansion of the state was causing irreparable damage to the national economy: 'Government must therefore limit its activities where their scope and scale harm profits, investment, innovation and future growth. It must temper what may be socially desirable with what is economically reasonable.'[16]

Writing of the politics which characterised the post-war period, she commented: 'No theory of government was ever given a fairer test or a more prolonged experiment, yet it was a miserable failure.'[17] The Thatcherite agenda was as much a repudiation of the record of the Heath government as it was of Wilson and Callaghan, a view eventually reflected in Thatcher's *post hoc* recollection of her time in the Heath Cabinet between 1970 and 1974: 'Ted Heath's government... proposed and almost implemented the most radical form of socialism ever contemplated by an elected British government. It offered state control of prices and dividends and the joint oversight of economic policy by a tripartite body representing the Trades Union Congress, the Confederation of British Industry and the Government in return for trade union acquiescence in an economic policy.'[18] Over time the governments of Harold Macmillan and Alec Douglas-Home came also to be seen as part of the 'problem' diagnosed by the Thatcher governments. As a radical project, Thatcherism was as opposed to the philosophy of actually existing One Nation Conservatism as it was to the practical results of social democracy, and Thatcherites made little distinction between the two.[19]

Much was made of the fact that former Tory Prime Minister Harold Macmillan had once emphasised the desirability of a system based upon both private enterprise and collectivism: 'an industrial structure with the broad strategic control in the hands of the state and the tactical operation in the hands of private management, with public and private ownership operating side by side',[20] a view that was anathema to Thatcherites. For Keith Joseph, the 'middle ground' carved out in the post-war settlement had served to force the Conservative Party ever leftward as a result of a ratchet effect determined by the policies of state intervention and the mixed economy, which proved 'a slippery slope to socialism and state control'.[21] The 'middle ground moved continually to the left by its own internal dynamic' as Tory ministers followed where Labour predecessors led.

Joseph argued that Conservative governments of which he had been a member 'were inhibited because we had accepted these policies as the middle ground, so that to criticise them would be regarded as "immoderate", "right-wing", "breaking the consensus", "trying to turn the clock back", in short, unthinkable, taboo. So, instead of remedying the

causes, we tried to suppress symptoms.'[22] The crisis of state authority
the Conservative government had therefore to address was one of ineffective governance, itself a product of the failure of the post-war institutional and political framework. In 1976, Joseph suggested that Britain
was 'over-governed, over-spent, over-taxed and over-manned'. He spoke
of a 'socialist anti-enterprise climate' characterised by the 'indifference,
ignorance and distaste on the part of politicians, civil servants and
communicators for the process of wealth creation and entrepreneurship'.[23] The post-1975 proto-Thatcherites considered the UK to be
unsustainable without the national wealth created by the entrepreneurial spirit, a spirit in their view long stifled by the post-war British state
which steadily destroyed the rewards upon which it thrived.

In his attempts to set a new framework for Conservative politics in the
post-1974 period, Joseph drew a clear distinction between analysis and
policy-making: 'Analysis should be in advance of policies, for whereas
policies must be circumscribed by what is politically possible at any
given moment, what is politically possible is in turn determined by
the climate of opinion among other factors.'[24] Joseph saw the failure
of the Heath government as originating in its inability to successfully
fight the battle of ideas. The nascent Thatcherites thought that the
Conservatives should set out their stall and fight for their ideas unashamedly in both government and in opposition: 'The climate of
opinion . . . is shaped by the battle of ideas and by experience. If socialists, irrespective of their place in the spectrum, press their views
vigorously, while we defer to what we believe to be the middle ground
consensus, we lose the opportunity to achieve a more congenial climate
for what we will need to be doing in the future.'[25] After 1975, Thatcherism ran against the status quo, and the window of opportunity it needed
arrived as the status quo was ever more discredited.

Historically, the ideas for which Thatcherism stood reflected an anti-
social democratic project (where social democracy is defined as characterising the state project enacted over the previous forty years by all
governments), one defined just as much as what it was against as what it
was in favour of. In displacing social democracy as a state project
Thatcherism has helped usher in a new form of politics characterised
by a post-social-democratic neo-liberal ascendancy. Of course, Thatcherite policy changes must be put in context: in many ways its political
agenda was not revolutionary but reformist and a certain continuity
prevails amid much change.

In the 1990s, the state continues to do many of things it did in
the 1970s, although in certain policy areas it does these things very

differently. But Thatcherism has sought to successfully redress the balance between the public and the private spheres. Again, aspiration is different from achievement. Thatcherism wanted to alter the world it inherited and tried to do just that. In some policy areas the Thatcher government succeeded spectacularly in developing means to secure its designated ends; elsewhere it failed or else fell short of developing coherent or rational objectives. Policy development was often a reactive form of firefighting designed only to paper over cracks in the body politic or to secure short-term gain for the government.

Although Herbert Morrison could foolishly (and typically) claim that socialism is defined by whatever a Labour government does, the temptation to define Thatcherism as the end product of whatever the post-1979 Conservative Party did should be resisted. As an ideologically informed project, Thatcherism offered the means to alter political relations. To reiterate: Thatcherism was a reaction against a status quo, a 'mix of prejudices' with both positive and negative characteristics. It can be initially defined in terms of what it was against just as much as what it was in favour of. It popularly conceived itself as being against the political form that post-war politics had taken. At the very heart of Thatcherism was an anti-statist project concerned with rolling back the frontiers not of the state *per se* but of the actually existing 'social democratic' state.

Thatcherite Conservatives were not against the state; they believed in its use for purposes they supported – developing a neo-liberal approach to the economy and neo-conservative ends such as hierarchy, law and order, and secure defence. Thatcher personally denied the charge that she was an anarcho-conservative: 'Never let it be said that I am laissez faire. We are strong to do those things which government must do and only government can do.'[26] Defence expenditure soared under the Conservatives. In housing policy, Thatcher was personally implacably committed to the defence (if not extension) of mortgage tax relief, a state subsidy strongly opposed by the Treasury. Simon Jenkins describes mortgage tax relief as 'the most glaring instance of her belief in the dominance of politics over economics and of social policy over the free play of market forces'.[27] Geoffrey Howe, Nigel Lawson, even Nicholas Ridley, all unsuccessfully attempted to win Thatcher over to its abolition. As Jenkins makes clear, Thatcher had little objection to public sector housing or to housing subsidy. '[She] was devoting more public money, including tax relief, to housing in real terms when she left office than in 1981.'[28] She was pro-subsidy for private ownership and renting in the Housing Association sector but objected to the promotion of local authority state-owned council housing typified by the pre-1979 status quo. Through the right-to-buy scheme and the sale of council housing the Thatcher government encouraged home ownership at the expense of housing provided directly by the state through local government.

Andrew Gamble's distinction between the 'free economy' and the 'strong state' effortlessly captures this dichotomy.[29] As Gamble demonstrates, Thatcherite ministers were committed to active interventionist government in the pursuit of their political aims: 'The problem for the Thatcher government was that its own diagnosis of the crisis of state authority constantly impelled it toward intervention.'[30] Thatcherites frequently demonstrated a strong belief in the efficacy of the state as a mechanism to achieve certain economic, political (and military) ends; no Spencerian nightwatchman state for them. It was the ends to which the state was a means that distinguished elements of Thatcherism from its predecessors: the reordering of the public sphere lay at the heart of the Thatcherite agenda. Thus, David Marsh's advice to reject a unidimensional approach to Thatcherism is well taken.[31] The economic dimension to Thatcherism does not over-determine the political or the ideological; nor does any one facet limit the contribution others made to the overall phenomenon. Each is interrelated. Where one dimension predominates it did so in tandem with other facets of the Thatcherite character. Of course, the ideas of the New Right were 'far from irrelevant to the content of [its] political practice', as Desmond King puts it.[32]

The ultimate objective of Thatcherism in government was to use the state to promote neo-liberal reforms in economic strategy. This anti-corporatist strategy came over time to be characterised by privatisation, deregulation and commercialisation of the state sector; accepting the primacy of market forces in the governance of the economy and all state-centred activity; encouraging the growth of the City and inward and outward capital investment; a flexible labour market; legislative control over trade unions. Redefining the role of the state was a necessary consequence of this. If Thatcherism is one response to the supposed devaluation of the social democratic paradigm (as defined by its inability to deliver economic growth, full employment and welfare policies), it sought to reallocate the costs of economic decline and restore economic fortune. It attempted to do so by means of the existing state (for example, by curbing public expenditure) and then later sought to recast the state (where it could be recast) in as close a neo-liberal (i.e. non-social democratic) guise as was politically possible or administratively practicable. Thatcherite policy may not have been uniform but it was relatively consistent in the goals it set.

Thatcherite desires to recast the public sphere (at three levels: centre, periphery, and local) in time came to embrace a strategy to in part privatise the state, hiving off its social democratic appurtenances in the form of the nationalised industries and elements of the pre-1979 public sector. It was easier to hive off the public sector than it was to deal with local government. The public sector (at the periphery of the central state) was under the direct control of the centre where local government was not. Here, three related objectives can be identified:

1 Redefining the economic role of the state by dismantling its corporatist features.
2 Recasting the industrial form and political purposes of the state.
3 Recapturing for the central state control over the capacity of the state (which was to be exercised in a neo-liberal form).

Thatcherism's criticisms of the inherited post-war state was a strategy to arrest the politics of decline by curing the supposed ills of collectivism. Policy was a method to reform the state regime and secure alterations in its role and function, just as twentieth-century collectivism reformulated the role of the state to regulate the market in a social interest. In contrast, Thatcherism displayed a neo-liberal attitude to the state, conceiving of its role as being to empower the market in an economic interest and (where possible) in a social interest (in that order). It was as much 'anti-social-democrat' as it was 'pro-neo-liberal'. The negative agenda of Thatcherism is as significant as its positive agenda. It can be measured by what it is against just as much as what it was for: anti-corporatism; anti-trade union; anti-public enterprise; anti-Keynesian. The deregulation, commercialisation and privatisation of the state sector was part of a neo-liberal state project, a policy of partially disengaging the state from the established social democratic forms of economic management.

One principle above all others underpinned the Thatcherite approach to politics and therefore government: that a measure of economic liberalism required the direct role of the state in economic life to be limited so as to provide the maximum opportunity for the free market to determine the production, distribution and exchange of those goods and services the state was not obliged to provide. As Jessop *et al.* suggest, 'The hopes of radical Thatcherism rested on developing and confirming the entrepreneurial society and popular capitalism as a hegemonic alternative to the Keynesian [their phrase] welfare state.'[33]

Here, empowering the market required a redefinition of the purposes for which the state would intervene in the economy (for example, anti-inflation strategies rather than to secure full employment).

One former supporter of the New Right, John Gray, describes Thatcherism as 'a modernising project with profound and irreversible consequences for political life in Britain'. In his view its impact has been such that it 'has permanently changed the terms of political trade ... [and] ruled out any return either to traditional conservatism of the right – One Nation Toryism, say – or to social democracy – a species of Croslandism or of Owenism, perhaps – on the left. There can be no going back to Butskellism.'[34] In his view, the post-Thatcherite outlook is therefore one that has to take on board the realities of the present situation, an economy and polity reshaped by global forces with the result that 'Keynesian macroeconomic policies and the Bevridgean welfare state are pillars of a status quo ante that has been destroyed irrecoverably'.[35] While Gray's normative suggestions for reform of this status quo need not concern us, his argument that the social-democratic project 'belonged to a historical niche that is gone beyond hope of recovery'[36] does, given it is a view shared by mainstream political opinion.

Whatever else, the idea that 'the remains of social democracy [cannot] be salvaged from the ruins of Thatcherism' indicates that Thatcherism has redefined the nature of politics (even if Gray himself places more emphasis on the consequences of the global bond market than the activities of political actors and economic circumstances). The Thatcherite phenomenon is neither inevitable nor are its policy prescriptions more modern that the outdated nostrums of the social democratic paradigm. There are no such inevitabilities abroad in political life. The status quo 'actually existing' Thatcherism engendered (or, for more structuralist-minded analysts, that engendered it) is the starting point for any successor project of reform (or, more likely, the object of administration as well as incremental tinkering by successor governments). Rather than being a product of modernity, a historical inevitability, one that reflects 'trends in the world economy which no government directs or controls',[37] Thatcherism made itself at the same time it was made. It is precisely because the phenomenon variously derives from:

1 the successful application of ideological doctrine to
2 develop practical means to
3 secure identifiable ends, that Thatcherism made a major contribution to the fashioning of a new status quo.

In certain areas it succeeded, in others it failed – overall, it managed to renegotiate the constraints it faced but only in a limited fashion.

Despite its many failures and unintended consequences, Thatcherism helped redefine 'the art of the possible', and its actual consequence (as opposed to being its identified objective) is:

4   The establishment of a neo-liberal economic and political agenda as the dominant paradigm to characterise British politics.

Having run with the grain of ideological developments (if against that of many political demands), the argument that the legacy of Thatcherism lies in a reconstructed 'state project' is an impressive one. For the most part experience shows that most past Cabinet Ministers are totally unaware of what an 'accumulation strategy' was and unsure if they were in favour of it or not.[38] But while there are a number of problems with the terms that state theorists employ (not necessarily the concept they denote), this position goes some way to accepting the fact that Thatcherism reflected an altered ideological discourse, one which encouraged the process of political change; its most potent appeal being the claim that there was or is no alternative to its vision of society. Its consequences are such that the ideals and prescriptions of the New Right have come to dominate the ideological playing field in terms of political economy and the distinction between the antonyms of state and market, individualism and collectivism. It is in the impact that Thatcherism has had on both practical politics and the political elite (none more so than its chief party political opponent) that it has had its greatest influence. The strategy of the Conservative Party was to win elections and implement policy. If it could make ideological converts among electors, all well and good; if not, securing office was the important aim.

Hegemony, as an explanation of Thatcherism conceptualised by Stuart Hall, has to engage with the political, electoral and economic objectives of the phenomenon rather than satisfy itself with an abstract theory of ideology wrongly suggesting that the success of Thatcherism lay entirely in its reconstruction of the political attitudes of civil society. It did not. Thatcherism did however succeed in remaking elite discourse: it fashioned a political agenda informed by neo-liberalism, creating proto-Thatcherites many of whom may well be politically active until, say, the year 2030. While the Conservative Party may be exhausted, Thatcherism continues apace. The Conservatives were, at one level, only a vehicle for the type of politics it was keen to enumerate.

In accepting that politics was indeed an 'art of the possible', the Thatcher government deployed a radical strategy often enacted (but not always) by pragmatic tactics; a flexible response' in which, once the government had determined to strike out in a particular direction, prescriptive remedies were introduced according to time and circumstances. All the time a common purpose underpinning government activity in the round was clearly at work. As Shirley Letwin suggests, most critics and supporters alike agree that 'Thatcherism amounts to something and that it has been going somewhere, or at any rate trying to go somewhere'.[39] Indeed, in identifying several objectives and a series of means to secure these designated ends, the Thatcher and Major governments discovered many others on their journey (and in so doing constructed different means to reach other identified ends). As such, leading Thatcherite actors began their careers in government in 1979 with (1) an awareness of what they believed was wrong with the Britain they had been elected to govern, and (2) an appreciation of the general direction in which they would like to steer the ship of state. Although they had the aspiration to reach a destination (and had an ideological perspective to structure their appreciation of it) they did not in 1979 (or in 1983) know how to get to where they would like to be, let alone know if it would be possible to get there.

As argued above, because Thatcherism is an inherently unsatisfactory term an initial distinction should be made between Thatcher and Thatcherism; between Thatcherism and Thatcherite; between neo-liberalism and neo-conservatism; and between policy arising from 'design' or 'project' and that which was 'accident' or 'pragmatism'. Five elements of Thatcherism combined to drive it forward as a political project after 1979:

1 a response to economic and political crisis;
2 a reaction against the political status quo;
3 an identified political objective (a strong state restoring the autonomy of the governing centre); which was coterminous with
4 electoral objectives (a strong state dominated by the Conservative Party).

As a programme to secure these objectives, Thatcherism was informed by:

5 a series of New Right ideological prescriptions, the success (in broad terms) of which benefited from the opportunities granted it by a discredited status quo.

Gradually, after 1979, Thatcherism came into its own. Policy development not only reflected these five elements but was also heavily influenced by questions of political and technical feasibility and electoral desirability. Thatcherite policies were shaped by political actors at the same time as they were the product of a developmental process; political actors learnt from experience and grew more bold in their approach. While the Thatcher period is one of immense change, commentators need to appreciate the continuities as well as the discontinuities. However, a great many policy reforms of the Thatcher and Major governments were indeed novel and new. Such was the force of the Thatcherite tide (and the ideological wind that helped propel it forward), that the mould of the political agenda was to be broken. During the course of the 1980s left-wing socialism was defeated; the collectivist values of reformist social democracy (temporally or permanently) were deemed irrelevant to the real needs of the modern world; the Tory 'wets' were routed; and Labour was cast into the political wilderness. In the century-long tension between individualism and collectivism, individualism advanced while collectivism retreated.

While few, if any, political actors possess a master plan, Thatcherite policy often reflected the political, ideological and economic initiatives of the Thatcher and Major governments. Naturally, timing, personality, circumstance and chance all played their significant part in explaining the policy change. The form a policy such as, say, privatisation took was certainly not devised by the Conservatives in opposition prior to being carried out in government. While it is wrongheaded to overestimate the coherence and the consistency of privatisation in its early years, it is equally misguided to suggest that the policy was the product of circumstance or else the result of a lucky accident. In short, privatisation demonstrates the preparedness of Thatcherite actors to take steps to liberalise the free market as the means to roll back the frontier of the social democratic state

Privatisation was claimed by its advocates to enhance individual freedom, make enterprise more responsive to the demands of the customer, decrease the public debt, weaken the power of trade unions and force industry to face the realities of the market place. It was the flagship of the much heralded 'enterprise culture' that ministers took office to promote, an innovation 'generally regarded as the textbook case of Thatcherite policy'.[40] As with other such examples, privatisation policy should therefore be considered in the light of the interaction between two variables: firstly, an ideologically based economic solution (New Right prescriptions for a new capital accumulation regime) and, secondly, a political opportunity (the legitimation crisis of social democratic politics). These two variables were mediated by a third, the political leadership necessary for any willing entrepreneur to pursue a series of objectives for political and electoral purposes. Hence, as did Thatcherism, privatisation developed as a process over time. Whereas thinking about what needed to be done was necessary, devising the actual means to secure the desired end was much more difficult. With regard to privatisation, the Conservative government faced the age-old dilemma confronting all serious political actors: put crudely, having decided (or, at worst discovered) where they wanted to go, ministers had to discover how and if they could actually get there.

To recap: Political and electoral factors external to government were a series of specific constraints on a policy initiative. A second set of constraints concerned political and administrative factors internal to government. Electoral politics, the internal politics of the government, and the administrative practicality of the reforms all impacted upon what the government could do, could not do, and what it actually did in regard to privatisation. Together these factors acted as a series of 'filtering mechanisms' that limited the ambitions of the Thatcher and Major governments. Whatever their changing tactics, the overall strategy of the Conservative Party remained constant. Despite the short-term vagaries of political life (even in the dark days of 1981 and 1984–6), privatisation is an example of a new policy advanced by a set of political actors who grasped the opportunities granted them. The perceived decline of the UK within the global economy encouraged the Conservative government to pursue the ideologically based free-market solutions they had come to favour. Central to this task was the overthrow of key assumptions which had informed the institutional framework upon which post-war political life had for so long rested. For proponents of Thatcherism the primary task was to roll back the frontiers of the social democratic state.

Under the tutelage of successive Conservative governments, neo-liberal prescriptions were to become for the 1990s what social democracy had been for the 1950s. Neo-liberalism was a philosophical doctrine utilised by the Thatcher leadership in its campaign against the supposed evils of the post-war collectivist state and its supposedly socialist works. The experience of the 1970s were the formative years of Thatcherism (as with its political alter ego, 'Bennism') while the 1980s proved the occasion to put ideas into effect in the form of policy. The proof of the pudding is in the post-Thatcherite eating: the political agenda of contemporary politics has altered and, in the context of the

UK, this is in large part the result of Thatcherism (as agency reflecting structural imperatives, a project enacted as a process over time). These changes did not happen automatically nor by chance. Although engineered under favourable circumstances with a fair wind and a generous tide, Thatcherism 'worked' because 'socialism' (read: social democracy) was deemed to have failed and Labour's 'Bennite' alternative was rejected. The Thatcherites won a short-term battle of ideas fought out on a political terrain influenced by strategic imperatives and short- or long-term events, judgements and decisions. A political agenda informed by neo-liberalism prospered as social democracy withered. In the war of ideas fought out in the twenty-five years after 1973, the politics favoured by contemporary Conservatism won out over the alternatives brought to bear against it. This is where the impact of Thatcherism is to be felt most keenly. The long-term influence of the politics it pursued is a result of the impact of Thatcherism as process, a political project simultaneously informed by an ideological doctrine and constrained by the dictates of statecraft, one eager to enact policy to reconfigure both state and society but responsive to political realities and electoral pressures.

5
Modernisation: The Transformation of the Labour Party

At the 1997 general election, Labour returned from the political wilderness. Its electoral landslide gifting it a Commons majority of 179, the largest in the party's history on 44.4 per cent of votes cast. None the less, with key exceptions involving the constitutional reform, Europe and supply-side modernisation, the agenda of the incoming Labour government reflects policies pursued by the Thatcher and Major governments. Political values preached by Conservative ministers – enterprise, self reliance, anti-statism – find contemporary reflection in the speeches of Labour ministers. The liberalisation of the market economy; the privatisation of nationalised industries, utilities and public sector companies; the divestment of public housing; the introduction of market liberalism to both the public sector and the non-market public sector; the binding of trade unions; the erosion of local government all collectively represented the wide-ranging redefinition of British political life engineered in the 1980s and 1990s and so serve to structure what Labour in government does.

Indeed, in sharp contrast to its past appeals, Labour's 1997 Manifesto echoed the economic priorities outlined in the 1979 Conservative Manifesto. Then the Tories committed themselves to: controlling inflation as first priority; curbing public expenditure; reducing the level of public borrowing; opposition to increases in direct taxation; restoring incentives to business and enterprise; and regulating trade union activities. In endorsing this the Blair government has taken up the economic objectives of the Thatcher and Major governments organised around four primary areas of policy reform: (1) Ensuring financial stability by promoting sound money and placing the reduction of inflation at the heart of both monetary and fiscal policy; (2) Placing the market at the centre of economic life through deregulation and the rejection of direct state intervention; (3) Privatisation of state-owned industries and utilities so withdrawing the state from direct control over economic activity; (4) Controlling trade union activity by legislation and (together with other measures) so disciplining the labour market.

The long march from the Labour Party led by Michael Foot to that led by Tony Blair is usefully explored in terms of a gradual, staged process altering Labour's programmatic stance and stated political objectives. Labour's transformation was born of a belief that the second, third and fourth successive Conservative victories in 1983, 1987 and 1992 illustrated a deep crisis facing Labour and the left of British politics, which meant that the party had to change and change quickly. Where the 1983 appeal came to be considered as dangerous and extremist, one that supposedly promised 'no compromise with the electorate', that of 1992 and 1997 were considered more suitable to offer Labour an electoral key to access the corridors of Whitehall. The period 1983–97 is one in which explanations of the changing Labour Party are to be found and understood; taken in the round Labour did not so much change or modernise itself as it was changed by the impact of events. In short, where Thatcherism has led, the Labour Party of Kinnock, Smith and Blair followed.

Modernisation: the extent of Labour's transformation

Labour's experience of defeat in 1983 is often suggested as a defining moment in the party's contemporary history, but pre-1983 is important in understanding what followed. The 1979–83 period saw a dramatic reaction to the 1979 defeat and the governmental record that preceded it in 1974–9. A left-wing-sponsored grassroots revolt was fuelled by trade union discontent with the Callaghan leadership. Headed by Tony Benn, who had opposed the direction of the Wilson and Callaghan governments from within the Cabinet, the Labour left wanted to commit the party to radical pledges to dramatically take British politics to the left. Whatever else may be said about the so-called 'Bennite' left (as problematic a term as Thatcherism), it too was a 'modernising' movement, one keen to advance a programmatic agenda and put right past failings evidenced in Labour's record in office in 1964–70 and 1974–9. In its own way, Benn's argument was as radical as that offered by Thatcher: Labour had failed because its tried and tested prescriptions were no longer up to the job; by itself the existing mixed economy and public expenditure had proved illusory at a time Labour widely believed that capitalism was no longer capable of sustaining the welfare politics upon which post-war Britain depended; actually existing moderate social democracy had proved far too cautious for Labour to deal with the political and economic crisis it faced. The proposed approach was a root-and-branch rejection of everything the Thatcher Cabinet stood for.

The National Executive Committee (NEC) and the Labour Conference came to represent alternative power bases to the Parliamentary leadership. Encouraged by the weakness of the Labour leadership and a demoralised right wing (the two being virtually synonymous), the 'Bennite' left pursued policy changes hand in hand with far-reaching constitutional amendments to secure the predominance of the extra-Parliamentary party by limiting the powers of the Parliamentary leadership. Faced with the perceived necessity to ensure its leaders would deliver on policy promises in the future, the left organised around a constitutional agenda embracing the mandatory reselection of MPs; the election of the leader and deputy leader under a wider electoral franchise comprising party members, trade union affiliates and Labour MPs; and granting control of the party manifesto to the Executive at the expense of the Cabinet or the Shadow Cabinet.[1]

These were all devices to bind the parliamentary leadership to the wider party and to ensure that Conference policy would be implemented by a future Labour government. The first two were successful by 1981, the third failed; in the event none would prove to have the significance many left activists had placed in them. With the exception of reselection these constitutional proposals were extremely moderate despite the excitement they generated at the time. By 1997 even the Conservative Party has committed itself to involving its membership in future leadership contests. Of course, at the time many of the proposed changes dealt with the likelihood of eventually changing the composition of the Parliamentary Party: reselection in theory could provide for the replacement of right-wing Labour MPs by left-wing party activists. Also, the extension of the franchise for the election of the leader was intended by many advocates to grant Tony Benn (or another left-winger) a greater advantage in any leadership contest given his disadvantage were any election to be confined to the right-of-centre Parliamentary Party. In the event this advantage was to be conferred not on Benn but on Neil Kinnock in 1983.

As is well known, Callaghan's government was the subject of heavy criticism from all sections of the Labour movement after 1979. The Parliamentary leadership was held to account for past misdemeanours perceived by the party at large. By winning trade union support the constituency-based left made the running at Labour Conferences between 1977 and 1982, typified by the adoption of unilateral nuclear disarmament and withdrawal from the then EEC as policy in 1980. Of course, the adoption of the Alternative Economic Strategy had long been party policy (while it had not been supported by the Wilson or Callaghan governments) and, although Labour's adoption of unilateralism was out of keeping with its traditional stance on defence matters (the party had only briefly supported unilateralism in 1960–1), Europe was never a clear-cut left–right issue. Conference had opposed joining the EEC in 1971 by a majority of 5:1 and, despite the majority of the Labour Cabinet being in favour of continuing membership, had supported withdrawal in the 1975 referendum by a 2:1 majority. As the left made the running, the Labour right was very much on the defensive. His authority weakened by his ejection from office, Jim Callaghan and his supporters found themselves in a minority on the NEC and at the Conference. Able only to object to its decisions rather than influence its deliberations, they were incapable of seizing Labour's internal agenda.

Once Callaghan finally stood down as leader in October 1980 Michael Foot surprisingly beat Denis Healey for the succession. Foot, a man of the left who had drifted to the centre for reasons of party unity, owed his margin of victory to the fact that Healey was thought too divisive by a number of his natural supporters. Callaghan timed his departure to forstall the election of any successor under the wider franchise to be agreed at a one-day Conference in January 1981; in particular he wanted to deny Tony Benn a successful run at the leadership. Aware he could not win any election confined to Labour MPs, Benn declined to stand for the leadership and backed Foot against Healey, but once the electoral college for leadership elections was established he sought the deputy leadership, the consolation prize gifted Healey the previous autumn. Widely portrayed as a battle for Labour's soul, the contest which ensued between Healey, *bête noire* of the left, and Benn, brought about an extended period of vicious Labour infighting which greatly exacerbated internal party tensions. Despite his efforts and his command of the support of Labour activists, Benn lost very narrowly by a margin of less that one per cent. While Benn's challenge had been welcomed by the broad left coalition he had assembled, it did divide the Tribune Group and helped create a group of 'inside leftists' led by Neil Kinnock. Their abstention in the deputy leadership ballot provided Healey's narrow victory.[2]

Labour's year of living dangerously, 1981, also saw the widely predicted defections of Labour's 'hard right' led by the self-styled 'gang of three', David Owen, Shirley Williams and Bill Rodgers, in concert with

Labour's longstanding would-be leadership contender, Roy Jenkins (then coming to the end of his time as President of the European Commission). In examining the origins of the SDP, Anthony King and Ivor Crewe quickly identify the Labour left (particularly the 'far left – the Trotskyites and their allies'[3]) as a significant element in bringing about the defection of some 10 per cent of the Parliamentary Labour Party. Variously describing elements of the Labour left as 'extremists' ('thuggish' extremists to boot, forming an 'unpleasant' 'mob' which 'appalled and disgusted' the Labour right, particularly 'passionate anti-totalitarians'[4]), King and Crewe none the less conclude that the principal objection of the would-be defectors was the influence that the broader Labour left had within the party: the policy and constitutional changes were not brought about by Trotskyists (of whichever persuasion) or by other would-be revolutionaries but by 'trade union leaders and constituency activists who held more or less traditional Labour-left opinions and who naturally wanted to see them become party policy... the shift to the left was what the majority of Labour Party members wanted'.[5] Clearly, the phenomenon of 'Bennism' did have deep roots within the broader Labour movement and as a result Labour's left-wing credentials were widely recognised in the early 1980s.

The contemporary modernisation thesis requires a belief that in 1983 Labour reaped the electoral consequences of straying from its programmatic traditions.[6] However the 1983 manifesto is not the aberration it is often presented as. Shorn of its defence and foreign policy commitments it does not mark a dramatic or sudden leftward shift in the party's practice compared to its developing policy stance of 1970–9; it did, however, sit ill with the record of the 1974–9 Labour governments (and the 1979 manifesto written by Callaghan and his adviser Tom McNally). The post-1979 economic and social policy stance was enacted within Labour's ideological tradition even if it marked a significant shift to the left. Labour's stance (adopted as much in response to the Thatcher government as a reaction to the perceived failures of the Callaghan and Wilson administrations) grew out of an incrementalist process that acknowledged the deficiency of actually existing social democracy and a need to modernise the reformist socialism established in the revisionist debates of the 1950s and 1960s. Arising from Labour's unsatisfactory experience of office in 1964–70 (and later 1974–9), Labour shifted leftward, as illustrated by the policy stances outlined after 1970 in *Labour's Programme 1973*; the February and October 1974 manifestos; *Labour's Programme 1976*. Both the interim 'manifestos' *Peace, Jobs, Freedom, Labour's Programme 1982*, and the 1983 manifesto clearly marked a shift to the left but were still drawn from the same ideological universe as, say, the February 1974 manifesto.

Despite the divisions and infighting which characterised the fightback of the Labour right against the left at this time, it is important to emphasise that Labour in opposition after 1979, left, right and centre, totally rejected the prescriptions of the Thatcher government. Its opposition to Thatcherism ran deep, and whatever differences divided 'moderate' and 'Bennite' Labour in terms of their alternative to the Thatcher government, outright hostility to all its works clearly united the party. Labour politicians such as Foot and Neil Kinnock, firmly of the left (although not as left as others within the party or the parliamentary party), were fully committed to an anti-Thatcher and, in essence, 'anti-Callaghan' left-wing appeal. In sharp contrast to the Thatcherite agenda, Labour's post-1979 economic policy reaffirmed a state-centric economic alternative, one that would manage the market economy by providing a framework to restrain capital and harness its power in order to solve social and economic problems. Rather than being the demand for a Soviet-style command economy it is often portrayed as, Labour's economic policy was to be enacted within a market framework. As Eric Shaw suggests: 'Labour's programme in 1983 amounted to a move toward accepting a predominantly privately owned economy, albeit one which subjected market forces to a complex system of state regulation.'[7] It was an approach which contained well-aired traditional Labour policy measures such as public-sector-led reflation, a corporatist state strategy, an interventionist industrial policy based upon government planning, competitive public ownership, and increased levels of public expenditure.[8]

While much has been made of the 1983 manifesto, the so-called 'longest suicide note in history', Labour's unashamedly left-of-centre economic programme was not fundamentally at odds with the general stance of Labour's Shadow Cabinet (with its right-wing non-'Bennite' majority) and the TUC General Council. Despite the continuing concerns of the Parliamentary Party (the redoubt of the Labour right not affected by the rise of the left), mainstream politicians like Denis Healey, Roy Hattersley and Peter Shore, then Shadow Chancellor, although extremely hostile to the 'Bennite' Left (and, invariably, Benn himself) and to policies such as unilateral nuclear disarmament, were broadly supportive of the economic programme of 1983 (if critical of the emphasis placed on expanding public ownership, planning agreements, disengagement from the then EEC, and other radical positions associated with an Alternative Economic Strategy). Whatever else divided them, left and right, Shadow Cabinet and backbenchers alike were committed to expanding the public sector, extending the welfare state and returning to full employment; 'getting more and spending a great deal' through taxation and borrowing was an integral part of Labour's economic case.

The left were to reap the whirlwind of Labour's landslide defeat in June 1983, a defeat which marked the beginning of the end for their campaign to refound the Labour Party. In hindsight, Tony Benn's narrow defeat for the deputy leadership in 1981 was both the highpoint of the left's fortunes and the beginning of the Labour right's successful efforts to claw back authority stripped away in earlier years. Under Michael Foot's successor, Neil Kinnock (and, in time, Tony Blair), both the organisational structures of the party and its policy and doctrine were transformed. The left was gradually weakened and its power within the party gradually whittled away; denied a majority on the NEC, its Conference base was slowly eroded and it was completely marginalised within the Parliamentary Party. As the left retreated, a revitalised Labour right (its ranks ever swollen by 'realigning' former leftists) advanced. By the late 1980s, Labour had gradually altered the cast of its policy. As a result, in contrast to past appeals, the party acknowledged that the role of the state in the economy should be confined to the provision of the fiscal and monetary conditions required to enable the market to facilitate economic activity.

Committed to 'enhancing the dynamic of the market, not undermining it',[9] Tony Blair has made it clear that excessive taxing, borrowing and spending were all things of the past as Labour ruled out increasing both personal tax rates and public expenditure in 1995–7. Building on the 1991 pledge of the Kinnock Shadow Cabinet that a Labour government would not 'spend or promise to spend what the country cannot afford', Labour under Blair firmly accepted the taxation and expenditure projections of the Conservative government in fiscal years 1997–8 and 1998–9. So-called 'tax and spend' policies, for so long the identified evils of Mrs Thatcher's political world view in the 1970s and 1980s, came also to be identified Labour's leadership in the 1990s as economic problems, no longer solutions.

Labour's transformation reflects a seemingly irreversible shift in the balance of power in favour of right-reformist neo-liberal politics at the expense of left-reformist social democratic politics. Its extent is illustrated by the changes wrought in Labour's ideological outlook and evidenced in policy. This long-drawn-out process of change was characterised by piecemeal and gradual policy qualification followed by revision in the 1983, 1987 and 1992 Parliaments. Labour's policy saw a dramatic alteration in its attitude to the changes brought about by the Thatcher government. Where Martin J. Smith defines this transformation as 'a post-Keynesian revisionism...for a different era which has learnt the lessons of the 1970's',[10] Eric Shaw more correctly suggests that the period saw 'the abandonment of Keynesian social democracy in favour of pre-Keynesian orthodoxy'.[11] Labour has come to embrace the arm's-length regulated market economy it was once pledged to directly manage and control.

Although cast in the guise of modernisation, the broad economic appeal outlined by 'New' Labour has little historical purchase on 'Old' Labour. Although it retains some affinity with 'Old' Labour, its policy far more closely reflects the preconceptions and prescriptions of the Thatcher and Major governments. In both 1979–83 and (to a far lesser extent) 1983–7, Labour's economic policy was geared toward providing for full employment and better quality public services through government-led reflation, direct management of the economy and an expanded public sector. Between 1983 and 1987, Shadow Chancellor Roy Hattersley demonstrated a marked bias 'in favour of public expenditure rather than personal tax cuts'.[12] A private Shadow Cabinet paper in July 1986 underlined Labour's commitment: 'The social, economic and political advantages of our proposals is that they will finance substantial improvements in health, education, environment and local government programmes as well as reducing unemployment.'[13] Here, as Hattersley later spelled out, Labour's position could be summed up in the phrase: 'Increased public expenditure good; public expenditure cuts bad.'[14]

This economic approach would win a Labour MP few friends at the top of today's party in government: such is the transformation wrought in the party, similar observations now find no echo inside 'New' Labour's high command. Rather than just repudiating 'Bennism', Labour now casts aside policy advocated by the most right-wing members of 'Old' Labour. The personal manifesto issued by Denis Healey in his defence of the deputy leadership against the challenge of Tony Benn in 1981 now makes interesting reading: Healey, a permanent fixture on Labour's right, committed himself four square behind Labour's then 'planned socialist alternative', calling for 'real increases in public expenditure' to 'implement an alternative economic strategy', the centrepiece of which would be 'the restoration of full employment'. In the international sphere, this committed Atlanticist described himself as a 'genuine disarmer' willing to support 'the cancellation of Trident' and the 'reduction of the level of defence expenditure'.[15] These traditional Labour commitments, all firmly within the party mainstream in 1981, were all explicitly cast aside by the Labour Party in the late 1980s and 1990s.

A sharply contrasting new economic discourse dominates Labour politics today, one 'articulated in the language of competition, efficiency, productivity, economic dynamism, profitability, and, above all, that of individual choice and self-fulfilment in the context of a market economy'.[16] Although concerned at the rhetorical level with the promotion of social justice (in common with all serious office-seeking parties in liberal democracies), 'New' Labour is principally concerned with strengthening the power of capital and allowing competition within the market to secure social reforms by virtue of 'trickle down' economics. Blair's designated image for his Labour Party is that it is a party for and of business, one that is 'safe', 'prudent' and 'sensible'; not 'extremist', 'dangerous', 'reckless', or 'profligate'. 'New' Labour today is careful to present itself as a party of an ill-defined centre, no longer a party of the left.[17] In economic terms the party has redefined its task as 'improving' the status quo entrenched by Thatcherism in office since 1979, not reforming the prevailing economic system let alone bring about a 'fundamental and irreversible shift in the balance of wealth and power in favour of working people and their families' promised (but not delivered) in the 1974 manifesto.

For the moment, one additional example may suffice to illustrate the extent of Labour's departure from past practice. In September 1985, a number of Tribune Group MPs argued the need for Labour to 'restate, develop and argue for socialist values in a way that can build popular support and convince the electorate that socialism is relevant to the problems of modern Britain'.[18] In suggesting that 'Economic power must be made publicly accountable through a system of social ownership, planning and industrial democracy, not merely to make the economy more efficient but to restructure it so that power and wealth are used for the public good rather than for a few individuals', this initiative would now be considered deeply unfashionable. Part of the effort of a 'soft' Labour left to distinguish themselves from the 'hard' left, the statement was signed by a number of present-day 'Blairites', among them Gordon Brown (of course better defined as a 'Brownite'), then a junior front bench spokesperson and Labour Chancellor of the Exchequer after 1997.[19]

The name of Tony Blair, although he certainly qualified as a realigning member of the Tribune Group, is notable for its absence. This statement was published in the Conference edition of *Tribune* and carried next to a two-page interview with Neil Kinnock. In addition it also declared a 'determination to disengage immediately from the nuclear arms race' and that 'Britain should retain the option of withdrawal from the EEC'.[20] In addition to Brown, other principal signatories to this declaration who held prominent positions in Tony Blair's Labour new government include: Margaret Beckett, David Blunkett, Robin Cook, Harriet Harman, Clare Short, Chris Smith, Gavin Strang (all members of the 1997 Labour Cabinet), three Ministers of State, Michael Meacher, Derek Fatchett and Mark Fisher. Labour's General Secretary in 1997, Tom Sawyer, and the current Chair of the Parliamentary Party, Clive Soley were also signatures. Indeed, in 1986, as a rising junior member of the Treasury team, Tony Blair argued that Labour should advocate 'a fairer distribution of taxation to ensure redistribution of wealth away from the wealthiest of our community to the poorest'.[21] It is inconceivable that Blair would advance this case today. Indeed, not only does he now argue the opposite: he makes a political virtue of so doing. Blair-led Labour eschews 'old style' redistribution based upon tax and spend policies; instead it is public committed to a low tax economy. At the 1997 election, Blair presented himself as 'the entrepreneur's champion'[22] and issued a 20-page 'Manifesto for Business' promising 'stable prices with an inflation target of 2.5 per cent or less, coupled with tough rules on borrowing and spending, and no rises in income tax'.[23]

In 1975, Margaret Thatcher's argument that government must temper what may be socially desirable with what is economically reasonable,[24] now finds a great deal of purchase within the Blair government. With regard to policy change, the issue of public ownership offers a useful case study with which the transition from 'Old' to 'New' Labour can be mapped out. In opposition during the 1979, and, to a lesser extent, the 1983 and 1987 Parliaments, Labour's economic stance reflected its continuing desire to extend public ownership and defend the existing public sector from the growing encroachment of Thatcher-led privatisation. This firmly held position altered between 1983 and 1997 as Labour came to reject public ownership, qualify its opposition to privatisation, and abandon its commitment to re-nationalisation. Where Labour's earlier stance evidenced its long-established ideological and practical attachment to the public sector, Labour moved to embrace a great many of the Thatcherite reforms it originally opposed tooth and nail.

From realignment through review: modernisation and 'New' Labour

In 1993, reviewing his time as party leader, Neil Kinnock intimated that he early on wanted to initiate changes in Labour's policy, a task supposedly identified in 1983 as part of a grand strategy to set the party back on a road to electability and moderation.[25] In fact, the historical record belies this claim: indeed, rather than being determined to immediately revise Labour's programme, Kinnock, in running for the leadership, declared 'I do not believe that our current body of policies needs major addition.'[26] With the exception of Labour's determined anti-EEC stance, nor did he propose any major subtraction. Under his leadership (and that of Tony Blair), Labour's withdrawal from positions previously staked out was neither sudden nor immediate. His later claims notwithstanding, Kinnock did not have such a plan to make these and other changes in 1983. The changes which came were both gradual and incremental; a cumulative process in no way part of some grand 1983 super-revisionist design, a strategy which did not exist at that point in time.

In detailing Labour's general shift away from its stance of the early 1980s, the years 1983, 1985 and 1987 stand out. The impact of the 1983 reversal set in only slowly as Labour quietly digested the extent of its defeat. It is in the general period embracing the 1983, 1987 and 1992 Parliaments that Labour's transformation can be mapped out. The immediate years following the 1983 election saw the beginning of the end of the 'Bennite' ascendancy. Internal political changes ultimately granted Neil Kinnock and his Shadow Cabinet and National Executive allies the executive authority they required to cautiously strike out to Labour's right. Rather than come to the leadership with a clear programme of reform, Kinnock ran as a candidate of the left in 1983 (albeit of a non-Bennite variety). Presenting himself as a younger and media-friendly version of Michael Foot, the new leader was to move from the 'soft left' to the Labour 'right' following his candidature for the leadership, when he had previously emotionally associated with Foot's policies.[27]

In November 1986, Margaret Thatcher gave an interview to the *Financial Times* dismissing Labour as an unreedemable socialist party and declaring her lofty intention to finish off socialism once and for all: 'I think you could get another realignment in British politics...after two more Tory victories.'[28] Tony Benn, when asked in conversation with another Labour MP if he had read Thatcher's quote, commented: 'Yes, but I think she'll have a job to outdo Kinnock.'[29] Challenged for being defeatist, Benn replied he was merely 'being realistic'.[30] This exchange demonstrated how the internal realignment within the Labour Party was perceived as early as 1986–7. Benn's dissatisfaction arose from his political disagreement with Kinnock and the leader's eagerness to side-line the Chesterfield MP in leading Labour circles. Benn's marginal-isation grew with Kinnock's determination to re-establish the leadership's executive command over the party. Both were greatly assisted by the emergence of a 'New Realist' current within the party and the disintegration of the Labour left that had coalesced behind policy reforms and Benn's candidacy for the deputy leadership in 1981. Labour's post-1979 left–right divisions greatly diminished in the face of the precarious electoral position in which the Party saw itself. The rise of a 'soft-left/right' coalition encompassing elements of the Tribune Group with the traditional Labour right inside the Parliament-ary Party was decisive. In addition, as Lewis Minkin argues, 'the TUC leadership sought to give full support to the parliamentary leadership . . . as it became axiomatic that the political running must be left to [this] parliamentary leadership'.[31] Central to these development was the defeat of the 1984–5 miners' strike and the abortive Labour campaign against ratecapping in 1985 which, for many, served to underline a weaknesses of the traditional left. The de-polarisation of party disputes was accompanied by a significant recomposition of internal factions following the 1983 defeat. These, in the wake of the apparent unstop-pable march of Thatcherism, all made significant contributions to the reassertion of leadership authority over the party.

Labour's gradual shift to the right was neatly symbolised by the expul-sion first of Militant and later of other elements of the left in 1985–6 and post-1987 (building on the proscription of the Tendency under Michael Foot in 1982–3[32]). Kinnock's strengthening opposition to the Labour left served also to pave his shift to the right. He appeared to relish taking on the various sacred cows of the left, denouncing what he saw as its timidity and its total lack of realism, setting up Tony Benn and the NUM leader Arthur Scargill as 'enemies within' to be denied office or influ-ence; 'bogeymen' whose isolation would itself prove Labour's new-found moderation and electability. After 1985, the emergence of an 'anti-hard left soft-left', illustrated by the shifting allegiances of Tom Sawyer, David Blunkett and Michael Meacher on the party's NEC, helped the leadership gradually establish a command over the party.[33] Its authority derived from an extended leader's office and the Shadow Cabinet backed up by the then very important NEC (on which Kinnock and later Blair established a reliable and ever increasing majority); a party headquarters (increasingly peopled with Kinnock and later Blair supporters); and the Party Conference where support from leading trade unions was ever more forthcoming after 1987.

Efforts to command the party were often thwarted by an insecurity born of a belief that the leadership may prove unable to carry the day at a Labour Conference. The principal occasions of Kinnock's defeat included: attempted changes to the re-selection of MPs (a move from a mandatory to a voluntary system) in 1984; his inability to stem the tide of support in support of the Scargill-led NUM in 1984–5; and Conference support for an amnesty for victimised and sacked miners and retrospective reimbursement of the NUM for fines levied over the duration of the strike in 1985. Apart from rebuffs arising from the Conference's desire to reduce the UK's defence expenditure to the Western European average in 1989, 1990 and 1991, the only major defeat Kinnock suffered between 1987 and 1991 was over his attempt to revise unilateralism in 1988 (he succeeded the following year). The authority of the Parliamentary leadership was at first necessarily limited and much effort was spent in internal coalition-building and constructing majorities on key party bodies. Kinnock's ability to lead were to be determined by the opportunities he had to successfully agenda set within his own party. These were at first limited, but after 1985–7 'the leader had acquired a grip on the party machinery which was an indispensable precondition for any fundamental change of course',[34] a process which has reached an apogee under Tony Blair's leadership: at the 1995, 1996 and 1997 Party Conferences Blair was undefeated (save for the membership's refusal to elect Peter Mandelson to the NEC in 1997), the first and only time such events had occurred in Labour's history.

Although always cautious, the Kinnock leadership did not immediately displace the Bennite agenda. Instead it constructed a qualified or 'watered down' version, one which reflected Labour's traditional social democracy and an anti-Thatcherite agenda based upon a moderated version of the 1983 appeal. Thus policy development in the 1983 Parliament was only an incrementalist shift away from the more radical agenda forged earlier. Given the institutional power of trade unions at Conference and the residual powers of the left in both its 'hard' and its 'soft' (travelling to the Kinnockite right) variants, Kinnock was reluctant to go where the party may not follow. As such, while existing 1983 commitments such as opposition to council house sales, immediate withdrawal from the EEC, and statutory planning agreements were quickly excised, in other policy areas the status quo was qualified rather than revised.

In the field of economic policy, while significant changes were made which went beyond repackaging the same policy, Labour continued to believe in the need to tightly regulate the market by state intervention. While the private sector would retain responsibility for capital accumulation, government would use its power to direct economic strategy for politically designated ends; still interventionist, but less interventionist than prior to 1983. Thus, at the 1987 election Labour placed government-led economic regeneration at the heart of its appeal. At the centrepiece of its programme lay a plan for jobs to reduce unemployment by one million in two years through public investment and an industrial strategy to plan the long-term structural development of the economy. While abandoning talk of returning to full employment in the lifetime of a Parliament (preferring instead to concentrate on more moderate aims), Labour promised to establish a neo-corporate National Economic Assessment involving government, business and trade unions in the discussion of economic policy and levels of investment, expenditure and consumption. It pledged itself to an aggressive, comprehensive industrial policy formulated with the direct purpose of facilitating government intervention in the economy and some degree of state co-ordination and control of the market economy. Managing the market was the key to what Neil Kinnock called in 1986 'social control of the market' to plan production and redistribute benefits, to secure economic growth and thereby achieve a number of socialist ends.[35]

At this time Kinnock made it clear that change involved 'a shift in attitudes and presentation, not a change in principles',[36] indicating a continuing association with a watered-down version of the 1983 appeal, one which recognised Labour's failure in office between 1974 and 1979. As Eric Shaw suggests, 'the general pattern of policy change from 1983 to 1987 [was]...a gradual retreat from more ambitious schemes of reform aimed (albeit often loosely) at a recasting of the social order and a return to the revisionist preference for pragmatic and largely consensual reform signalling the abandonment of any sustained challenge to the power and privileges of business.'[37] In the event, Labour's third consecutive election defeat in 1987 combined with the forward march of Thatcherism to encourage the leadership to abandon attempts to moderate the 1983 appeal in favour of its wholesale revision. Where Labour's 1987 pitch was not light-years away from its 1983 appeal (or indeed the broad commitment to economic management that characterised both the 1959 and the 1974 Labour manifestos), the economic approach established after 1983 culminating in the Blair manifesto of

1997 is proof positive of a dramatic shift. Here, the process of policy qualification and dilution which characterised the 1983 Parliament was ultimately replaced by policy revision, a two-stage process encompassing the 1987 and 1992 Parliaments, typified by the outcome of the Policy Review process of 1987–91 and the post-1994 Blairite reformation.

The Policy Review was in many ways the precursor to 'New' Labour, the flagship of the initial 'New Model' party fashioned by the Kinnock leadership. Between 1987 and 1991, it was the mechanism by which Labour's policy stance was altered and the authority of the leadership boosted. Working with the Shadow Cabinet and, when necessary, the 'contact group' of trade union leaders, the Parliamentary leadership became an Inner Core Elite within Labour's highest counsels, its authority such that the opportunities for non-leadership groups to exercise influence over the Labour Party were to be increasingly circumscribed in subsequent years. Couched in the language of earnest review based upon the subscription of ideas and opinions designed to enable Labour to address itself to the needs of the time, the Review process had a simple agenda: it was, in short, not so much a review as a revision of policy, one conducted not merely as an attempt to reapply timeless principles to a modern setting but to respond to perceived changes in the nation's political and economic outlook. Shorn of the intention to radically alter the balance of power within the economy, the 1987 manifesto still placed great emphasis upon the importance of planning the market economy to generate growth and reform its inefficiencies. The Policy Review gradually abandoned this approach in favour of a bolder endorsement (although, when compared with the post-1994 Labour strategy, a somewhat qualified one) of the market mechanism, a process illustrated in the yearly reports submitted to successive Labour Conferences.[38] Over the three full years of the Review, two policy documents were produced by the Review Groups: 'Social Justice and Economic Efficiency' in 1988, and 'Meet the Challenge, Make the Change' in 1989. These were presented to the Shadow Cabinet and agreed by a comfortable majority vote of the NEC. All were endorsed without amendment by the Labour Conference courtesy of a compliant trade union block vote.

In 1990 and 1991 further 'distillations' of the Policy Review entitled 'Looking to the Future' and 'Opportunity Britain', this time heavily influenced by selected members of the Shadow Cabinet, were agreed by the NEC and again endorsed by the autumn Conference. Policy having been successfully reviewed by 1989, the Policy Review machinery ground to a halt although the Review itself continued: policy-making was now almost entirely the preserve of those Shadow Cabinet members whose proposals bore the imprimatur of the Parliamentary leadership. Each policy statement was presented to Conference in a process that had almost as much to do with political communications as it had to do with policy formation. By publicly launching each stage of the Review in a blaze of free publicity the leadership's policy would be presented to the party as an effective *fait accompli* as the chosen corporate image, and the slogan under which the new document was launched provided the theme under which Labour would campaign in the spring and summer and would structure the presentation of the Party Conference in the October.

After 1987, Labour gradually abandoned its commitment to planned action by government in concert with all sides of industry to deal with the problems of the market economy. No longer was it suggested that the market was a good servant but a bad master. The idea that the framework within which economic life proceeds must be substantially determined by government was ruled out. Subject to its responsibility to put in place a responsible fiscal and monetary regime conducive to the workings of a dynamic private sector, it no longer fell to government to determine levels of employment, reform the supply side, or generate sufficient demand. In contrast to previous Labour thinking, the market was said to be both self-regulating and self-correcting, and by itself not wholly responsible for major social and economic divisions. In his introduction to the 1989 Report of the Review, Kinnock stated that the 'economic role of government' should 'help the market system work properly where it can, will and should – and to replace or strengthen it where it can't, won't or shouldn't'.[39] By 1991, he argued that 'the old ideologies – command economy at one extreme, crude free market economies at the other – do not work'.[40]

At the rhetorical level of its policy pronouncements, Labour continued to acknowledge long into the 1980s that the market unaided may not be able to deliver a strong and modern economy. Should the private sector depend upon public sector involvement, the market had to be monitored and regulated in a social interest (if no longer managed in the traditional sense). Thus, early reports of the Policy Review included commitments to some degree of state regulation and control; less than previous but a greater degree than was eventually found in the 1992 and 1997 Labour manifestos. Despite the emphasis placed on interventionist investment in training, research and development and regulatory management, the idea that '[t]he role of the state in economic management was thereafter to be an enabling one, performing tasks which the market was unwilling or unable to accomplish'[41] was a perspective common to policy statements in 1987–91 which was not to be maintained; a 'halfway house' marking the transition away from Labour under Foot and early Kinnock toward that eventually presided over by Tony Blair. For Blair's Labour Party, the role of government is confined to allowing the market economy to work well At the 1997 election, Blair declared his intention was to 'enhance the dynamism of the market, not undermine it',[42] expressing the belief that 'the post-war Keynesian dream is well and truly buried'.[43]

The political direction in which Labour was travelling is unmistakable after 1989 and the attitude it takes to the reforms pursued by Thatcherism in office is central. In 1989, reporting on the then most recent stage of the Policy Review, Peter Kellner wrote: 'Instead of being a party which found the market guilty until proven innocent, [Labour] was now a party that regarded the market as innocent until proven guilty.'[44] Having granted the market the right of the presumption of innocence in 1989, Labour under Blair after 1994 was to firmly declare it wholly innocent of all (indeed, any) charges brought against it in respect of either economic efficiency or social justice. Early stirrings of Labour's rapprochement with the *realpolitik* of Thatcherism can be evidenced in Kinnock's post-1985 attempts to redefine Labour as a 'party of production', one keen not merely to 'distribute with justice' but also 'produce with efficiency'. This appeal gradually became a common theme in Labour's economic stance after 1986 ('Improved distribution of wealth, however necessary and justifiable, cannot long exceed improved production of wealth'[45]) and grew in strength as the years passed and, as Labour increasingly diluted its attachment to redistributive policies.

Influenced by his economics adviser, John Eatwell (later created a peer at Labour's nomination), Kinnock was persuaded after 1987 to emphasise the argument that Labour could make the existing market economy work better than the Conservatives. As the deregulated market place figured larger in Labour's economic plans, it marked a shift away from its traditionalist commitment to state intervention to reform the market mechanism in favour of establishing a framework which would complement the workings of the market. Here, 'reform' of the market is confined to a 'light touch' regulation; the commitment to 'redistribution' over time dramatically overshadowed by the commitment to 'production'.

Despite the relative success of the Policy Review in reorientating Labour away from its election agendas of 1983 and 1987, the party once again crashed to defeat in April 1992. Faced with an electorate willing to 'hold on to the Conservative nurse for fear of something worse' in the midst of recession, John Major's Conservatives played the high-taxation, high-spending anti-Labour card and surprisingly won. Kinnock duly fell on his sword on the morrow of his party's defeat and, following a relatively unprotracted leadership contest, the Shadow Chancellor John Smith was elected in his place, beating Bryan Gould by a margin of 9 to 1 in July 1992. Close Kinnock supporters such as Tony Blair and Peter Mandelson, the party's Director of Communications 1985–90 and MP for Hartlepool since 1992, all 'modernisers' committed to taking Labour to its right, considered Smith's leadership, despite his many abilities, to be suspiciously 'old' Labour. Powerless to prevent his accession, the modernising tendency none the less rejected the notion of 'one more heave', a belief that Labour had only to persevere and wait for a coming election victory; they favoured implementing a more fundamental agenda of party change.

Although Blair and Gordon Brown prospered under Smith's leadership (becoming Shadow Home Secretary and Shadow Chancellor respectively), Mandelson, wholly disliked by Smith, found himself totally frozen out of the party's inner circles. Despite the career advancement of men like Brown and Blair, the two years of Smith's leadership proves in retrospect to have been something of a hiatus for the modernisers. Ever the conservative (small c) politician, Smith was wary of the 'project', the sobriquet applied to modernisation and the 'New' Labour agenda, and unwilling to endorse policy reforms urged upon him by the Blair and Mandelson tendency. He firmly set his face against the idea of revising Clause Four and reportedly 'blew his top' in 1993 when one member of his Shadow Cabinet, Jack Straw, publicly advocated doing so. While prepared to put his leadership on the line in the successful battle to secure the passage of 'One Member One Vote' (OMOV) through the 1993 Labour Conference in the teeth of trade union opposition led by John Edmonds of the GMB, Smith only did so because it was 'unfinished business' left over from the Kinnock regime, a policy he had committed himself to during the 1992 leadership contest.

Many Labour modernisers considered that Smith demonstrated decidedly 'old' Labour credentials in making concessions to trade union opinion on rights at work and the commitment to using the state to return to full employment,[46] but while he may not have significantly advanced the modernisers' agenda nor did he undo any of the Kinnock reforms. In hindsight, Smith's leadership was a period of consolidation, one modernisers privately refer to as an interregnum where their 'project' stalled (if it was in no way reversed). It was only in the wake of

Smith's death and the elevation of Tony Blair, moderniser *par excellence*, in his place that the emergent reform project was placed firmly back on track. Where Smith wanted to consolidate the Kinnockite status quo in an attempt to reconstitute the grand old party of, say, Gaitskell or Callaghan, the modernisation agenda was predicated upon the belief that the enterprise culture fashioned by Thatcherism in office structured what Labour should do in opposition and could expect to do in office.

As Leader of the Opposition in 1994–7, Blair was everywhere. The long-established frontrunner to replace Smith once Gordon Brown fell on his sword, he came to office with favourable press coverage, buoyant poll ratings (both for himself and his party) and showed remarkable success in leading his party from the front (symbolised by his success in revising Clause Four in 1995 and winning the endorsement of party members for the 'Road to the Manifesto' document in 1996). Blair's leadership was characterised by his commanding his party and seeing it follow (a position he was to skilfully contrast with what he saw as John Major's inability to do likewise in the latter stages of the 1992 Parliament). His time as party leader marked yet a further (but not that dramatic) shift away from Labour's pre-1987 position. Indeed, despite all his efforts, no dramatic shift under Blair since 1994 can be identified (other than a far-reaching tightening of a pre-prepared ratchet); 1994 was not a 'year zero' for the Labour Party because Blair's reforms were built on the firm foundations established before he came to the leadership. Although his tenure of the leadership saw a steady shift in economic and industrial policy it was a shift marked by continuity with the altered political world view of the leadership of the then 'new model' Labour Party fashioned under Kinnock.

As a process, Labour's shift certainly involves an amount of serial disengagement with past practice, but it is not a series of 'disjointed breaks which suggest that the phenomenon had fundamentally different (as opposed to distinct) characteristics at different times. In identifying distinctive stages in the emergence, rise and consolidation of what is now referred to as the 'Blairite' agenda, the process of Labour's transformation can be evidenced. In periodising Labour's transformation, a five-stage shift away from the policy stance of 1983 can be evidenced:

1 High-tide: the advance of the left halted, 1981–4
2 Interregnum: Kinnock's quest for control, 1984–5
3 Realignment: the right consolidates its authority, 1985–7
4 Transformation: the Policy Review and after, 1987–94
5 Consolidation: the Blair reformation, post-1994.

Each of these stages had a cumulative effect and all were contributory factors in bringing about Labour's transformation. None can be taken in isolation; all had a collective impact. Here, in the wake of the stalled rise of the Labour left of 1970–84, Labour's modernisation (itself a word that dates back only to the early 1990s; one in vogue only since 1993) is part of a process. It is not in itself an action. To take any key period in isolation at worst obscures and at best only partially maps out the process of change.

Labour's transformation over time reflects a period of transition. As with the chonology of Thatcherism the remaking of Labour has been a 'process' enacted over time, one adjudged in terms of 'stages' with several distinctive points of origin and motivating factors. Hence, there is nothing intrinsically inconsistent in identifying 1983, 1985, post-1987 and 1994 onward as significant 'moments of transition'. They are not by themselves point(s) of origin given that Labour's shift is a staged process. Here, enacted against the backdrop of Thatcherism, a series of key periods (or staging posts) can be identified including the 1983, 1987, 1987 and 1992 General Elections; the shift in the Kinnock leadership in 1983–5; the Policy Review of 1987–91; and the Blair reforms post-1994. Together, these all contributed to the change from the party Labour was in 1980 to that it had become in 1997. With regard to the alteration of the party's politics after 1987, 1988–91 (the Policy Review) and 1994–6 (the Blair 'reformation') are as significant as (but only because they are related to) the 1983, 1987 and 1992 election cycles. Rather than look for one point of origin, a more profitable approach maps out various staging posts in order to fully explore and explain the complex process underpinning Labour's transformation.

6
How and Why Parties Change: Identifying Environmental Contexts

Between 1977 and 1997 the Labour Party offers a textbook example of party change, a process whereby the party altered its appeal and abandoned previously held positions in favour of a new and reformed programme. Given the 'fundamental assumption...that parties enter government to influence policy making and to control policy implementation',[1] the question is: what endogenous and exogenous factors determine or otherwise influence the policy agenda that parties follow? What determines the attitudes of parties? How does such party change manifest itself? More particularly, how does party change come about?

Studies of party change across time usually consider the transition from one functional type of party to another. Otto Kirchheimer developed a theory of the historical transition of parties from institutions of mass integration based upon social cleavage groups into organisations that appeal beyond the sectional group they had previously and exclusively represented, a shift from sectionally based to catch-all parties.[2] More recently, Angelo Panebianco has postulated the transition over time from a 'mass-bureaucratic' party stressing ideology and belief, to an 'electoral-professional' organisation emphasising issues and leadership.[3] Here, change is defined as the transition from one party form to another: party change usually distinguishes between party types involving distinctive forms of secular change in the nature of political organisation.[4]

Where the party retains its original form, party change can be broadly illustrated by changes in what is best described as its 'public identity'. A public identity enables a party to define and represent itself to the electorate (and other political parties) at large. Changes in this public identity are evidenced in the programmatic appeal the party offers, its identified political objectives and the political strategies it employs.

Change is thus effected when parties 'change', 'modernise' or 'repackage' their political image, 'update' their policy appeal or else 'jettison' past convictions and ideological baggage. From this perspective, a party alters its stance on a particular political question or else with regard to a whole range of issues. This public identity is not fixed and unchanging; nor is it wholly fluid, determined as it is by historical appeal and tradition. Due to a variety of institutional, political and socio-economic influences, party change is an inevitable consequence of an organisation stimulated by the environment in which it is located and responsive to external and internal factors brought to bear upon it. Change affects party behaviour in altering what the party does and seeks to do. It affects not only how the party perceives itself but also (more importantly) how it is perceived by others. *Party change is a dynamic process, an ongoing event, a process subject to fluctuation marked by the passage from non-change to change, where the type, rate and degree of party change is characterised by a serial progression from stability toward transformation through adaptation.*

In discussing the reactions of parties faced with a record of poor electoral performance, Pippa Norris and Ivor Crewe suggest a variety of options available to them: '[Parties] can respond to a "declining market share" by adjusting their policy products, launching new ones, advertising more effectively, raising the entry barriers for new competitors and so on. Whatever their strategy, the initiative lies with party elites, not ordinary voters.'[5] An analysis of party change is very distinct from an examination of party system change because parties are objects worthy of study in their own right, not just simple expressions of social forces: party systems are the product of interacting political parties.[6] The processes underlying party–electorate interaction is a major determinant in party change, but it can also be separated from the stability of the system within which parties and voters interact. Peter Mair correctly draws a distinction between party change and party system change:[7] each political party is an independent actor, one with a significant degree of autonomy within the party system, not necessarily structurally dependent upon other forces. Of course, a dramatic realignment (or a systemic collapse) of any party system would result in dramatic party change. A process of individual party change may have no adverse impact upon the prevailing party system. Indeed, quite the reverse, when party adaptation reinforces that system and prevents a breakdown.

Perceived changes in Western European parties have provoked many academic observations (and not a little speculation) about the prospect of a system realignment. These usually involve a discussion of party change in the light of electoral volatility, party and partisan dealignment, and possible system fragmentation. *However, party systems may prevail at the same time that political parties evidence an ability to change demonstrated by alterations in their strategy or appeal.* Although no dramatic realignment leading to system fragmentation may be evidenced, parties do change. Change does not have to take place across the party system but can be confined to individual participants within the party system when the characteristics of the party system remains unchanged. As Peter Mair argues: 'Electoral developments, ideological change, organisational revitalisation, and so on, are all important aspects of party change, but they are appropriate indicators of party system change only when they also begin to have a bearing on the pattern of interactions which characterise the system itself, or, in other words, when they have systemic relevance.'[8]

Although 'party system change occurs when a party system is transformed from one class or type of party system into another',[9] a well-attested law of inertia applies to party systems. Once established they tend to prevail however altered they may be across time by political processes.[10] The system (unlike its component parts) is rarely subject to any grand realignment. Able to adapt or modify their positions, parties can deflect or absorb pressures likely to threaten the party system, so 'preserving the underlying format of the party system despite social change or the emergence of new issues'.[11] This denotes a continuity of party systems from the hyper-stability identified by Stein Rokkan to the less-well-founded but relatively stable systems seen today; they are altered but not necessarily changed. Certainly, systems are subject to an element of adaptation (defined by alterations in the parties that compose the system) but such party change rarely promotes a grand realignment where the mould of the system is broken and its total form recast. The rise of issue voting and the weakening of party association in its wake brings with it instability within the electoral party system. This may in itself provide an impetus for party change, but, as distinct from promoting change among the parties that comprise that system, it does not alter the parameters of the prevailing party system.

Deterministic accounts of party and party system change which erroneously lump the two together offer little illumination into the process of party change; they offer no insight into the dynamics of political change within the UK party system where party change (as defined above) is an independent variable, quite separate from party system change. While stable voting patterns between established parties (where support for one increases at the same time it decreases for the other) reduce the potential for party system change, electoral instability may well affect a particular party rather than the party system itself. The impact of changing political alignment (mediated through the process of party competition) may well mean that the alignment of a party *within* the stable party system will alter at the same time that the system itself remains fundamentally stable.[12] Despite the volatility of the 1970s and the 1980s – the so-called 'decade(s) of dealignment', the advent of three-party politics within the two-party system – the form of the British party system was not fundamentally altered.

Between 1970 and 1992, two-party aggregate support declined from some 90 per cent to 75 per cent due to rising electoral volatility demonstrated in the rise of third-party politics (and nationalism in Scotland and Wales). Here, February 1974, 1983 and 1987 stand out. The post-1987 period has seen a return to 'normal' with two principal parties seeking office within a three-party political system: 'Overall, seen within the constraints set by the electoral system, post-war changes in society and electoral behaviour have failed to change the general two-party format.'[13] While a party system provides the parameters within which established parties operate, it is marked by continuity not dramatic change, and reflects adaptation over time rather than dramatic transformation (for example the transition from two- to three-party politics with nationalist parties represented at the margin); the adaptative capacities of political parties is striking. Here, it is the nature of the political alternatives (the appeal offered by parties and the strategy they advance to communicate their intentions) that is redefined while the form of the party system remains intact. Party change need not alter the parameters of the prevailing party system.

After 1983, Labour, despite assertions to the contrary, lived to fight, lose, lose again, and eventually to win handsomely in 1997. Despite the dramatic setbacks of the 1980s, Labour not merely survived but went on to prosper. For sociological and psephological reasons Labour's status as second party (the opposition party in Parliament for the entire 18 years of the Conservative rule) was maintained. Despite the challenge of the SDP/Liberal Alliance in 1983 and, to a far lesser extent, 1987 this was never seriously in question (although Labour's ability to win future elections certainly was). Unlike the displacement of the Liberal Party by Labour in 1918–29, the contemporary Labour Party retained a political hold on sufficient electoral support to warrant its continued existence (but not the ability to successfully office-seek in 1979–92): Labour's post-1983 record suggests that parties are more permanent institutions that many commentators sometimes allow. Realignment is not always around the corner. The UK party system held firm in terms of the forces it represented (as distinct from the ratio in which they were represented) in Parliament (if not necessarily in the country). This situation arose courtesy of the prevailing party system just as much as by the single member plurality electoral system.

By contrast to party system change, party change within the prevailing party system is a far more common phenomenon. The public identity, the electoral and political appeal parties offer within the party system are dramatically affected by, say, the unfolding events of a twenty-year period. That they change while systems prevail is attested by an empirical assessment of the Labour and Conservative Parties in recent history. Thus the simple serial proposition that social change = electoral change = party change = party system change should therefore be rejected. The third variable, party change, can be provoked by political change as it is enacted within a stable party system. Where party system continuity is thus 'conditioned by both forces of persistence or change and the adaptive capacities of parties',[14] party change is often a precondition for the survival of an established party system, not necessarily an illustration of system breakdown: given that a variation in party behaviour need not involve party system change, party change is a staged process of varying degrees of serial adaptation, but it is one within the same structure where the rules of the game, in this instance the structure of the party system, remains continuous even if it becomes more volatile.

Exploring the past from the vantage point of the present grants any commentator the benefit of hindsight. Hindsight suggests that the party's continued existence is a product of its persistence. While this is accurate, this explanation is itself insufficient. An explanation of why a party continues in existence must be advanced: The fact that Labour did not disappear does not imply that it could not have disappeared. After 1983 and 1987, the Labour elite did worry that their party if not electorally dead in the water was a considerable distance from winning office at subsequent elections. Labour modernisers increasingly counselled against the notion that the party had simply to bide its time and wait its turn in the revolving door of the electoral process. From this perspective the beginnings of Labour's transformation was obviously in part promoted by the impact that electoral outcomes had on its office-seeking capacities. Although the type of change promoted as part of this process of transformation was dependent upon other circumstances, repeated defeats did encourage a changing Labour elite to change their party; they were worried that Labour had to adapt for fear it would not prosper. Here, the party system was instrumental because it affected the strategic choices of party actors. It must be noted that because the Labour elite feared their party would disappear they were determined to maximise its office-seeking capacities. Although preferable to extinction, surviving within the system was insufficient; prospering was the objective. While electoral outcomes may have promoted Labour's change *per se*, they did not specify the actual form that these changes would in fact take.

In their path-breaking electoral study of the 1960s, Butler and Stokes located three dimensions of political-electoral change: (1) replacement of the electorate over time; (2) alterations in the electorate's enduring party alignments; and (3) change in the electoral response to the immediate issues and events of politics. While they over-emphasised the role of each individual elector (when aggregated) at the same time as they downplayed the role of ideas, they did recognise that 'the sources of electoral change are to be found in the electorate itself only in the most proximate sense'.[15] They rightly suggested that political scientists need to 'look beyond the electorate to its environment'.[16] Of the factors that determine party change (not merely electoral change), the reaction of the party to the environment in which it is situated is central. Environmental contexts set the parameters within which parties act by constraining their strategies, limiting options, and structuring available choices: 'external stimuli' matter. The environment of a political party embraces the following interrelated dimensions:

1 governmental-institutional (the form of the state, the rules of the constitutional system, election law and system, electoral cycles);
2 political-ideological (the form of ideological engagement, the climate of opinion, policy orientation on the part of actors and electors);
3 political-electoral (electoral outcomes, public opinion, the party system, electoral pressures);
4 socio-economic (economic factors, social composition, demographic considerations).

Together these may be defined as a series of arenas in which resources are exchanged and where parties interact with each other and other social and political actors. *Of these environments two are of particular significance: the political-ideological and the political-electoral. They provide two closely interrelated factors which provoke party change as a reflection of wider political change.*

Angelo Panebianco observes that 'Electoral defeat and deterioration in terms of exchange in the electoral arena are classic types of external challenges which exert very strong pressure on the party.'[17] In electoral terms, each party exists only in terms of the relationship historically formed with electors and other political parties: its political-electoral environment is affected as patterns of political attachments are challenged by alterations in the substantive attitudes of voters to parties. The electoral environment counts: parties are all too often forced to react to changing electoral circumstances; change can be the response made following party competition when defeat within the electoral cycle is interpreted to 'require' the unsuccessful party to reconstruct its appeal. Alternatively, victory may vindicate the successful party and drive it on. There are of course a series of constraints that impinge upon party activity, among them, for example, the fact that experience of office and opposition bring with them very different external influences, as do different electoral outcomes.

Much of the contemporary literature on party and party system change focuses on the impact that the electoral environment has upon party identity.[18] Most environmental explanations of the changing form of party competition derive from the socialisation model devised by Butler and Stokes. Ivor Crewe and Bo Saarlvik suggest that the British electorate underwent a partisan and class dealignment in the 1970s and 1980s;[19] Mark Franklin emphasises the importance of issue voting in the wake of the decline of class identification;[20] Himmelweit *et al.* describe the electorate–party relationship in a consumer–producer relationship;[21] and Heath *et al.* argue that party-led political activity is more influential in bringing about political change than changes in the sociological composition of the electorate.[22]

The impact of electoral politics upon party change cannot be underestimated. It is widely suggested that party change is to sustain an electoral position considered (or demonstrated) to be in doubt; a reaction to a sustained electoral shock. The weakening of party association (and the concomitant rise in issue voting) gives parties the opportunity to appeal to electorates previously beyond their influence, bound as they were by ties of association and partisan identification to opposing parties. It also questions the ties of association that parties have previously established with sections of the electorate within the party system. A decline in party identification and a rise in issue voting has a dual effect: it creates a turbulent electoral arena, 'one in which the "belonging" vote is reduced and the "opinion" vote greater... the greater the proportion of "opinion" over "belonging" voting, the greater the (potential) electoral fluidity and thus the greater the degree of environmental uncertainty'.[23] Forced to compete for votes within a more deregulated electoral marketplace, parties are obliged to organise themselves in response to electoral demands. They have to build electoral support and cannot take for granted traditional support they previously could rely upon. Parties are thus more likely to adapt to changes in the competitive environment in which they are located.[24]

Because party change involves the realignment of a party within a continuing party system the interaction of electors and parties is significant: '[T]he electoral base of a party will change as the society itself changes, either as a result of socio-economic change or demographic change. The politics of party will also be subject to modification over time, in response to changing needs, changing demands and changing constraints.'[25] This phenomenon is often alluded to: it is, of course, a reflection of political and not just electoral facts. Because electoral phenomena reflect political rationale, explanations must uncover not only how electoral environments change but how parties react to these changes and subsequent political consequences. Obviously, variations in electoral support are explained by a number of variables, many of which are sociological (if not psychological) in origin, involving social class, demography, occupation or even political or ideological value orientation. The impact of these variables may be long-term rather than short-term, but they clearly involve a shift in the level of electoral attachment to party organisations.[26] While electoral factors have a significant impact on parties obliged to market themselves in the quest for electoral support the political-electoral environment is but one type related to other environments, each of which impacts upon a given political party.

With regard to electoral impacts on UK party change since 1979, much has rightly been made of the four consecutive electoral victories of the Conservative Party.[27] Election outcomes are important in promoting party change; the historical course of British politics has been affected by the fact that the Conservatives won four consecutive elections at the same time that Labour lost them. Robert Harmel and Kenneth Janda propose a useful typology by which election outcomes as impacts upon parties can be classified: (1) calamitous; (2) disappointing; (3) tolerable; (4) gratifying; (5) triumphal.[28] Applying this typology in the UK, the four general elections to 1992 could be defined in regard to the outcome for both Conservative and Labour parties: 1979 was disappointing for Labour and gratifying for the Conservatives; 1983 calamitous for Labour and triumphal for the Conservatives; 1987 calamitous for Labour and triumphal for the Conservatives; 1992 disappointing for Labour and gratifying for the Conservatives. These electoral outcomes all had significant impacts upon each party and the calamitous defeats of 1983 and 1987 have been defining moments for the Labour Party (as well as spurring on Thatcherism).

Where Harmel and Janda associate change with past electoral performance (in their view this is 'a necessary, though not necessarily sufficient, condition for party change'),[29] they only factor in the impact of electoral performance over the two-year period following an election. After this period they assume erroneously that the impact of the election ceases. Cumulative impact is a very significant factor they overlook.[30] For reasons established in the previous chapter, Labour's interpretation of its 1983 defeat was not as significant in 1985 (in terms of party change) as it was in 1995 following the experience of both the 1987 and 1992 defeats. The outcome of the 1987 and 1992 elections, the first in particular, reinforced the impact of the 1983 election defeat and the implications that sprang from it. For the Blair circle today the memory of the 1983 election result as much as that of 1992 is an important incentive underlying the modernisation project. Cumulative electoral shocks across electoral cycles are therefore extremely important in promoting party change: it is significant not that Labour lost one election but that they lost four. Of course, Labour did not alter its appeal immediately on the morrow of defeat in June 1983 nor in April 1992; it did so over time as each successive external shock was registered internally. Dennis Kavanagh suggests that 'parties adopt or disavow policies not only to win forthcoming elections but also as a response to past electoral outcomes'.[31] Certainly, they do both simultaneously: office-seeking parties react to electoral defeat in order to forestall future defeat.

Of course electoral defeat is only one external stimuli among many. Adopting Harmel and Janda's typology of electoral outcomes, it is important to distinguish between 'calamitous' and 'disappointing' elections. A 'calamitous' election is one evidenced by a large loss of seats or votes; a 'disappointing' election a sharp rebuke recorded by a small loss/ minimal gain when sizable gains are expected. The distinction between these is a matter of degree, but both signify political defeat and exclusion from office. A comparison between Labour's 'calamitous defeat' in 1987 with the 'more calamitous defeat' of 1983 is a case in point. This illustrates that Harmel and Janda's expectation that a calamitous election result should promote change more readily than a disappointing election again misleads. Labour changed more dramatically in the wake of the 1987 and 1992 defeats than it had following the 1983 reverse: cumulative effects matter, dependent upon the manner in which external stimuli are interpreted by the party as an organisation. As such external stimuli such as repeated electoral defeats do not of themselves automatically result in party change. Other factors contribute.

By themselves, electoral factors (defeat or victory) are not the only factors involved in the process of party change. It is too simplistic to assert that defeat in an electoral cycle automatically impels a party to undergo a process of change in the way that night follows day. Parties may be forced to change when they have performed badly in an election but this is not an instant reaction. Party change is akin to a juggernaut turning, a slow process where adaptation over time rather than a rapid reaction is the norm: the form that party change takes is produced by factors other than electoral outcomes. Political–ideological–electoral environments unfavourably affecting a party provide external stimuli which can encourage party change. Such external stimuli, an external event or events producing a shock of some form, usually take the form of an unfavourable electoral outcome, an ideological shift in public policy, an elite realignment across party or else a combination of all three. Such external shocks usually present themselves as a trend, a measurable and verifiable shift over time.

Of course, the impact of any environmental context or external shock cannot be assumed. Parties are to some extent free agents; they do not react to an external stimuli but choose when and how they respond to it. In his study of the origins of party change from one organisational form (mass-bureaucratic) to another (electoral professional), Panebianco suggests that change is the product of an 'external stimulus' either environmental or technological which joins forces with 'internal factors' such as leadership change, an alteration in the governing or dominant coalition which governs the party. External stimuli as interpreted by the party internally provide a change incentive; external stimuli are not merely the given rationale or the universal explanation of party change. Rather, party change is the product of an internal response to external circumstances; it is, in short, for the most part leadership-led, evidenced in a shift in the outlook of party elites. A hypothesis can be easily advanced which associates party change with poor electoral performance, but the instigation of party change can only be fully understood in reference to the manner in which the party internalises its external experiences; by itself an external stimulus is an insufficient explanation for party change. As Harmel and Janda observe, 'While the good reason (i.e., stimulus for change) may be externally induced, the designing and successful implementation of a responsive change will be highly dependent upon internal factors.'[32] In short, the significance of the environment (as perceived by any political actor) is heavily influenced by an intra-party response which realigns the party in line with perceived changed circumstances.

Over time the outcomes of the 1979, 1983, 1987 and 1992 general elections all collectively impacted upon Labour. An internal party reaction to an environmental context is facilitated by a 'significant authority', usually the dominant coalition within the party, most obviously the leadership, but perhaps a faction with the ability to oppose the dominant coalition.[33] It is commonly suggested that party leaders decide if a party should change in light of prevailing (usually electoral) circumstances but their ability to instigate change is dependent on a number of factors. Party leaders are not always free to impose their will. Although never entirely autonomous the degree to which they are free to define the party identity is contingent on a variety of exogenous and endogenous circumstances. These circumstances change over time depending on the political and organisational composition of the party they lead. It is easier to initiate change where strong leadership structures apply than where the periphery or sub-leadership elites enjoy a degree of autonomy. Over the past twenty years the Labour Party exemplifies a transition from an organisation with 'severely limited leaders' to a party with 'strong leadership structures', one where the Inner Core Elite is able to determine the direction in which the party travels.

The instrumental difference between party leaders and other party actors in terms of their ability to steer the party ship of state cannot be stressed too highly. The course of the 1980s demonstrates that once free to act it is leaders, elites and sub-elites and not followers that with periodic exceptions have their hand firmly on the tiller of the party ship. They control the rudder of the boat subject to the various internal constraints brought to bear upon them. Because external environments impact upon parties, electoral defeat(s) can serve to empower the party leadership. Of course, at the same time it can damn the individual party leader made to pay the price for defeat. Michael Foot's loss in 1983 paved the way for a new executive leadership under Neil Kinnock. Kinnock was obliged to resign as leader following Labour's defeat in 1992.

Conversely, Labour's electoral weakness served to empower its leadership. The more pronounced the defeat, the more power was granted the Labour leadership. Labour's modernisation was sold to the party not as an end in itself but for a definable purpose: winning office at subsequent general elections. Thus, because the party was prepared to grant its leadership the autonomy it craved, the Kinnock–Blair elite was able to gradually refashion Labour's appeal. No criticism, however

well intentioned or constructive, was welcomed. Nor was internal opposition, dissent or disunity tolerated because it was deemed to interfere
with Labour's electioneering efforts led by its leadership.

Party change may therefore be considered a price well worth paying
for a long-awaited electoral advance. How is this sold to the membership? The significance of the primary goal(s) of a particular party cannot
be underestimated. The internal motivation which underpins party
change as a reaction to an external environment is therefore a significant factor in any explanation of party change. Parties may change
because they decide that their present public identity prevents them
from achieving their objectives. Here, the question of primary goals
arises. Party objectives are based upon a series of designated ends
reflected in the set of primary goals emphasised. The rational choice
tradition of explaining party competition focuses on three established
models of competitive behaviour in which political parties can engage:
vote seeking; office seeking; and policy seeking.[34]

A distinction between vote seeking and office seeking cannot be
made with regard to each of the two major parties in the United Kingdom. For the major contenders for government office under 'two party
politics in a disguised multi-party system', they amount to the same
thing; coalition government is more than an exception within a plurality electoral system conferring office exclusively in terms of granting
parties with the largest minority of the vote a majority vote in the
legislature. In the UK the breadth of electoral support needed for office
may be quite small. Office seeking and policy seeking provide two
distinctive forms of party behaviour. Firstly, office seeking leads the
party to develop strategies for winning elections in the quest for executive office. Secondly, policy seeking requires strategies which articulate
issues and ideology as specified by perceived group interest. Both are
interdependent forms of behaviour, present simultaneously within any
political party and, depending on time and circumstances, one or other
may be dominant. In distinguishing office- and policy-seeking Budge
and Keman suggest that four considerations apply: (1) office is valued
for its own sake; (2) office is considered a means of advancing policy; (3)
policy is valued as a means of achieving office; (4) policy is pursued for
its own sake.[35] Of course, for reasons advanced here these are not
necessarily exclusive: parties can demonstrate a mix of the two and
thus party strategy is often a trade-off between competing interests.

Neither pure office seekers nor pure policy seekers, major parties do
not exist in order to either win and hold governmental office as an end
in itself or to introduce distinctive public policies: they do both. Parties

can seek office not just for office maximisation but also for the purposes of policy influence. Few mainstream political actors publicly seek office by expressing the desire to hold office as an end in itself; equally few actors would claim a desire to policy seek at the expense of office maximisation.[36] The relationship between office seeking and policy seeking is one of complex interdependence. Separately and collectively, both objectives are significant and are present within any political party in a structured but changing relationship of dominance and subordination. It is contemporary political circumstances (external factors) and the balance of power within the party organisation (internal factors) that determine the actual relationship between these goals at any one moment.

The twin goals of vote maximisation and policy advocacy are mutually interdependent but may well therefore be expressed separately in an antagonistic relation: one will come to the fore at any given time depending upon the internal and external factors that impinge on the organisation. The dominant goal motivation depends upon the particular stimuli. The view that electoral defeat is considered a factor in party change presupposes that electoral success in itself is the primary goal which motivates party activity; equally, policy failure in office can lead parties when in opposition to prioritise policy seeking. The prospect of office after years of opposition may act as compensation for a party unwilling to policy seek in the manner it did previously. Here, the primary goal of office seeking has become the dominant objective. Similarly, a party ejected from office in the wake of an indifferent or poor record in government may find the leadership the subject of internal criticism in light of its perceived failures. Here, policy seeking may come to the fore as the party attempts to react to the loss of office. This is evidenced in different forms by Labour post-1979 and the Conservatives post-1974 in the wake of the perceived failures of the Heath, Wilson and Callaghan administrations. On both occasions office seeking strategies advanced by the leadership inner circle were seen to be flawed and policy seeking strategies promoted in their place as the dominant objective. Hence, party change can be measured as a process of selecting as a dominant objective one primary goal from another.

Having prioritised office seeking as their dominant objective, parties are likely to accept the need for party change in the pursuit of this goal at the expense of radical policy seeking in line with traditional ideological predilections; the more pronounced their electoral failure the more likely (and the more dramatically) they are to change. A prescriptive programme of action is advanced (most usually by the dominant coalition) to solve the 'crisis' of the party and negotiate obstacles in its path in order to secure the preferred objective. If, as is usual, the external stimuli (as internally perceived by the dominant coalition) that has brought about the party crisis is electoral in origin this will inevitable result in the leadership offering an office seeking strategy in place of a policy seeking strategy deemed to have been the author of the party's misfortune.[37] Thus party change is facilitated by external pressures as they are internalised by the party itself: the prioritisation of one primary goal over another is dictated by the party's internalised reaction to its external environment. Together, these endogenous and exogenous factors provide the dynamic for change[38] but exogenous factors are key. To recap: If change is induced by exogenous factors, then critical actors within the party must first perceive environmental impacts and assess their probable effects.

A theory of inter-party competition driven party change

The experience of defeat in 1979, 1983, 1987 and 1992 led the Labour Party to prioritise office seeking over policy seeking. Its interaction with its environment lay at the heart of its modernising project. Of course, the impetus for change may be identified where electoral factors are deemed to promote party change but the rationale that dictates the form that change takes is not; further investigation need to be initiated. How should a party successfully seek office? Which policies should it seek to promote? Electoral outcomes convey two specific messages to the defeated political party. First, that the party has lost. Second, the manner of defeat (as interpreted by the party itself) is explained. Hence, electoral defeat provides an external stimulus provoking party change by leading the party to interpret the rationale for change where electoral pressures convey political impacts to parties.

The political-electoral environment often reflects a dominant political-ideological environment. In the case of Labour's transformation, a specific ideological reaction was seen to be a 'necessary response' to its electoral predicament. Electoral outcomes communicate political changes and so Labour's accommodation to the neo-liberal politics advanced by actually existing Thatcherism was to prove a reflection of an altered politics which found expression in the political outcomes of the 1983, 1987 and 1992 general elections. Labour's defeats provoked the party to modernise itself, by changing in order to embrace many of the changes that had been undertaken by the Thatcher and Major governments. Having on its own admission lost the 1980s and the early 1990s, Labour's gradual acknowledgement of an alteration in its electoral environment went hand in hand with the perception of a shift in the ideological climate of British politics, the one reinforcing the other. Over time, party change affects the party's location within the ideological continuum that characterises the prevailing form that party competition takes within the electoral marketplace.

As conservative organisations likely to adapt themselves to perceived changes in circumstances in as familiar a fashion as possible, parties do not change frequently or easily. They owe much to the political tradition deriving from the *familles spirituelles* from which they arise. A party historically of the left moving to the right rarely becomes a party of the right, or vice versa. While a party of the left can move to the right, it may occupy an ideological space that is still to the left of its right-wing opponent. It is exceptional for established parties of left and right to leapfrog one another on an ideological space. Prisoners of their history (and of their identified electorates), parties are often obliged to act tomorrow in keeping with the tradition of what they did yesterday. Here, should the Conservatives move leftward they still present themselves as a party of individualism, the property owning democracy, while Labour, should it move rightward, has still to offer a political appeal which meets its electorate's desire for social reform to secure the 'good society'. Of course, nothing is entirely fixed. In particular, it is conceivable that the Liberal Democrats, hitherto a centrist party to the right of Labour and the left of the Conservatives, could position itself to Labour's left as Labour moves rightward in economic and social policy.

A party's propensity for change is coloured by its 'genetic code': its historical background, past ideological associations, traditional identity and the various expectations voters and political commentators have of it. Any internal challenge to a reform programme advocating party change is usually based upon three criticisms: (1) it is a break with continuity and a rejection of traditional practice; (2) a betrayal of traditionalist first principles; (3) it undermines party identity and its basic political mission. Internal constraints that inhibit the freedom of manoeuvre open to advocates of change include: (1) the expectations of other party actors (sub-elites; activists and members); (2) traditional appeal and genetic code; and (3) the internal balance of power within the party favouring either the leadership or other political actors. In contrast, a number of claims are advanced in defence of a reform strategy: (1) maintaining continuity; securing traditional values in a modern setting, applying fundamental values to, say, the politics of the 1990s; (2) fidelity to abiding and established principles; (3) preservation of party identity; and (4) achieving collective goals, usually ensuring the electability of the party. In the case of the Labour Party advocates of change have been careful to associate themselves with these claims listed here. The less constrained the party leadership, the more negative the impact of environmental stimuli upon the prioritised primary goal, the more likely party change will be.

If social structure determines electoral choice, parties are at best mere bystanders in the electoral process who will have marginal effects on electoral outcomes. They would have no purchase on preordained, determined electoral preferences. If, on the other hand, short-term forces dominate, then such outcomes can be strongly influenced by party strategies when electoral attitudes are open to influence. If it is accepted that party strategies are so influential, a series of theoretical questions follow: To what extent can political parties affect electoral outcomes? Can they exercise control over the process of party competition and so influence the political terrain upon which that competition takes place? An effective analysis of party competition should consider the impact that wider political change has upon the mode of interaction that characterises the relationship between parties and electors. The roles of electors and political elites are inextricably linked; the sociology of politics too often focuses on the political consumer at the expense of the political producer; it should account for both. As Giovanni Sartori argues, 'a party system is only a response to the consumer's demands but it is equally a feedback of producer's options. There can be no consumers without political entrepreneurs, just like there cannot be political entrepreneurs without customers.'[39]

Parties are the beneficiary of public support where voters individually make collective choices by choosing between options presented to them. The importance of an electoral marketplace lies not just at the moment of electoral choice but through party competition across elections when a series of elections provide cumulative snapshots not only of electoral preferences but also political outcomes over time. Party change may be a response to electoral outcomes but also a response to other types of change that alter the external environment in which the party is located. Party competition is a necessary part of the elective process, a two-way process of engagement in which voters communicate their opinion of party appeals and parties express their intentions. Here, electors respond to the promises offered by parties at the same time as parties criticise the promises offered by their opponents. Neither voters nor parties are autonomous. The form of party competition is not set by voters alone but is subject to the interaction of parties with electors and, crucially, the interaction of parties with other parties: this is all too often ignored. The electoral responses of voters as much as the promises offered by parties are shaped both exogenously and endogenously. Where political actors lead, citizens as electors may or may not follow and vice versa.

The actions of political parties, successful or otherwise, impact upon their political opponents. Here, because party competition is a finely balanced 'political eco-system' where the actions of participants have consequences (both intended and otherwise), the dynamic of competition clearly has an effect upon parties. As intermediate organisations between citizens and the state, parties are not a dependent variable.[40] As organising structures which seek to link electors to government, parties are the cornerstone of the entire process, a bulwark of the stable, albeit gradually evolving, party system. Identifying the source and dynamic of political change in relation to political parties requires analysis of the process of party competition. Institutionalist explanations (the role of the state and its institutions; the environmental governmental-institutional arena) usually have a permanent impact on the roles that established parties play; any explanatory value they have is in an analysis of long-term stability rather than medium or short-term change. Sociological explanations (the influence of social structures) are a different matter. Together with political explanations (electoral and elite opinions, attitudes and values) they cannot be taken as given; but do have an impact on why and when parties change and how they can make a contribution to political change.

Parties win and lose in the process of party competition. In a two-party system, should party A win party B must lose. The explanations of success and failure are necessarily objective but are evaluated subjectively by commentators and analysts and by parties themselves. Party competition is a mediating force in facilitating political exchanges between parties and the electorate. As an important factor in political change, it is an arena within which resources are exchanged and where rival philosophies may battle it out. Here, some win while others lose. Two-party competition presupposes a hierarchy of winner and loser; it has a significant effect upon political outcomes. Clearly, party competition matters.

Anthony Downs argued that parties follow voters by taking a position on a set of issues and tailoring that position according to calculations of electoral advantage. Downs's proximity model placed the dynamic of electoral competition in a rational choice framework which suggested: (1) each voter can be represented by a point in a hypothetical space which when aggregated represents the distribution of voter preferences; (2) the policy stance of each party can be located in the same space; (3) voters judge parties on their proximity to their own preference profile and cast their vote accordingly; and (4) parties in turn adjust their appeals to reflect this median voter preference profile to maximise their potential vote to gain governmental office. In Downs's model parties are vote-maximisers and voters are interest-maximisers; both behave analogously to producers and consumers in an economic marketplace.[41]

The Downsian model suggests that median voter convergence grants sovereignty to the voter as consumer whose electoral preferences are pre-determined; as a result, parties, in order to secure electoral advantage, reflect voter preferences. The key assumptions and predictions of this model include rationality; proximity; and that parties locate to the median voter's dimensionality. Predicated upon a belief in voter preferences being unaffected by party competition, the original Downsian model saw office seeking as the only feature of party behaviour. There are of course limits to this model. Contra Downs, parties do not always respond to voter preferences as determined by voters themselves; they are not free to simply accommodate voter preferences whatever they may be. Vote maximisation (where parties office-seek to the exclusion of everything else) is an ideal expectation because parties also represent certain policy perspectives. They also policy seek. Gaining elective office, a necessary precondition for policy influence, is commonly both end and means, not simply, as Downs would have it, an end in itself. It is one primary goal among many.

Parties are different and, while capable of engineering dramatic shifts in their public identity over time, they have identifiable beliefs and traditions that act as a brake on the fluid opportunism identified in the Downsian model. Parties rarely agree upon a given policy package on the same political issue: not all points in the policy space are open to all parties.[42] This relates to the notion of a genetic code outlined above, one which acts as a brake on change rather than preventing it taking place. The core proposition of the Downsian model of party competition that party leaders are always and everywhere rational vote maximisers and never policy-seeking ideologues should be rejected. Parties do not always formulate policy in order to secure election as Downs would have it; nor do they always seek election in order to implement policy. Both office seeking and policy seeking objectives, whichever comes to the fore, are dependent upon the situation in which the party finds itself. In the early 1980s, Labour and Conservatives did not position themselves closest to the point of median voter convergence on the basis of a pragmatic appeal, one ill-distinguished from their chief competitor. Instead they gave preference to what might loosely be termed ideology over pragmatism and abandoned the pre-1979 political 'middle ground'. Downs's argument that parties are not bearers of policy agendas but simply seek to reflect existing electoral preferences is wrong. Parties do not necessarily formulate policies to win elections but can win elections to implement policy. The assumption that voter preferences are fixed and unchangeable has been the subject of sustained criticism. The phenomenon of Thatcherism itself creates considerable difficulties for the Downsian model.

Preference accommodation (the classic Downsian model) has been challenged by a theory of preference shaping where, rather than simply alter their policy stance in line with voter opinion, parties can attempt to change voter opinion in line with their own favoured policy stances. Patrick Dunleavy's preference shaping model of party competition argues that parties can attract electoral support by developing, shaping or changing political choices in their favour.[43] In similar vein the directional voting model offered by Rabinowitz and MacDonald also suggests that parties can generate a stimulus for voters to vote for them. Controlling for 'extremism' they argue that: 'The more intense a candidate is on an issue the more the candidate generates interim support or opposition with regard to that issue. By taking clear, strong stands, candidates can make an issue central to [electoral] judgements about themselves.'[44] Dunleavy suggests that 'using state power for partisan advantage allows party leaders to keep their existing policy commitments and ... devise public policy measures that will change in a direction favourable to their party purposes the shape of the curve showing the aggregate distribution of preferences'.[45] He identifies four main strategies in which parties can use political actions to secure partisan advantage: (1) Engineer favourable changes in the social structure; (2) Target particular groups for special treatment; (3) Use state power to change what voters want or what they see as feasible; (4) Alter existing institutional arrangements in ways that confer partisan advantage.[46]

If, as Downs would have it, electoral preferences are fixed and cannot be changed by party competition, parties demonstrate their suitability to meet those preferences rather than change them. Here, they simply find out what electors want and offer it to them. Of course, voter preferences are not static but change over time. If voters do not have fixed policy preferences parties can influence what these preferences are. As a result, voter preferences can be determined by party competition not simply by voters themselves: 'The aggregate distribution of preferences is not autonomous from the process of party competition, but may be influenced by party strategies to some degree in both the short and the long term, as well as by a wide range of factors external and internal to the society being analysed.'[47] Parties are instrumentalist institutions in this process. Rather then react to electoral demands they can shape electoral wishes by offering promises and appeals or by criticising those offered by their opponents. They can therefore advance either reactive and/or proactive strategies dependent upon the situation in which they find themselves.[48]

Although it is suggested that electoral processes 'should therefore be studied as a system in dynamic equilibrium, in which parties propose and voters dispose in sequential interaction',[49] voter demands must be distinguished from party promises. While involving exchanges between parties and electors, party competition does not necessarily imply that they are independent of one another. Parties do not just do what electors instruct them to do; they offer alternatives from which, ultimately, electors choose.[50] Hence, should parties respond to existing preferences (as they perceive them) and change their public identity, the manner in which they respond to these preferences is open to question. Most often, parties (together with other political actors such as intellectual commentators, opinion formers, media critics) and not electors set the agenda, as political issues, handed down from above, are a mechanism by which political elites address the mass. Electoral choices are not freely made, but largely given: the invitation to choose between one of two party alternatives for government is a limited choice, all the more so if the policy packages on offer from each alternative are largely similar. A clear distinction (absent in Dunleavy's work) can be made between electoral preferences and available choices. Hence, an elector casts a vote for one party rather than another not necessarily because that party meets his or her preference but because that is the choice made available to them.

Liberal democratic theory presupposes that for voters to take meaningful decisions they must understand the options on which they are voting. These options are presented to the electorate and not by them: they are given as aggregated packages and not as specific and separate items – within the electoral process voters choose to support parties not particular policy options. Choices are different from preferences. For example, a restaurant diner is free to choose between eating beef (if he or she is foolhardy) or pork, but cannot have fish if it is not on the menu. Here, the restaurant constrains the choice the diner makes, not actively shapes the preference. Choice and preference are constrained (if not actively determined) in every electoral process. Parties can matter: contra Richard Rose, parties can sometimes make a difference even if their influence only extends to constraining the choices that electors make. All choices are predetermined; should an individual wish to buy a car but be unable to afford a Rolls-Royce they have to choose between, say, a Mini Metro and a Volkswagen Golf. A preference cannot be met but a choice can be made: always a preference is constrained by the choices that can be made. Because political parties define problems and offer remedies, the vision of popular control over public policy offered by the responsible party model is heavily circumscribed. Precluded from directly expressing their views with any real precision, citizens are at best able to influence policy only indirectly through an electoral choice not of their own making.

Not simply a passive respondent to external pressures, the political party can be a key player in shaping political issues to initiate an appropriate and favourable public response. Indirect links between electors and parties are mediated through the process of party competition, and so the electorate is often placed in the role of jury, adjudicating between rival claims, and in so doing offering office seeking parties an incentive structure that eventually impacts upon their behaviour. Preference accommodation strategies remain a viable option for a party which prioritises office seeking over policy seeking. They are available to the party which cannot successfully preference shape. Unable to re-shape the electoral universe in their own likeness, parties are obliged for office seeking reasons to alter their policy seeking strategies.

It is important to emphasise that, however important it may be, party competition is not reducible to electoral outcomes alone; voting behaviour is one thing and party competition another. Electoral outcomes are often an expression of political change and not just an explanation of it. Dunleavy argues that within party competition 'parties choose tactics; in doing so, they help to define the political agenda and shape the choices that voters confront'.[51] His model defines the objective of party power within party competition as the ability to alter or influence voters' political expectations, their normative evaluation of public policy or their perception of political realities. But, in addition to influencing voters, parties can also influence one another. Parties also 'shape the choices that other parties confront' and so party competition can alter or influence party expectations, evaluations of public policy, and perceptions of political realities. Rather than act as prisoners of electoral realities, parties, in attempting to reshape voter preferences (and, just as crucially, in altering public policy), impact upon one another: they can act as a vehicle by which political change is effected.

Political realities can be shaped by interactive parties seeking either successfully or unsuccessfully to influence political opinion through party competition. Party competition, party-driven rather than simply voter-driven, is influenced by a 'top-down' process. In assuming that social determinants are influential in explaining electoral or political change, political explanations cannot be ignored. Although parties can be the agents and not just the prisoners of their own fate, they can also be the prisoners of other parties which successfully shape the environment in which party competition takes place. Where parties reshape electoral preferences in their own favour, they impact upon their party competitors. Where electoral predilections are considered to have changed in a manner favourable to one party and unfavourable to another, the penalised party will be forced to reassess its chosen strategy.

As argued above, poor electoral performance by itself, taken in isolation, is not sufficient to explain when, why and, most significantly, how parties change. Victory has its own incentives much in the same way as defeat. To reprise electoral impacts outlined in the previous chapter: a triumphal election crowns the performance of the winning party at the same time as a calamitous election sees rivals vanquished; a successful election outcome vindicates the stance taken by the victorious party, confers a mandate for its programme and damns the unsuccessful loser. Cumulative effects are important. Parties experiencing triumphal elections may be able to set an agenda demonstrated by the vindication of their programme and appeal at the same time as that of their rival(s) is dismissed. On both occasions, successful and unsuccessful parties are influenced by the outcome of an election. Party competition is therefore a form of 'elite actor interaction'. In contrast to the classical Downsian model (building upon that of Dunleavy), a model of party competition-driven party change suggests that while electors do influence parties, parties also influence electors and influence other parties.[52]

In shaping electoral preferences parties can forge a new 'political map' by way of establishing an electoral dominance, one that allows them access to office and leverage over government policy. In so doing, where dramatic change results from a party being able to policy seek through successful office seeking, they can help reshape the political landscape. Where a party does not set out to consciously preference-shape, party realignment within an existing political space presupposes it follows electoral preferences and responds to an altered electoral universe reshaped in the process of party competition. However, the idea that parties change their policy package, hoping to create a new identity that appeals more to voters, is only one side of the coin. In terms of explaining the impact of party competition on the wider political environment, party success (and the reasons which account for it) is as important as party failure: which party wins, why they win and what they do as a result of winning is probably as important as who loses. Within a two-party system, where one party is seen to successfully preference-shape at the level of the electorate (as attested by its ability to successfully office seek), an unsuccessful party will be obliged to respond to that success and to its own failure to succeed. Successful parties can and do map out a dominant agenda. Exceptionally they can make a major contribution to the process of political change as evidenced in alterations in the dominant political-ideological environment.

Party change engineered through party competition can reflect wider political change. The model of party competition outlined here combines both preference accommodating and preference shaping strategies. Where Dunleavy's model presumes that a successful political party can pull the position of the median voter in the direction of its choice by changing the aggregate distribution of preferences so altering the electoral environment, other parties who are unable to alter the aggregate distribution of preferences are obliged to take note of the changed environment. As a result, the defeated political party faces two choices: either to seek to re-influence the preferences of the electorate or to accommodate to the electoral environment as shaped by its successful opponent. Preference shaping parties therefore co-exist alongside preference accommodating parties. This process, described as the 'politics of catch-up', bridges the gap between the classical Downsian and the Dunleavy model of party competition. Arising from their interactions with electors (and other parties), parties do alter their position in a competitive space (as the Downs model suggests); some parties can successfully preference shape (as Dunleavy argues), while others can alternatively preference accommodate. The relationship between parties (in contrast to that between parties and electors) is one both models need to address.

The choice between preference shaping and preference accommodating strategies dictates party behaviour. Dunleavy rightly suggests that existing models of party competition offer too positive an image of electoral competition based on voter sovereignty: 'The preference shaping model offers us an account of party competition in which the shape of public opinion... is determined endogenously within the competitive process.'[53] While Dunleavy applies this concept to the elector–party relationship it can also apply to a party–party relationship. If the object of elections for office seeking parties is to win state power (put more moderately, office and the fruits that go with it), party competition provides an environment within which parties learn how to do things and adapt their strategies accordingly. If it is rightly 'logically necessary' to review the assumption that voter preferences are exogenously fixed,[54] we are also obliged to consider how parties relate to one another in the construction of the political agenda; the policies, ideas and values upon which party competition is so often based. 'Multiple factors influence how party leaders choose between preference and preference accommodating strategies, rooted in the characteristics of the party systems and institutional arrangements of different countries.'[55]

Adopting a 'directional approach' leads a party to select policies which reflect a political value system derived from a long-term ideological purpose. Conversely, the selection of a 'positional approach' sees a party 'sell' itself by more closely aligning its policy 'product' to what are seen to be prevailing electoral tastes. These are not necessarily preferences expressed in electoral opinions but preferences as expressed in electoral outcomes. The choice parties make between 'directional' and 'positional' behaviour is dependant on circumstance. A 'directional party' will seek to pull the optimum point of the median voter across the political scale to either left or right. The 'positioning party' (that which, when faced with a successful 'directional party', is unable to significantly alter voter perceptions in sufficient numbers to win an election) will, in time, acknowledge the changed political terrain and move to catch up with the new position in which the realigned median voter finds themselves.

Of course, the tools and paraphernalia of electoral campaigning must be distinguished from party competition strategies; while compatible, the two are not the same thing. Campaigning practices are available to any party irrespective of the choice of a preference shaping or a preference accommodating strategy. The objective of any election campaign is to enhance the public identity of the party at the same time as unfavourably affecting that of their opponents. Electors interpret (and, more significantly, can have interpreted for them) these public identities. Here, 'value' issues can draw distinctions between parties where policy platforms may not: the appeal 'it's time for a change' or the claim that one party rather than another can 'make Britain great again', can make all the difference between a successful or an unsuccessful office seeking strategy. Public relations strategies, political marketing and personalised leadership are all part and parcel of the modern election campaign irrespective of the actual party competition strategy that is being followed: a theory of election campaigning is not necessarily reducible to one of party competition.

Adapting Dunleavy, then, the nature of party competition involves parties selecting between preference shaping and preference accommodation strategies so choosing the preferred method according to an assessment of political realities. A 'catch-up' model of party competition suggests that successful preference shaping parties so realign the perceived location of the median voter that unsuccessful preference shaping parties are obliged to preference accommodate. It assumes that parties either adopt preference accommodation in order to accommodate to the median voter or preference shape to alter the position of the median voter in the party's favour. However, parties may adopt a positional strategy and so choose to preference accommodate not just in response to altered electoral preferences but as a reaction to the success of their political opponent. In explaining the success of the Thatcher-led Conservative Party after 1975, a distinction must be made between the influence exerted on the electorate and the impact that the Thatcherite project has come to have on the political elite; none more so than its principal competitor for public office, the Labour Party.

7
Party Competition Driven Party Change: The Politics of 'Catch-Up'

Thatcherism has so permeated the political life of the nation that the influence of its value-based political ideas enacted as policy has had considerable impact on political and not just electoral developments. Yet no permanent coalition of voters endorsed the Thatcherite project and evidence points to the fact that at the level of the electorate the fabled 'Great Moving Right Show' was largely illusory: there was 'no Thatcherite electorate, no Thatcherite party'.[1] Despite the electoral success enjoyed by the Conservatives, persuasive claims are made that Thatcherism did not fundamentally alter the nation's political values. Clearly, certain social democratic values retained strong support among the public even at the height of the Thatcherite boom (as evidenced in opinion research on such matters as collective provision, welfare, and social responsibility).

A MORI poll published by *The Independent* on the tenth anniversary of the 1979 election victory illustrated that a majority of the public did not share many of the core principles of Thatcherism.[2] An earlier MORI poll in June 1988, as Ivor Crewe suggests, demonstrated that given the choice between 'a "Thatcherite" and a "socialist" society the public opted for the Thatcherite model on only 2 out of 5 dimensions, and then by small majorities... After nine years of Thatcherism the public remain wedded to the collectivist, welfare ethos of social democracy.' Crewe argues that, with the exception of privatisation, Conservative values failed to grow among the electorate between 1974 and 1987.[3] Whatever its success in the electoral and other fields, Thatcherism did not succeed in the long term in reforming popular opinion on key political issues. Such were its ambitions that it hoped to 'build new coalitions of interest, to win the battle of ideas for a radical change of direction and the dismantling of old structures and old priorities'.[4]

Of course, its achievements often did not match its ambitions. Although its ambitions extended beyond winning office, Thatcherism's ability to successfully office seek provided it with the opportunity to policy seek in government. While its electoral support was never so secure as to make it an hegemonic project, Thatcherism utilised its electoral base to pursue significant reforms in both the state and civil society.

The lasting consequence of Thatcherism demonstrates that party competition theories which simply examine party–elector relations may not in themselves fully illuminate the contribution that party competition makes to the process of political change (as evidenced in party change). Party linkages provide a core focus for an evaluation of the political consequences of Thatcherism, as distinct from the impact that Thatcherism had on electoral attitudes. The consequential interaction of parties can be only indirectly influenced by electoral outcomes. Here, parties may follow electors or follow where competitor parties lead. While electors can influence parties (Downs) and parties influence electors (Dunleavy) they also influence one another (subject to the fact that the interaction of parties with electors facilitates the interaction of parties). Party competition involves a set of intra-party interactions at the same time as it involves a series of party–elector relationships. Because these two processes are interrelated and help determine political outcomes, party competition can be a crucible of political change both within and between parties. An assessment of the dynamic (and impact) of party competition therefore requires an inter-party focus.

In analysing the impact of Thatcherism, too much should not be made of its electoral reception. The work of Stuart Hall on 'authoritarian populism' can misleadingly suggest that the ideological intentions of the Thatcher government were part and parcel of a strategy to wholly transform electoral opinions.[5] The objective of Thatcherism was to gain influence over the ship of state by establishing an electoral grasp on the levers of power. In this sense, contra Hall, a reliable electoral base rather than a political hegemony was fashioned in the first instance. Thatcher wanted to win hearts and minds but knew than the conversion of the mass to the ideals of Thatcherism was a hard task. Political considerations prompted the Thatcher government to devise strategies to secure election and re-election but a hegemonic project directed at the electorate was not the 'be all and end all' of Thatcherite politics.

In many ways the idea of a public hegemony envisaged by Hall was an illusion; what was sought was a reliable electoral base, and ministers were happy that an electoral poll of 40–44 per cent of those voting was not merely sufficient for their ends but could grant a landslide (or at worst a working) parliamentary majority. Rather than just recast electoral perceptions, Thatcherism was engaged in a battle with political opponents, principal among them existing social democracy and a left-leaning Labour Party threatening to undo many of its reforms. The political (and administrative) elite as much as the mass electorate were the ultimate audience of the Thatcherite drama. In this perspective the construction over time of a Thatcherite hegemony was to be directed ultimately at the level of the political elite rather than at the mass hegemony suggested by Hall.

Thatcherism demonstrates that office seeking and policy seeking can be part and parcel of competitive party behaviour. The Conservatives were concerned with winning sufficient electoral support so as to achieve the level of parliamentary representation that brings governmental office. Rather than being simply an end in itself, office was the means to influence policy outcomes: For a policy seeking party, party competition can be structured toward these designated sequential ends: office seeking to policy seek. A party unable to gain office because of its policy seeking profile may therefore content itself with office seeking. The determinants of party change are therefore rooted in party competition and related to political change evidenced in public policy and dominant ideological belief-systems. Political parties come to reflect, reinforce and, to some extent, determine political-electoral and, as significantly, political-ideological environments.

The role of ideas on political or policy change is significant. Together with socio-economic–political interests and circumstances as mediated by the interdependent role of actors and institutions, ideas can make a difference but, by themselves, ideas are not enough.[6] While circumstances (defined positively as an 'opportunity' for a 'new' approach to replace an 'old' discredited one; negatively as the absence of such an opportunity), interests, and institutions interact with one another in the promotion (or the prevention) of change, ideas (as often theory-laden as they are objective) do reflect political change as well. Ideas (subject to the interplay of interests, institutions, and circumstances) do impact upon the changing nature of public discourse, the currency of political and administrative actors. At one level, interests, institutions and circumstances provide the marketplace for ideas; some are successfully 'sold', others remain unsold.

Ideas can be aggregated into a macro-collectivity, usually described as a system of ideas. For want of a better term this can be considered an 'ideology', a way of looking at the world. While ideas are not necessarily reducible to an ideology (which designates both beliefs and actions;

defining what 'should be' at the same time as it describes 'what is'), ideology provides a structure of beliefs which fashions political values and opinions and shapes public policy. It underpins the strategies and tactics employed by political actors in (1) defining problems; (2) offering solutions; and (3) devising practical methods of policy formation. At one level a broad definition of ideology embraces such theories as capitalism, socialism, communism and fascism; this may be defined as macro-ideology. In contrast, a lower-level form of ideology, a micro-ideology such as social democracy or neo-liberalism, individualism or collectivism, governs the preconceptions of governing (and would be governing) actors that determine policy selection within a society characterised by a macro-ideology. For example, neo-liberal or social democratic, capitalism remains capitalism be it a feature of the Britain of 1959 or that of 1999. Political change is manifested in the transition from one dominant micro-ideology to another; a set of cognitive maps which inform working political ideas, structure policy agendas and influence political attitudes at the level of both elite and mass. Defined as a 'system of ideas' or, more concretely, a 'set of assumptions' about contemporary politics and its attendant policy options, a dominant micro-ideology can indicate where actors and institutions are located within a political spectrum stretching from left to right in socio-economic terms.

As political actors, parties can (under certain circumstances) either shape or reflect political realities, just as other parties act as weathercocks signalling the way the ideological wind blows. The political consequence of Thatcherism lies in the new political middle ground over which it presided, a changing micro-ideological space between parties (where it shifts, either narrowing or increasing) which reflects party change and is in turn related to wider political change. Party change is therefore a response not just to cumulative electoral defeats but can also be a reaction to an altered political terrain. Hence, a dominant micro-ideology provides a compass by which parties are obliged to navigate their procession thought political and economic straits, a response characterised by the dominant political ideas associated with an opponent able successfully to policy- and office-seek at the same time as the unsuccessful party was unable to do so.

Defining the political middle ground

In altering its political appeal (for whichever reason) and relocating along the competitive spectrum, a right-of-centre party will move to the left and a left-of-centre party will move to the right. Henceforth, this forms the political terrain upon which contemporary party competition is acted out and is defined as the middle ground: a political middle ground which, rather than being fixed, shifts (and is shifted) within the ideological continuum stretching from left to right. In contrast, the median 'centre ground' is fixed, a hypothetical point on a spatial model equidistant between extremes of left and right. The political middle ground is fluid, a movable point on the same space between alternate poles. What is commonly referred to as the centre ground is this political middle ground, a constantly shifting construct. Here, one should refer to *a* middle ground rather than *the* middle ground to distinguish this point: it is a common error to suppose that 'median' equals 'moderate'.

The political middle ground is characterised by socio-economic distinctions of left and right. Clearly, the UK party system (and political differences) are organised around this most basic dimension in party ideology. For example, Arend Lijphart identifies four main dimensions of this particular axis across which the left–right spectrum is spread:[7]

1 state versus private ownership of the means of production;
2 the extent of the government role in economic management;
3 the level of political redistribution of economic resources facilitated by government;
4 the level of development of the welfare state.[8]

Here, (1), (3) and (4) form the core issues which bound the left–right political divide in the UK. This demonstrates a spatial model of a left–right dimension along which individual parties locate and shift along the horizontal axis according to political circumstance and environmental context. The environmental stimuli that generate party change are usually considered to be electoral in origin. Clearly, given that party competition is predicated upon electoral exchanges, this is a major factor, but, as will be explored below, the 'political stimuli' to which parties respond involves wider factors such as changes in micro-ideological politics which, when related to electoral outcomes, impact upon parties and result in party change.

The recomposition of political activity, evidenced in party competition in terms of political shifts to the left or the right of the spectrum, reflects the *existence* of a political middle ground around which parties locate themselves. The *formation* of this middle ground is a quite separate matter. Parties, in following electors, can shift their position on the political spectrum in keeping with the aggregate distribution of preferences (i.e. they go to where the electors are). Equally, parties can change their position in keeping with what they see as an altered status quo where politics, as the art of the possible, has been redefined by parties (and other factors) which, as political actors, engineer political change. Because a party has followed where a party has led (where it is deemed electoral realities have been successfully reshaped), political debate is conducted upon the political terrain set out by the successful political party and so the successful political party has contributed to the transformation of the political stance of its electoral opponents. Movement along the ideological spectrum creates this party political middle ground. It can be a response to a party following electoral preferences or a party following a successful opponent (and not necessarily a party following a majority, or a sufficient minority, of the electorate under the plurality rule applying in the UK).

Here, unsuccessful office seeking parties accommodate not necessarily to the demands of the electorate but to the pace set by the successful party; one successful party, able to combine policy-seeking with office seeking, can contribute to the reconstruction of the political agenda which influences what governing actors (and would-be governing actors) do. A changing political 'middle ground' is bounded by a set of parameters in which parties come to accept what is possible and what is not possible for them to do. These parameters are clearly drawn within a process of party competition. The phrase 'middle ground' is in need of constant redefinition, just as that of 'left or right of centre', the phenomena it describes, is the subject of continuous change and modification. Hence, the political middle ground maps out a continuity zone; a micro-ideological space on which a competitive equilibrium is characterised by party acceptance or endorsement of the values, attitudes and opinions which find expression in problem definition and policy selection (cf. Figure 7.1).[9]

The Downsian model's presupposition of a policy equilibrium (one marked by policy convergence rather than total policy instability) offers a useful insight into party behaviour where parties follow parties not necessarily electors. Although Downs offers an unrealistic picture of parties willingly modifying their policy stance, preference accommodating parties can do so in response to a competitor party able over time to use the privileges of office to successfully policy seek. Such policy seeking parties, exemplified by the Thatcher-led Conservatives, can lead opponents to adopt a 'positional' rather than a 'directional' strategy so influencing electoral choices and engineering changes in party preferences.

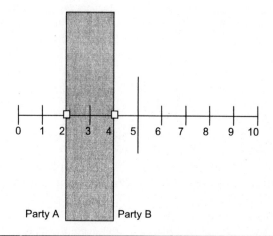

The political 'middle ground' maps out a continuity zone dependent upon the location of principal office/policy seeking parties. It maps out a micro-ideological space around which they are located. Here, it is the the space between points 2–4. The median point, in the above diagram point 5, is an equidistant space between two extremes; this is the hypothetical centre which is fixed and unchanging. In contrast, the political 'middle ground' marked out by the location of competitive parties is fluid, a movable point on the same space between alternate poles 0–10. What is commonly referred to as the centre ground (the space around which parties are located) is in fact this political 'middle ground' and not the centre as median point. Given that parties locate themselves within an ideological continuum, a political 'middle ground' reflects the party's location via its principal competitors. The closer Party A is to Party B the more consensual the political situation. The location of the political 'middle ground' reflects wider political concerns. A shifting political 'middle ground' (when compared to an unchanging 'centre' ground/ median point) is an indication of the extent of political change reflected in the altered parameters of political activity in terms of policy selection and problem definition and the related framework of ideas and values.

Figure 7.1   Distinguishing a political 'middle ground' from the median 'centre ground'

When a policy agenda is seen to have been successfully set by party A, party B must respond in either a negative or a positive fashion. Here, because party A has influenced the parameters of public debate and party B accepts the reordered status quo, party A sets the pace by leading from the front so influencing the dominant mode of political activity and constructing, shaping, changing or developing the political choices of parties engaged in the search for electoral support. If the successful

political advocate can reconstruct public agendas they will do so by
defining objectives through certain values. The Thatcherite creed of freedom v. equality, private activity v. collective association, and individualism v. collectivism was part of an effort to apply normative beliefs as
influenced by a micro-ideological agenda. Of course, certain normative
beliefs are more powerful than others: the more successful the normative belief (as evidenced by the electoral success of the party that
advances it) the more widespread it may become. This is demonstrated
by the success of social democracy after 1942 and by the Thatcherite
version of neo-liberalism after 1982. The politics of 'catch-up' demonstrates that in certain cases one party (against the background of its wider
environment) shall have taken the lead and the other followed.

Assuming that the viability of a micro-ideological agenda can be
demonstrated, electoral outcomes are very important in determining
which competing micro-ideological perspective is able to carry the day
(should, as rarely happens, antagonistic perspectives compete with one
another; continuity within a changing micro-ideological consensus
across party alternation in office is more often the case: the collapse of
the centre in 1970–83 is an exceptional case). Although electoral bases
are very significant environmental variables (given an unchanging if
volatile party system) which directly affect vote- or office-seeking strategies they only indirectly effect what a party actually does in terms of
its response. Here, given a record of relative failure, the question of how
to successfully office seek may all too often be a reaction to the prevailing wisdom of the day, the *zeitgeist* that prompts a party to engineer a
particular change in its political attitudes as reflected in its policy stance.

Party convergence (as a reflection or catalyst of political change) is
evidenced in party change. Labour's profound transformation since
1983 reflects wider political change and suggests the party has come to
accept the terms of a post-Thatcher settlement characterising the micro-
ideological terrain upon which party competition is enacted. In discussing the impact and consequences of Thatcherism a comparison with
political developments following Labour's electoral victory in 1945 is
instructive. At that election, the wartime experience (fostered to some
extent by the Wartime Coalition) had encouraged some form of collectivist spirit based upon a sense of unity and common purpose within the
British electorate. This had demonstrated the ability of political actors
to achieve desired social ends through the better organisation of the
state. The electorate then chose to endorse Labour, the party it believed
was best placed to fulfil these aspirations.[10] The resultant Labour
landslide swept what was considered a backward-looking, out-of-touch

Conservative Party from office. With the brief exception of 1924 and 1929–31, the Conservatives had been in office continuously since 1916.

Cast into opposition, the Conservatives found themselves forced to reassess their entire political strategy in the light of this electoral cata-strophe.[11] According to one then-influential Conservative politician, Rab Butler, 'the overwhelming electoral defeat of 1945 shook the Con-servative Party out of its lethargy and impelled it to rethink its philoso-phy and reform its ranks with a thoroughness unmatched for a century'.[12] After 1945, the Conservatives claimed to recognise how powerful Labour's political philosophy had become – it provided a doctrine and a vision to which they had, in Butler's words, 'no author-itative answer or articulated alternative'.[13] The Conservative Party's attempts to renew its electoral appeal saw it shift to the left, the endorse-ment of the social democratic ethos of the Labour government symbol-ised by the adoption of the Industrial Charter in 1947.[14] For Butler the Industrial Charter marked a fundamental change of direction for the Tory party (albeit one in keeping with Conservative sense of traditional 'One Nation' politics): 'giving the party a permanent but painless face-lift', one that would 'counter the charge and the fear that [the Tories] were the party of industrial go-as-you-please and devil-take-the-hindmost, that full employment and the Welfare State were safe in our hands'.[15]

Here, according to Butler, the Conservatives wanted to 'present a recognisable alternative to the reigning orthodoxies of socialism – not to put the clock back, but to reclaim a prominent role for individual initiative and private enterprise in the mixed and managed economy'.[16] This era of the (in)famous 'Mr Butskell' (an unhelpful phrase for reasons explored below) saw the reconstruction of political debate around social democratic, Keynesian economic principles. Although both parties con-tinued to strongly differ with each other, competing as they were for the right to form the government, this competitive edge was softened by this general agreement on such issues as government management of the economy, the mixed economy, full employment, welfare policies and the increasing centrality of the corporate state.

By the 1950 general election, the Conservatives may have attacked the Labour government as dangerous and extremist. They may well have championed their 'defence of individual freedom' against the Labour government's 'alien, centralised state control' but, nevertheless, they had come to unquestioningly endorse the social democratic attitudes upon which the post-war settlement was based. While remaining true of the tenants of 'reform Conservatism', the party of Churchill, Eden and Macmillan thus followed where Labour had led; the strategic assumptions they made and the key priorities they followed throughout the 1950s and 1960s were broadly in keeping with social democratic politics owing much to the political developments of the 1930s and 1940s and dramatically consolidated by Labour in office post-1945.

In 1974, Keith Joseph criticised this post-war political convergence, explaining the persistent shift to the left by the Conservative Party in terms of a 'ratchet effect': (1) Labour in office promoted 'socialism'. (2) This was accepted by the succeeding Conservative government and thus a political 'consensus' was formed. (3) The Conservatives were replaced by another Labour government which pursued more radical and egalitarian policies and so moved the political 'centre ground' even further to the left. (4) When, in due course, the Conservatives returned to office they would again accept this left-wing 'centre ground' as the new status quo and so reinforce an ever left-leaning 'consensus'. As the Conservatives moved leftward by this process, so too did the 'middle ground'. While Joseph's account places far too much significance on the ability of the Wilson-led Labour governments to set the agenda others follow, his argument does relate closely to the 1945–55 period. As the Conservative Party moved to its left in the wake of the Labour landslide of 1945, so Labour has moved to its right after 1983. The intention of both parties was initially to fashion an electoral strategy to appeal to the voter who did not vote Conservative in 1945 nor Labour in 1983. After 1983, Labour's primary task, the leadership constantly proclaimed, was to recognise changing circumstances and accept the need to change accordingly; to 'rethink its philosophy and reform its ranks', an approach set out by Rab Butler in 1946 in the successful effort to persuade the Conservative Party to do likewise after 1945.

Given the significance of the political-ideological environment (the form of ideological engagement, the climate of opinion, policy orientation on the part of actors and electors), its interaction with the political-electoral environment is an important factor in explaining party competition driven party change.

Assume two actors in a two-party system, party A of the right and party B of the left, competing on an existing political middle ground X. This status quo is altered over time by party A which, being able to successfully office seek and policy seek, is able to transform the status quo so that political activity is no longer configured by party competition around the politics characterised by political middle ground X. Party B, offering a markedly different micro-ideological agenda to that of party A (or else maintaining its location at political middle ground X), is faced with the political reality of party A's success. Such is the nature of the shift of political opinion away from the previous status quo that party A is able through electoral endorsement and policy success to consolidate the changes that have been made. Faced with this challenge, party B is able to make one of two choices: (1) to attempt to shift the terms of the political debate away from the position staked out by party A; or (2) to accommodate to the project initiated by party B. Should party A choose the second course of action, party change will be evidenced in the party's shift across the political spectrum away from political middle ground X (or the alternative position it had carved out) to occupy a position closer to that of party A which then becomes political middle ground Y as characterised by the gradual accommodation by parties A and B to the new, altered status quo. This characterises the process of catch-up; party B follows (for whatever reason) where party A has led.

Here, party competition is significant in that it facilitates and encourages party change; in so doing it acts as an agent of wider political change. Of course, continuity rather than change is the feature of the political middle ground; dramatic change is the exception and not the rule. Thus, the Thatcher-led Conservative government succeeded in refashioning the political middle ground as a 'directional' agent able to alter the political landscape. By combining office with policy seeking, it was able to pull the British political spectrum to the right, a phenomenon copperfastened by Labour's playing the politics of catch-up post-1983. Catch-up reshapes a party's public identity as it is represented in the political marketplace. Dependent on circumstance, parties can choose between a 'directional' or a 'positional' strategy as internal assumptions and external environmental influences determine whether a party attempts to preference shape or preference accommodate. Either can come to the fore in a party strategy at any particular conjuncture; in turn, the choice will reflect the primary goal, office seeking or policy seeking, which has been prioritised. If it is accepted that the political landscape of Britain has been reshaped to transform the nature of the political game, parties have to react accordingly. This is attested to in the Downsian model (which assumes that electors transform the electoral landscape) and also in the Dunleavy model (which supposes that parties as actors can alter electoral preferences). More infrequently, however, successful political parties cannot simply engineer changes in electoral behaviour but also establish a dominant agenda and alter the behaviour of political opponents. In so doing the process of party competition will, in time, help shape the political terrain upon which competition takes place. A successful party will therefore have transformed the political stance of others as an unsuccessful party

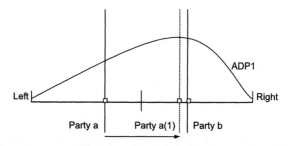

1

This is the classical Downsian model: Party a is forced to relocate within a spatial model to capture the median voter and successfully office seek. Party b is more in tune with existing voter preferences, and given that preferences are fixed and unchanging its continuing electoral success is guaranteed if Party a fails to relocate to position a(1) in order to increase its electoral popularity.

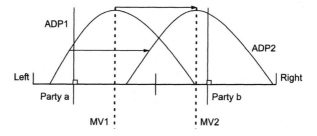

2

This is Dunleavy's alternative to Downs, the 'preference-shaping' model. Here, Party b has succeeded in altering the Aggregate Distribution of Preferences (ADP) in its favour, as evidenced by the shifting position of the Median Voter from MV1 to MV2. It assumes that voters can be persuaded to alter their electoral preferences in line with the programme appeal offered by Party b by a variety of positive and negative inducements. Here, Party b will be able to successfully policy and office seek.

However, parties need not always be influenced by electoral considerations. Office seeking parties all too often policy seek in line with the given policy agenda/political paradigm of their day (one which can be influenced by a party opponent). Party competition is enacted on an inter-party agenda within which electors adjudicate between competing appeals rather than decide for themselves. The shaded area in the diagram below indicates the competitative space once Party a has relocated to position A1.

Figure 7.2 Beyond Downs: preference-shaping and 'catch-up' party competition

responds not necessarily to the demands of the electorate but to the pace set by its successful opponents (cf. Figures 7.2 and 7.3).

To briefly take a comparative example: Where, in ideological terms, stands US President Bill Clinton? As the first Democrat re-elected to the

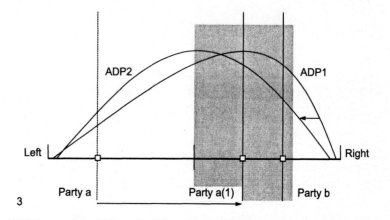

Rather than follow electors, parties can follow other parties: in this diagram Party a shifts its position in response to party B. The Aggregate Distribution of Preferences shifts slightly leftward while Party a shifts rightward in an effort to catch up with Party b. In programmatic terms, party competition can be a form of 'elite actor interaction'. Building upon the Dunleavy model (in contrast to the assumptions of the classical Downsian model), parties cannot just influence electors but may also influence other parties. Parties may alter their location within an ideological space not just in reponse to electoral preferences but as a reaction to the political agenda successfully articulated by a party opponent which is able to successfully combine office seeking with policy seeking and so make a significant alteration in the political status quo.

This process, the 'Politics of Catch-Up', bridges the gap between the classical Downsian and the Dunleavy model of party competition. Preference accommodation and preference shaping are only two strategies open to any particular party. Here, parties can alter their competitive space in the search for votes OR they can attempt to alter the position of the median vote (and with it the Aggregate Distribution of Preferences) in their favour. A model of party competition driven party change suggests that a party unable to successfully preference shape may be obliged for office seeking purposes to alter its spatial location in favour of the electoral terrain mapped out by its party opponent. In addition to preference accommodating strategies, parties can engage in 'Catch-Up' in order to respond to the perceived success of its party opponent.

Figure 7.2 Beyond Downs: preference-shaping and 'catch-up' party competition (*cont.*)

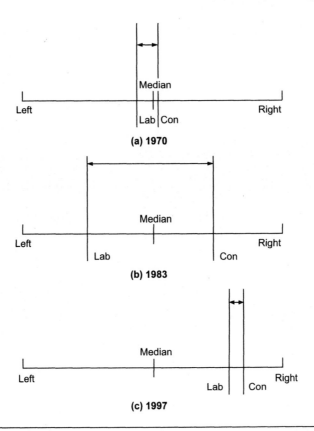

NB: Alternate poles to left and right are illustrative only: they form part of a continuum.

Figure 7.3 Party convergence and the changing political 'middle ground', 1970–97

White House since Roosevelt, is he closer to FDR or Ronald Reagan? Dick Morris, the election consultant who advised Clinton in the run-up to the 1996 campaign, dreamt up 'triangulation', a much lauded 'strategy' (particularly by Morris himself) by which Clinton moved away from traditional Democratic politics and positioned himself nearer Republican terrain established since the mid-1970s. In his memoir, *Behind the Oval Office*, published after his fall in the wake of a much publicised indiscretion, Morris characterised 'triangulation' thus:

I had studied the Republican Party from within as one of their con-sultants. If you are within their field of fire, they are deadly. Raise taxes, go soft on crime, oppose work for welfare, weaken the military? They're all over you yelling 'liberal'. If you wander into their line of fire, they're going to kill you every time. But they have no other game plan, no other way to win. If you come around behind them or alongside and don't raise taxes, if you are tough on crime, and want to reform welfare, use the military effectively, and cut spending, they can't hit you. A tank can rotate its turret, a Republican can't.[17]

Here, laying out a vote/office-seeking strategy, Morris's portrayal of US Liberalism (which strikes one as a vulgar Republican stereotype) is pre-sented as a series of *de facto* negatives for a Democratic candidate. To successfully office seek, Clinton has to fight on Republican issues. Where stands the traditional Democratic agenda of social reform? The outcome of Clinton's anti-traditional liberal stance meant that he ran on a proto-Republican policy ticket. Who then set the agenda on which the fall campaign was based? And thereby the agenda of the second term of the Clinton Presidency? The 1996 Democratic platform (while addres-sing traditional Democratic concerns – read US shibboleths – such as the 'good society' and the 'American values of fairness, decency and equal treatment') more reflected a moderate version of the 'Gingrichite' 1994 'Contract With America' (moderated because Clinton for electoral rea-sons clearly ran to the left of the Republican campaign in 1996 as in 1992) than it did the liberalism that variously characterised the do-mestic policy of the Roosevelt, Truman, Eisenhower, Kennedy, Johnson, (and even) Nixon, and Carter administrations. Rather than avoid the Republican line of fire, as Morris suggests, Clinton has climbed into the Republican tank turret. Parallels can easily be drawn in the UK case.

   The electoral purchase of any party strategy (preference accommodat-ing or shaping) is a significant factor. One interesting question is that the post-'Bennite' Labour Party did not simply develop a moderated social democratic agenda arguably where the political preferences of the electo-rate were located. Instead Labour embraced many of the neo-liberal reforms introduced by Thatcherism in office. Here, its transformation was enacted against the backdrop of contemporary politics; hence, in addition to being an electoral ploy to win office, Labour modernisation was a response to a dominant micro-ideological agenda made present through party competition and the success Thatcherism had in setting out a political agenda. Because 'catch-up' politics is mediated through party competition it reflects and generates the dominant political agenda, the dominant micro-ideology which serves to define the set of political ideas, attitudes and values that arise within political discourse.[18] Put crudely, where dramatic change is evidenced in the transition from one form of political middle ground to another, one party contributes to the agenda, the other accommodates (in some way) to it. As an abstract reflection of political activity, the agenda may be described as the broad appeal which defines the attitudes political actors are likely to strike when they attempt to engage with those issues promoted to public attention.

This framework of political ideas and values within which political activity takes place reinforces the attitudes which find expression in political, economic and social policy. The political middle ground focuses the parameters of political activity which are thus accepted as given and unchangeable by political actors and within which policy is developed. Should a successful party help establish these parameters, they will have contributed to a dominant political agenda through competition. Political success (winning elections and implementing policy change) can therefore construct, shape, change or develop the political choices not only for individual electors but also for competing political elites. The successful political advocate can reconstruct the political agenda to the detriment of its political or ideological opponents. Electoral success is one thing, political success quite another. The former Labour leader, Harold Wilson, won four elections out of the five contests in which he led his party but (despite recent attempts at rehabilitation) his governments are widely considered a great disappointment.

The political middle ground underpins the dominant political agenda subscribed to (to some extent) by all political actors thus demonstrating political change. Political change is therefore a broader phenomenon than electoral change; the two are often conflated. They are interlinked, but electoral change may be all too often a reflection of political change which may be far wider: political and economic change is informed by micro-ideological change realised in public policy change. This presupposes that a dominant political agenda exists (which overshadows subordinate, less influential agendas) and has come to redefine, colonise, or otherwise alter an existing political project. This political agenda can evidence electoral purchase, in that it enhances rather than impedes the office-seeking capabilities of the political party associated with it (or a variant of it). To some extent party competition is able to help generate a political agenda which is capable of: (1) determining elite (not necessarily popular) political opinion; and (2) influencing the set of policies (the ideological predisposition that informs policy choice) presented by political actors to the public in the form of administrative choices. Of course, political agendas may not be shaped by party competition alone. While it is a very important factor in the promotion of party change, party competition is only one important factor in the process of political change. The importance of party competition to political change lies in the way it can act as a agency of change, a 'transmission belt' which thereby facilitates a process of change wider than party change. Influenced by party competition (and other factors), party change is related to political change. It too can be a response to a prevailing 'climate of opinion', a 'catch-up' reaction where one party feels itself obliged to follow another; an acknowledgement that the parameters which bound the ideological space within which parties locate themselves has changed and that accommodation to this form of political change (evidenced in party competition) is necessary.

Party competition driven party change involves a process of convergence around a new political middle ground, one fashioned not merely by electoral demands (as suggested by Downs) but by parties that either have successfully preference shaped in the past or have managed to set (or associate themselves with) a political agenda to which other political actors become obliged to accommodate. For the most part elections are important external stimuli in themselves but particularly as harbingers of political change evidenced by an alteration in the microideological proclivity of the political nation and the need for the unsuccessful party to respond to this. Party change is therefore a product of the pattern of competitive interactions between parties and the electorate and between parties themselves. Realigning elections such as 1906, 1945 and, taken together, 1979, 1983 and 1987, while infrequent, do provide a snapshot of opinion and signpost political change.[19] Of course, what happened *after* (and as a result of) those elections is far more important. Party competition clearly affects the ideological universe within which parties are located. This approach to party competition assumes not only that office seeking becomes the dominant objective of a political party but that parties alter their policy seeking behaviour in line with what is deemed to be the dominant mode of policy seeking.

The pattern of party competition is a significant factor in the generation of political (and therefore party) change as a process over time. While not the only factor, external stimuli (such as electoral defeats), not necessarily natural phenomena, can be the product of party competition. This argument posits an association between party–voter linkages and party–party linkages. Both have a direct influence on the pattern of competition between political parties and together impact on the process of party change. As a process of catch-up, party change can therefore illustrate far wider political change evidenced in the shift over time from one micro-ideological paradigm to another. If parties are adaptive organisations, changing their appeals in light of the changing predilections of their electorate, they also change in response to the parameters bounding the competitive ideological space as marked out by their successful (party) competitor.

This is not necessarily (1) a case of 'If-You-Can't-Beat-Them-Join-Them' (although this is necessarily a feature of any catch-up strategy) but it is, at the very least, a (2) 'We-Can't-Beat-Them-With-The-Approach-We-Have-Followed-Up-To-Now-So-We-Need-To-Change-Our-Strategy' approach, one adopted when one party feels itself obliged to follow where another is seen to have successfully led. In any case, strategy (2) invariably promotes the adoption of strategy (1) in some form even if the catch-up party claims an association with the political agenda advanced by its political opponent for its own reasons and purposes. Directional and preference shaping strategies change electorate predilections within party competition. Should party B feel obliged to adapt to environmental changes engineered by party A that are perceived to penalise (the office seeking) party B, then party B is more likely that not to embrace the need for party change assuming that the impact of this environmental change is internalised by a dominant coalition able to successfully promote a strategy for change.

Party change is therefore a variation in behaviour arising from the political consequences of strategic party interaction. Who wins and why they are perceived to have won an election are as important as the fact that a party lost an election (or a number of elections). Environments are influenced by party competition (but, of course, not only by party competition), and party change is therefore a process of adaptation to circumstance and events; one in which change is the product of the internal response to a set of external stimuli. Parties can shape their environment: equally, parties can be constrained by an environment or even by an environment that has in part been reshaped by its political competitor. Accordingly, party change, a response to an altered policy universe, can be provoked by other parties acknowledging that a fundamental micro-ideological shift has been engineered in the form of political debate.

Explaining Labour's transformation: modernisation and the politics of 'catch-up'

David Marquand initially suggested that Labour, under Kinnock and Blair, rediscovered its political roots: 'The great aberration of postwar

Labour history came in the 1970s and early 1980s when [its traditional appeal] was temporarily abandoned. What Kinnock and Blair have done is to bring the party back to its roots. They have not invented a new tradition. They have reinvented an old one.'[20] This is also a view held by Andrew Gamble: 'Three general election victories over a divided and increasingly demoralised Labour Party ensured that it was a free market strategy that determined the agenda . . . [Having abandoned its 1983 programme, Labour] returned to its social democratic traditions and embraced economic policies which accepted capitalism, embraced the profit motive, the role of markets and the importance of competition and the consumer.'[21] It is impossible to endorse these views. Marquand later qualified the above comment, observing that 'We know what the new regime is not; we don't yet know what it is. Patently, it is not socialist. It is not even social democratic or social liberal . . . Like the Thatcher government before it, New Labour espouses a version of the entrepreneurial ideal of the early 19th century.'[22] This later comment acknowledges that Labour's extraordinary political realignment clearly reflects both a sharp and a dramatic shift in the contemporary political agenda. Old labels have been qualified, others invalidated: for many, the very term 'New' Labour is 'deliberately designed to distance the party from its past'.[23] While much of the remaking of Labour was designed for electoral purposes it also marks a significant shift away from past Labour practices; almost a deliberate attempt to shrug off the ideological baggage of the past.

Leading moderniser, Peter Mandelson, an influential Minister in the Blair government, suggests that 'Lazy or superficial commentators describe the party's process of change as merely "taking Labour to the right" . . . But this is the simplistic view propagated by New Labour's opponents.'[24] Yet, that Labour has moved to the right since 1983 is undeniable, its shift evidence of the transformation wrought in the British political scene in recent years. Writing in 1992, Perry Anderson offered the following observation:

> [Labour's] new programme accepts the basic parameters of the Thatcher settlement, in much the same way that the Conservative government of the 1950s accepted the parameters of the Attlee settlement. It does not seek to extend the public sector or reverse privatisation to any significant degree. It does not propose to raise the overall level of taxation, but promises to adjust its incidence in a mildly more egalitarian direction. It does not substantially depart from the laws that now regulate industrial action, while rendering them a little more

favourable to trade unions. It does not abandon the British nuclear deterrent. All these changes of the Thatcher years are uncontested.[25]

Under Blair the party has gone further and faster. One former Labour insider, Bryan Gould, a member of the Shadow Cabinet at the elections of 1987 and 1992 (and briefly a rising star of Kinnock's 'kitchen cabinet'), drew the conclusion that Labour came to ape the Thatcherite agenda: 'I think the position taken by Labour's leaders in the late 1980s and into the 1990s was a position of surrender... an acknowledgement that really we had lost the argument, that a Thatcherite agenda had been established to which we could only accommodate, [one that we] couldn't change... fundamentally.'[26] Contrary to the view first expressed by David Marquand, 'New' Labour's ideological pitch involves the eclipse of a Labourist social democratic appeal. Modernisation (itself a politically loaded term for 'change') is not simply a repudiation of 'Bennism' but a wholesale re-evaluation of past Labour practice. Distinguishing between ends and means, the contemporary politics of the Labour Party are in no way a return to normality following ideological excesses in the late 1970s and early 1980s.

In their book, *The Blair Revolution*, Peter Mandelson and Roger Liddle make much of a 'Bennite' aberration of the 1970s and early 1980s, a 'blip' which cast Labour into an electoral wilderness.[27] From this perspective Labour lost the 1983 election rather than the Conservatives having won it (little mention is made of the 1979, 1987 and 1992 elections). The modernisation thesis requires a belief that Labour reaped the electoral consequences of straying from its programmatic traditions. However, for reasons argued earlier, the 1983 manifesto is not the aberration many would have us believe. Shorn of its defence and foreign policy commitments it certainly marks a leftward shift in the party's practice but the economic and social programme of the post-1979 policy stance, part of the post-1970 Labour mainstream, was enacted within Labour's ideological tradition. The contemporary policy of the Labour Party is not.

The 1950s revisionist *par excellence*, Tony Crosland, argued that the dislocation of private wealth and social poverty, while not entirely reducible to the profit motive of the market, was redeemable by the political decisions of government which decided the level of taxation and the direction of public expenditure. The revisionist milieu was shaped by Keynesian economics, the mixed economy and the corporate state, part of a political consensus based upon 'full employment; public ownership of the basics of monopoly services and industries; state provision of social welfare requiring in turn high public expenditure and taxation; and economic management of a sort, via a large public sector and a reduced role for the market'.[28] Egalitarianism was the objective of the social democratic project and the Keynesian Welfare State was the method to secure that objective.

In 1974, Crosland reiterated his core beliefs in the revisionist case and spelled out the need for detailed egalitarian policies involving 'a determination to "bash the rich", by a wealth tax, a gifts tax, [and] the public ownership of land'.[29] He argued that because the end socialism sought was equality, Labour should prioritise the relief of poverty and social squalor; secure a more equal distribution of wealth; and improve social conditions by means of the expansion of housing, health and education programmes: 'These objectives, which are in Labour's central tradition of conscience and reform, call for a reallocation of resources and a redistribution of wealth. They require high taxation and public expenditure and rigorous government controls. This is the basic divide between Left and Right; a divide which a Tory government [that of Heath] is now joyously revealing.'[30] Crosland consistently argued that only through increasing social expenditure and redistributing wealth could Labour champion social equality and mount an attack on poverty. Firm supporters of the use of governmental power to constrain the workings of the unfettered market, the 1950s revisionists argued that only through the use of governmental power to constrain the workings of the unfettered market and increasing social expenditure could Labour champion social equality and mount an attack on poverty.

Labour's social democratic perspective on the mixed economy presupposed that while resources are allocated by the market, public power should alter certain market outcomes and constrain market forces for public ends; Croslandite revisionism reflected this. The prime elements in this social democratic lexicon were economic growth; redistribution; higher social expenditure; competitive public ownership (when necessary on grounds of economic efficiency; and equality. With the exception of a commitment to economic growth these are elements notable by their absence from the agenda of 'New' Labour. Noel Thompson suggests that a reading of the recent economic literature of the Labour Party indicates the extent to which a new economic discourse dominates one 'articulated in the language of competition, efficiency, productivity, economic dynamism, profitability, and, above all, that of individual choice and self-fulfilment in the context of a market economy'.[31] Croslandite revisionism by contrast posited a regulated, controlled, tamed, *reformed* market, one that the Labour Party was committed (in opposition if not always in government[32]) to manage through the apparatus of the social democratic, corporatist state. This involved a commitment to the control of market forces by government intervention as the means by which Labour would secure its identifiable ends.[33]

All such objectives and methods, part of the Labour mainstream in the 1970s, would now find few public supporters among Blair's Labour Party. The twin engines of Croslandite revisionism, progressive taxation and increasing public expenditure, have been called into question by New Labour: Crosland's ends and not just his means no longer form part of Labour's agenda. The former deputy leader (and self-appointed keeper of the Crosland flame) Roy Hattersley argued before Blair became Prime Minister: 'These days the Labour Party...commits itself to ending the redistribution in favour of the rich, but feels that it cannot redistribute in favour of the poor. The Blair government will be decent, compassionate, efficient and honourable. But it will not be socialist.'[34] Indeed, Hattersley has made the same observations ever more frequently, both before and since May 1997. In February 1997, in a *Guardian* review of a book on Crosland, he observed that most of the Blair Shadow Cabinet number among the 'apostles of the notion that the free market provides the best redistribution of resources and guarantees the greatest efficiency'.[35] Hattersley's opinion of 'New' Labour is a marker of its politics: redistribution, high rates of progressive taxation and increased levels of social expenditure have all been ruled out under Blair leadership. Egalitarianism, for one thing, no longer counts among Labour's objectives.[36] Of course, as Hattersley often fails to point out, Blair has followed a well-worn path mapped out under Neil Kinnock's leadership.

'New' Labour considers Crosland's belief that '[t]he state now regulates (or seeks to regulate) the level of employment, the distribution of income, the rate of accumulation, and the balance of payments; and its actions heavily regulate the size of industries, the pattern of output, and the direction of investment decisions'[37] both unfeasible and undesirable. The idea that a 'passive state has given way to active, or at least the ultimately responsible, state; the political authority has emerged as the final arbiter of economic life'[38] is also rejected for the same reasons; social democracy is dead. 'New' Labour is decidedly post-Crosland. It is not a re-invention of Gaitskellism nor a return to social democracy. Put crudely, in terms of a spatial model of ideological comparison, Blair stands far closer to Margaret Thatcher than he does to Tony Crosland (cf. Figure 7.4).

David Owen, one of the original Gang of Four to defect from Labour in January 1981, may well be described as the first non-Conservative Thatcherite. As leader of the SDP after the 1983 election, Owen worked hard to take his depleted grouping to its political right, calling for 'a new synthesis, a combination of what are too often wrongly assumed to be incompatible objectives',[39] a rapprochement with many of the elements of Thatcherism in the economic (if not yet in the social) sphere. Owen's concept of the 'social market economy' set the theme for an appeal based upon the primacy of the market in economic affairs.[40]

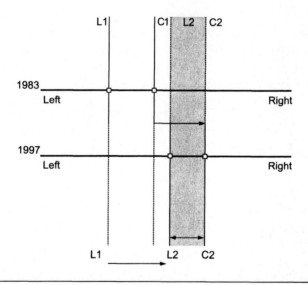

1.   The shaded area marked L2–C2 marks out the political 'middle ground' in the ideological space stretching from left to the right in 1997. This is the area of 'contestation' that currently divides Labour and Conservatives in terms of their political differences: it illustrates the political ideological 'terrain' around which contemporary politics is fought.
2.   The distance C1–C2 indicates the direction in which the Conservatives have travelled in the period since 1983. Building on the foundations established in the 1979 and 1983 Parliaments, the Thatcher and Major governments continued to shift their party alignment to the political right.
3.   The distance L1–L2 is the distance travelled by the Labour Party since 1983. This spatial area (highlighted by an arrow indicating the distance travelled) is that conceded by Labour in the period to 1997. Labour's shift to position L2 was influenced by the Conservatives moving location from C1 to C2. It is this shift that characterises the Politics of 'Catch-Up'.

Figure 7.4   The politics of 'catch-up' as illustrated on a spatial model of party competition

His utterances in the 1983–7 period bear an uncanny resemblance to much of what Blair says today. Owen critics, Ivor Crewe and Anthony King, describe him as having wanted to reconstruct British politics 'on to a new post-Thatcher basis, one which . . . a high level of social reform would be added to an emphasis on competition, the free market and free enterprise'.[41] Seeking to embrace 'Thatcherism with a Human Face' (or to become, as Denis Healey once sniped, Mrs Thatcher in a trouser suit[42]), Owen attempted (with some political success but little electoral advantage) to market the phrase 'tough but tender' as illustrative of this new approach, one combining 'competitiveness and compassion' and 'the social market and social justice'. These phrases, heavily laden with symbolism, marked an attempt to bridge the gap between an opposition party previously of the centre and the Thatcherite juggernaut.

In actuality and to the dismay of his colleagues in the Gang of Four (as early as 1984 Roy Jenkins was making his well-known distaste for Owen clear in his private warnings that the SDP should not take a 'junior Thatcherite approach'), Owen saw a need to build upon Thatcherism not bury it. His 'social market economy' was a reaction to a changed politics, one in which neo-liberal attitudes appeared to be setting the political agenda. Here, this appeal to a kindlier, gentler politics acknowledging the centrality of a state-led social policy in addition to market-driven economics was a distinctive pitch, one intended to harness opponents of the uncaring winner-take-all nature of Thatcherism to supporters of its radical, modernising spirit. The 'social market economy' considered the market as an essential tool to achieve economic success which itself could not provide for social harmony. In the event, should both elements of this approach clash, it was the primacy of the market in economic and industrial life that was to prevail. By 1987, Owen continued to refer to the notion of 'social justice' but increasingly spoke more of his commitment to a market unhindered by government intervention.[43]

In the eyes of one former director of policy of the Liberal Party, Owen came to be identified 'as one more footsoldier in the forward march of the New Right'.[44] In the event, the SDP political adviser closest to Owen, Danny Finklestein, joined the Conservative Party together with a small group of adherents from the 'Owenite' SDP just before the 1992 general election (Owen himself was to endorse John Major at that election). From the Social Market Foundation, Finklestein went on to become the Conservative Party Head of Research in 1995. Owen was the first opposition politician to recognise an attraction in the Conservative agenda.

His willingness to embrace the economic agenda of Thatcherism led to him being attacked as well as praised from all sides for being a 'closet Conservative'.[45] In many ways, Owen now strikes one as a prototype Tony Blair, a Blair Mark I, initially designed by Margaret Thatcher (where the Blair model was also engineered by Neil Kinnock).[46] His political leadership of the ailing SDP was a reaction to the neo-liberal agenda of Thatcherism and an early indication of the way the political wind was blowing.

Owen's political legacy is, of course, limited. Owen went the way of all flesh through the lack of a political base while acknowledging the intellectual force represented by Thatcherism, and recognising, as does Blair (and ultimately as Neil Kinnock did), the need to accommodate with it. As SDP biographers King and Crewe suggest: 'The SDP did not teach the Labour Party to be a modern, centre-left party. Neil Kinnock did – assisted, if indirectly, by Mrs Thatcher.'[47] Quite what is meant by the phrase a 'modern, left-of-centre party' is unclear; it is often more of an assumption than a fact. King and Crewe do not specify this other than to demonstrate the common perception that the Conservatives are right-wing (or, at times, ultra right) while Labour is left-wing (at times, ultra left) and centre-parties centre. By themselves such terms as left, right, and centre (to say nothing of the phrases 'sensible' or 'modern') are meaningless. Irrespective of party traditions all parties are more or less left-wing or more right-wing depending on the nature of contemporary politics. The 'centre' is not fixed; it shifts sometimes to the left and sometimes to the right. The present-day centre (the 'sensible' place for 'modern' parties to supposedly position themselves) is to the right of that occupied in the 1940s, 1950s, and 1960s.

Is social democracy in fact imprisoned within an unredeemable past? David Coates, a critic of Labour both 'old' and 'new', suggests 'New' Labour is not in fact terribly new.[48] He argues that there have always been two main groupings within the Labour Party: 'social reformers (keen to subordinate the power of private capital to progressive social ends) and bourgeois radicals (keen to modernise the local industrial base)', established versions of 'modernisers' and 'traditionalists'.[49] While Coates's attempts to categorise 'New' Labour as 'Just the Same Old' Labour is mistaken, his categorisation of these groupings (never as distinct as he would suggest; key political figures of the Labour right, Crosland, Gaitskell, Evan Durbin or even Roy Jenkins, for example, embraced both distinctions at certain moments in their careers) does underline the reality of 'New' Labour: 'The politics of Labour's social reformers have always focused on redistributing power (and resources) from the privileged to the poor. The politics of Labour's bourgeois radicals have always focused on strengthening the competitiveness of local capital, from which to glean surpluses for welfare provision without major policies of income redistribution.'[50]

Although the attitudes which cast Blairite economic policy may not be as 'fundamentally novel' (to use Coates's phrase) as modernisers would have us believe, the fact that the party no longer reflects, even marginally, the specific agenda of what Coates describes as 'Labour's social reformers' demonstrates a great deal about the transformation in the Labour Party. Equally, the programmatic appeal enunciated by 'Labour's bourgeois radicals' (if we can describe 'New' Labour modernisers as such) has little in common with 'Old' Labour practice given that its economic prescriptions reflect a neo-liberal rather than a social democratic mould. Attlee, Gaitskell, Wilson, and Callaghan (all 'bourgeois radicals' to Coates's way of thinking) were, in aspiration if not achievement, committed reformers with radical ambitions. This is why Roy Hattersley has seen his party shift to his political right while he, as true today to the revisionist philosophical beliefs he had when first elected to the Commons in 1964, has remained more or less in the same space on the ideological spectrum.

Although concerned at the rhetorical level with the promotion of social justice, 'New' Labour is principally concerned with strengthening the power of capital and allowing competition within the market to secure social reforms by virtue of 'trickle down' economics. For critics of the Labour project such as Coates, Blair's politics are a rejection of past Labour practice: 'Tony Blair seems determined to establish Labour's electoral credentials by demonstrating the party's distance from the unions, and by eschewing any vestigial class appeal. His rhetoric of stakeholder capitalism allows no space for the creation of new state institutions of planning and control, and puts him well to the right, not simply of Will Hutton but even of a former Social Democrat like David Marquand.'[51]

Labour's transformation is not simply an accommodation to 'political realities', nor a reflection of 'modern politics'. Where Tony Blair suggests that '[t]he totalising ideologies of left and right no longer hold much purchase',[52] the case made that left-wing 'totalising ideologies' are no longer relevant is born of actually existing politics, the product of interacting political and economic actors against the background of political, social and political events. Here, we may assume that Blair believes that mainstream social democracy or reform liberalism, not just old-hat command-style economy socialism, falls into this category.

It is not an automatic fact of life that is simply arrived at. Labour's transition is a reflection of the impact of Thatcherism and its direct influence on the pattern of mainstream ideological politics. Here, the suggestion of Jessop *et al.* that Thatcherism is a failed economic project serves to obscure its lasting consequences. The idea that Thatcherism 'proved more adept at rolling back the frontiers of the social democratic state and the gains of the post-war settlement than at rolling forward a new state able to engage in an international race for modernisation in the next wave of capitalist expansion'[53] may persuade, but the hold that Thatcherism has exerted upon contemporary politics demonstrates the lasting success it has had as a political project.

In contrast to Blair's politics, Labour's revisionist agenda of the 1950s demonstrated the firm purchase of the party's traditional approach. Where Crosland *et al.* advocated a reform agenda involving a recasting of the party's public identity by devising a new approach which would secure Labour's age-old objectives, the Blair agenda evidences a quite different purpose. Writing on Gaitskell's political world view in 1959, his most recent biographer, Brian Brivati, concludes: 'For Gaitskell, democratic socialism had evolved to a point at which the tools existed to provide a more equal society through a combination of public ownership (in a variety of forms and decided upon a basis of efficiency); demand management (with an awareness of the disincentive effects of high taxation); and physical controls, either through indicative planning (national plans and targets) incentives or, as necessary, through directive measures (further nationalisation).'[54] This world view reflected the political milieu within which Gaitskell was located; the modernity which fashioned his political outlook: it is one which finds no reflection in the politics of Tony Blair.

In his speech to the 1959 Labour Conference, Hugh Gaitskell declared his party in favour of 'social justice, an equitable distribution of wealth and income...a "classless society"...[where] the public interest must come before private interest'.[55] In contrast, Tony Blair's speech to the 1996 Conference indicated the refashioning of language since 1975: 'A society of opportunity. A society of responsibility...the Decent Society, a new social order for the Age of Achievement'.[56] In opposition and now in government, Blair's language is often symptomatic of the Thatcherite project: setting out to reclaim such Tory words as 'Freedom, Choice, Opportunity; Aspiration and Ambition', he often suggests that Labour's mission is 'not to hold people back but to help them get on'. In his eyes, Labour is committed to entrepreneurship as much as to equity.[57] Indeed, only through entrepreneurship (combined with the government safety-net Winston Churchill and other non-socialist historical figures often made reference to) can equity be likely to be secured.

As did Thatcher, Blair associates himself with words like 'freedom', 'achievement', 'people', and 'individualism'. His willingness to do so reflects Thatcherite success in helping recast the language of public discourse. While such normative principles do have a significant purchase in traditional Labour politics (and all are principles Labour should eagerly be associated with), Blair too often gives the impression he is not so much re-acquiring them as Labour values as appropriating them in their given Conservative (read: Thatcherite) form. Such quintessential Labour concepts as 'the state', 'collectivism', 'public provision', 'solidarity' have all been deemed negative and out of date. That Blair and his party are willingly entering into Thatcherite territory indicates the fact that, as Stuart Hall suggests, 'Thatcherism discovered a powerful means of translating economic doctrine into the language of experience, moral imperative and common sense, thus providing a philosophy in the broader sense . . . This translation of a theoretical ideology into a popular idiom was a major political achievement.'[58] To a considerable extent, this 'popular idiom' found expression by the mid-1990s in the language within which all parties express their political intentions: whatever else, Blair's politics are proof positive of that.

None the less, both Gaitskell and Blair in their very different ways demonstrate that Labour, in the words of Ralph Miliband, has long been 'concerned with attempts at a more efficient and more humane administration of a capitalist society' in contrast to (as Miliband himself would have preferred) seeking to 'adapt itself to the task of creating a socialist one'.[59] Labour's task has always been one of managing capitalism: when faced with the choice between securing the profitability of the private sector and strengthening capital over social reform and the redistribution of wealth and power Labour has always chosen the latter. This is the distinctive function of Labour both past and present. But the purposes identified by 'New' Labour are different from the agenda of 'Old' Labour. The economic policy instruments borrowed by the Blair government do little to manage capitalism in line with the social justice agenda with which Gaitskell and his ilk were happy to associate themselves. For the Gaitskellite revisionist: 'There was a belief, not merely in the occurrence of major changes in the structure of contemporary capitalism, which are not in question, but in its actual transcendence in its evolution into an altogether different system and, needless to say, a much better one.'[60] While wanting capitalism to work better for everyone and, should it prove possible, ending poverty, much as moral reformers would like to do away with sin, the Blair government gives every impression of being content to accept (even if it wishes to reform) the ideological status quo inherited from the Thatcher and Major governments.

8
A Theory of Consensus Politics

A theory of consensus politics should embrace notions of stability, continuity and, most particularly, a concept of change. It can offer an insight into governing across election cycles and the alternation of parties in office. It can demonstrate how policy development is a product of 'agreement on procedures and broad policy goals with contained disagreements about methods and means'[1] and, in the transition from one consensus to another, provoke an appreciation of shifts in political opinion across time. It may also promote an understanding of both policy and political change as an alteration in governing political agendas informed by dominant political ideas. The idea of consensus in political historiography usually 'describes the overlap between the economic, foreign and social policies of both Labour and Conservative governments'[2] throughout the post-war period until its breakdown in the 1970s.

For David Marquand, 'From the mid-1940s to the mid-1970s, most of [Britain's] political class shared a tacit governing philosophy',[3] a philosophy evidenced in a post-war political milieu shaped by a semi-collectivist political outlook characterised by a significant degree of state management of the economy, a commitment to full employment, the mixed economy, and the welfare state. Here, political attitudes to government were characterised by an acceptance of state intervention realised in levels of state economic intervention hitherto unimagined (with the exceptional period of the statist prosecution of total war in 1939–45 and, to a far lesser extent, in 1915–18). A semi-collectivist ethos (when compared to the pre-1930 status quo), a key feature of political life and government activity, was a hallmark of a theory of the state that came to be widely shared by political actors and public administrators, one common to both Labour and the Conservative Parties. As Marquand makes clear, this shared adherence to a social

139

democracy 'did not cover the whole spectrum of political opinion, of course; nor did it prevent vigorous party conflict. The two great parties often differed fiercely about the details of policy; on a deeper level, their conceptions of political authority and social justice differed even more. They differed, however, within a structure of generally-accepted values and assumptions.'[4]

The various distinctions between Labour and Conservatives in the 1950s (the highpoint of the post-war consensus) easily provoke examples of division and disagreement. Divisions over Suez offer one particular case in point, as do the personal contests between Macmillan and Gaitskell and later Wilson, Home and Heath. To agree with one critic of consensus, Nicholas Deakin, general elections were indeed to some extent 'bitterly contested between opponents advancing sharply different views of how the economy and the welfare state should be managed';[5] on issues of domestic (and foreign) policy government and opposition front benches did clash repeatedly; the key fact (reflected in the sentence struck by Deakin) is that divisions centred upon questions of how the economy and the welfare state 'should be managed' and to what ultimate end.[6] It was assumed by government and opposition alike that some form of Keynesianism and the existing economic norms of the 1950s, 1960s and 1970s were permanent features of the British political scene; these were 'guiding assumptions' that determined the stance of political actors of whichever party. Traditional policy differences were subsumed by these 'guiding assumptions' as the ideological gap between the parties narrowed as politics was characterised by a 'progressive centre' influenced by the politics of the centre-left distinct from those of the right or the left. Keynes and, to a much lesser extent, Beveridge were symbolic forces in post-war politics, actors whose ideas were eventually appropriated by a Labour Party keen to discover additional methods of translating their wish list of the good society into practical politics in 1945–51.

The objectives to which each government pursued full employment policies is of course open to question; Labour was more likely to declare itself in favour on grounds of equity and workers' rights, the Conservatives on grounds of individual benefit and economic efficiency. Although the record of the Labour government was castigated by the Conservative Party in opposition, the 'guiding assumptions' of the Attlee administration (reflecting foundations established during the Wartime Coalition) were broadly endorsed by the incoming government led by Churchill after 1951 (and subsequently by Eden, Macmillan and, after a short and half-hearted hiatus, Heath). Rab Butler, the architect of Conservative post-1945 rapprochement, described it as an adaptation to the reality of the 'mixed and managed economy', albeit one which reflected an intention to introduce elements of an 'non-socialist' enterprise society.

While the Churchill–Eden–Macmillan administrations did little to turn back the pre-1951 collectivist status quo, Conservative successes in the 1951, 1955 and 1959 general elections did ensure that the collectivist agenda offered by the Labour Party had 'come so far but gone no further'. Road haulage and steel may have been denationalised, physical controls relaxed, rationing abandoned, and Treasury policy liberalised, but the Conservatives contented themselves with the management of the situation they inherited (and ultimately reaped the benefits of the emergent 'affluent society'). The phrase, 'there is probably no alternative' is one that has some significance when applied to the attitudes struck by Tory political actors in the 1950s. They may, as some say, 'have held their noses' while making an accommodation to an altered status quo, but change they certainly did. Eager to promote the 'property owning democracy' within the status quo they inherited, Conservatives may have stemmed the collectivist tide, but, with partial and incremental exceptions, did little to dramatically reverse it.

Understanding consensus politics

The debate on the post-war consensus (or, as some commentators would have it, the non-consensus) embraces both contemporary history and political science. Paul Addison's path-finding work, *The Road to 1945*, first published in 1975 (and issued in a second edition in 1994), credits the post-1940 Keynesian revolution and the experience of the Labour/ Conservative Wartime Coalition under Churchill with the emergence of a 'social democratic consensus', eventually set in concrete by the actions of the 1945–51 Labour government (wartime measures included the 1941 Budget; the Beveridge Report of 1942; the 1944 Education Act; the 1944 Full Employment White Paper).[7] Arguing that consensus 'was an exercise in containment', a process committing both Conservatives and Labour to common principles of post-war policy, Addison suggests that after 1945 'whichever party was in office, the Whigs were in power. Party conflicts were compromised, and ideology relegated to the margins of government, by countervailing factors which impelled all administrations toward the middle ground'.[8] This middle ground less reflected the absence of ideology than the dominant predilections which governed the actions of political actors as evidenced in their selection of policy and their identification of objectives. Essentially, all major parties co-existed in a social democratic universe in the 1950s and 1960s. As a result this post-war consensus reflected the reality that 'whether ministers were Labour or Conservative, they were borne along by a belief in the state as a modernising instrument'.[9]

The notion of consensus has as many detractors as it has advocates (indeed, at present it is more fashionable to number yourself among the first rather than the second). Ben Pimlott, among others, has argued that consensus is a myth, 'a mirage, an illusion that rapidly fades the closer one gets to it',[10] and the power of a rising revisionist case against consensus has been attested by the grand old man of the thesis, Paul Addison, who refers to 'a rising generation of historians who stress the primacy of party and ideology and that fundamental differences divided them'.[11] Such 'revisionist' historians and political scientists question the whole notion of consensus by stressing the differences between Labour and Conservatives as separate and distinct political parties characterised by the continuing conflict of political values and interests. They see Labour as the party of socialism and the Conservatives as the party of capitalism.[12] Kenneth O. Morgan also questions the idea of a broad consensus after 1945 as 'perhaps a later construct which requires qualification. It does not conform to much of the record of events, to the personal recollections of those active at the time, or to the voters' contemporary conception of themselves.'[13] Anthony Butler complains that the issue of the post-war consensus has not yet been purged from political debate. Offering himself as another candidate to 'flog this dead horse', he suggests that consensus, a concept 'too dangerously malleable for political analysis', offers no firm purchase to distinguish between myth and reality.[14]

If the actual term 'consensus' has clearly fallen into some academic disrepute by the mid-1990s, much of this is due, as Anthony Seldon suggests, to 'confusion about what exactly is meant by it'.[15] In his discussion of the post-war consensus, James Marlow suggests that the idea of consensus is an unexamined assumption in both historiography and political science: 'For such a taken-for-granted notion, it is...ill defined, poorly explicated and inadequately analysed.'[16] This is a very fair comment, one that, given the historical record, suggests to this author the need for the concept to be reformulated rather than abandoned. As the debate stands, the idea of consensus has often been misused as a result of its under-theorisation and the all too common assumption, given the origin of the term, that its primary feature is a common agreement between political actors and public administrators on the ends the state is obliged to meet and the means it employs to reach them. Operationalising a theory of consensus politics may therefore be a worthwhile and relevant contribution to the explanation of political continuity (as well as to the promotion of sustainable change). Consensus (as applied in its post-war variant) is most definitely a problematic issue in political historiography and unpacking the term is all too necessary. The problem is often one of reading history backward, one which clearly implies an agreement (of sorts) between parties but obscures the question of what type of 'agreement' characterises a consensus; how much dissensus means no consensus? Although the word 'consensus' is Latin for agreement, its use in post-war political history less implies agreement than, as Seldon would rightly have it, 'a set of common assumptions and a continuity between the policies pursued by both the main parties when they were in power. It does not mean that there were not disagreements; there were many. But it does suggest that the differences in the policies practised when the parties were in office were relatively small rather then fundamental.'[17] The notion of consensus is all too often used without being defined in any precise or meaningful way. This approach invariably encourages damaging false assumptions. The problem with the idea is that, as with the term 'Thatcherism', we are stuck with unsatisfactory terminology coined in the past. Consensus is, frankly, a deeply unhelpful term (although the ideas which lie behind it are not), a phrase which can obscure that which it was originally employed to illuminate. Consensus as a concept should be applied in a redefined, precise and meaningful way.

A clear distinction must be drawn between the post-war consensus (of which so much has been written) and consensus politics in general. Here, reference to a consensus is the operative form as opposed to discussion of the consensus. Rather than one ideal historical consensus there are a number of consensuses, each distinct from its predecessor and distinct from its eventual successor. Where the tide ran in favour of semi-collectivist politics in the 1940s and 1950s, the 1980s and 1990s have witnessed a tide swell of support at the level of the political elite in favour of economic liberalism. Hence, consensus (in the plural) is a series of 'general agreements' prevailing over time and subject to incremental modification. Policy is largely based upon normative values that structure outlook; should these normative values change or be altered in some way, for whatever reason, parties may move apart from each other in policy terms. As Addison suggests, 'the history of consensus is far more fundamental in politics (though less discussed) than the record of party strife'.[18] One, of course, has both. Inter-party strife is not merely commonplace, it is rife; part and parcel of any competitive party system and as much a feature of the party system in the 1940s and 1950s as the 1970s and 1980s. Office seeking divides parties and so 'conflict' as 'disagreement' remains an endemic feature of an adversarial and partisan political system.

The suggestion that a political consensus is a set of 'commitments, assumptions and expectations'[19] shared by political actors which transcend party conflicts and provide the framework within which policy decisions were made, offers a valuable starting point. Consensus thus denotes a high level of acceptance at the level of the political elite about the legitimacy of a chosen and existing set of political practices. Consensus should not be taken to imply total agreement. A crude analogy may usefully illustrate a laboured point: Should a couple (married or otherwise) agree after much discussion to purchase a house in, say, North London, a consensus is formed between them. Both now accept that a move to South London, North Glasgow or Outer Mongolia is off their personal agenda. Although they agree on this matter they may well disagree strongly (how violently they disagree would depend on the nature of their association) on such other matters as the colour of the front door, the choice of wallpaper in the bedroom, the distribution of room space or even the allocation of domestic chores. Hence, the idea that consensus exists, as Pimlott suggests, 'not when people merely agree, but when they are happy agreeing',[20] that it is a 'harmony', is not so much a myth as an unsuitably straw man. Consensus, as the concept should be used, does not imply total agreement.

Thus, Dennis Kavanagh and Peter Morris suggest that the post-war consensus existed in the form of a set of 'parameters which bounded the set of policy options regarded by senior politicians and civil servants as administratively practicable, economically affordable and politically acceptable'.[21] Disputation and ideological difference between parties were often the stuff of electioneering, distinguishing between competitors for government office; and political leaders, when they disagreed on major issues of substance, did so over questions of objectives if not the choice of methods. Under any consensus, parties will broadly accept or actively endorse a series of policy options they regard as given, unchangeable and therefore politically acceptable. A theory of consensus politics is not reducible to 'an agreement of opinion' nor does it take the form of deliberate or conscious bipartisanship: rather than assume complete and total agreement between parties across political issues the concept presupposes that an adversary style of politics will continue and may well prosper. Consensus does not simply reflect a policy coincidence but implies a broad association as an agreement on general principles which inform the policy decisions parties make. All parties will continue to seek electoral preferment by mobilising electoral support through the process of party competition.

If consensus is evidenced by continuity across party government over time, nuclear defence policy since 1945 provides a useful instance of the shared attitudes that characterised the governmental decisions of either party. (1) In 1947, the Attlee government secretly commissioned the construction of the atomic bomb. (2) In 1959–63, the Macmillan government began modernising the independent nuclear deterrent by exploring the possibilities of the ill-fated Blue Streak and Skybolt projects, eventually purchasing Polaris from the US through the Nassau Agreement brokered with the Kennedy Administration in 1963. The incoming Wilson government took possession of the submarines. (3) In 1977, a sub-committee of the Labour Cabinet agreed the Chevaline programme to modernise Polaris, and Callaghan agreed at the Guadalupe Summit in 1979 to the principle of siting US Cruise and Pershing missiles in Western Europe. (4) In 1982, the Thatcher government negotiated the purchase of Trident from the US, and the Labour opposition having (left and right) opposed the decision from 1979–89 eventually pledged to commission the fleet. Here, with the exception of Labour's policy turn toward unilateral nuclear disarmament in 1960–1 and 1980–9, both parties, in government and out, have firmly accepted the principle of the nuclear deterrent and the geo-political world view upon which it was based. On the testimony of one participant, the full 1974–9 Wilson and Callaghan Cabinet held only one discussion on this question in the five years in office, such was the assumption that the policy was incontestible: modernising the existing deterrent was considered by a small *ad hoc* sub-committee of a Cabinet Committee.[22] Consensus on specific policy cannot be questioned; it reflects a status quo just as a changing consensus indicates a degree of political change.

Criticising the now wholly and totally outdated notion of adversary politics pioneered by S.E. Finer in the 1970s, Richard Rose argues it is incorrect to assume that 'party government in Britain would be characterised by an abrupt oscillation in public policy, with the direction of government swinging from well on the right to well on the left and back again in the course of a decade'.[23] Developing the idea of a moving consensus, Rose suggests that parties rarely make a difference and that incoming governments, rather than deploy a partisan approach, are bound by the status quo they inherit: 'On grounds of party doctrine, whether the Conservative or Labour Party is in office should make a big difference to patterns of public expenditure. In practice, the growth of public expenditure has shown a steady secular trend upwards through the years, varying little with the complexion of the party in office.'[24] Of course, while Rose correctly draws attention to the continuities between party governments that lie at the heart of any theory of consensus he does not take into account the opportunities for change than occasionally arise: parties can (but often they do not) make a difference. Witness the Thatcher-led Conservative Party.

Misreadings of history and misinterpretations of the rationale that underlay the actions taken by political actors cloud the debate on consensus politics generally (to say nothing of the historical debate on the post-war consensus). The notion of consensus that has followed on from the Addison school of thought needs to be re-evaluated. It is not the case that whichever policies were introduced became part of this post-war consensus, nor that parties were Tweedledum and Tweedledee composites. Contradiction is as much a feature of the true consensus as is association; change amid continuity and disagreement amid agreement are factors which should complement rather than question a theory of consensus politics. A theory of political consensus has nothing in common with the idea of a social consensus, one predicated upon a mutual harmony between all parts of an organism, a condition where different parts of the same whole integrate together in a form of mutually beneficial co-existence. A political consensus is not analogous to a form of cohesive interdependence between parts of a social system. The term 'consensus' need not be usually employed as a descriptive (or pejorative) term. It does not mean nor should it imply a uniformity of belief or behaviour. Nor does it presuppose a homogeneous conformity among all political actors of whichever political origin.

Ben Pimlott too quickly questions the entire edifice of consensus: 'It is easy to take for granted hard-won reforms, and to forget how bitterly they were contested at the time. When one policy triumphs over another, it is tempting to regard the change as inevitable and as part of a progressive, consensual evolution. Yet the reality of radical reform is that it has seldom come without a fight.'[25] Certainly Pimlott correctly draws attention to the difficulties that any ideas-based reform (be it from the left or the right) experience in the transition from heterodoxy to orthodoxy. This applies to the rise of neo-liberalism just as much as to the rise of social democracy. Pimlott correctly argues that 'Labour's [1945–51] programme was fiercely resisted and furiously resented'[26] but Labour 'won' the post-war argument by the fact that it helped refashion the status quo. In short, Labour appeared to be making the political running; smarting from their electoral defeat (and fearful of another), the Conservatives felt obliged to alter their appeal in line with this new status quo and beginning their moderate reform agenda within it. Equally, the post-1979 reforms of the Thatcher government were the subject of fundamental disagreement between Labour and the Conservatives in the 1979, 1983 and, to a far lesser extent, the 1987 and 1992 Parliaments. Labour's opposition to the Thatcherite project had literally to be seen to be believed in 1979–87 (as did the less intense disagreements between Labour and Conservatives in 1945–51). One difference is that the Conservative opposition (in terms of the alternative policy it offered) to Labour in 1945–51 was weak and half-hearted compared to Labour's avowed attempts to eradicate Thatcherism root and branch in the period, say, 1979–86. Both were, of course, ultimately unsuccessful.

A more sophisticated analysis of consensus suggests that it is seen as a form of settlement, not simply an 'agreement' marked by the absence of 'disagreement'. Consensus as 'settlement' offers a more satisfactory framework of reference.[27] Where Colin Hay argues that a settlement generally refers to the 'relationship between the state, economy, civil society and the public sphere that was to emerge and become institutionalised in post-war Britain',[28] a consensus embraces less a state regime than a settlement as a re-definition of politics as an 'art of the possible' reflected in party stances. Hay would both agree and disagree with this: 'It is important to emphasise that the notions of post-war settlement and post-war consensus, despite their superficial similarity, cannot be conflated. They refer to fundamentally different objects of analysis. Thus while the former refers to the broad architecture of the state and its modes of intervention within the economy, the private sphere and civil society, the latter takes as its referent the ephemerality of daily politics and hence the nature of the governmental process'.[29]

This is a distinction between settlement and consensus that makes much of the fact that a notion of settlement implies a difference between a state regime and the political system. Thus reference to the post-war settlement in this scenario suggests that 'the creation of the mixed economy and the welfare state during the post-war Labour administration laid the foundations for the economic and political settlement between capital and labour in the next two decades'.[30] Hay limits his discussion of consensus to a 'tightly specified topic', one based upon 'policy goals; policy means; policy outcomes; political style; the presentation of policy to the electorate; and even the range of policies excluded from the political agenda'.[31] While agreeing with this specification of consensus it is hard to see how this is unrelated to the idea of settlement. Defining a settlement in relation to state theory is necessarily one thing. But it can also apply in the form of a political convergence between political elites, as is typified by the similarity of political actor strategy as realised in policy convergence. Hay does recognise that consensus can be considered to be an 'epiphenomenon of settlement' where 'an elite consensus could be said to exist in as much as the structures, practices, boundaries and responsibilities of the state regime are taken as circumscribing the politically possible, and as setting the context within which political projects can be conceived'.[32] The two phenomena are closely related.

A consensual settlement, within which policy is enacted, is the result of implicit and unstated 'guiding assumptions' shared across parties, an 'agreement' existing in the form of a 'framework', one that reflects a prevailing political orthodoxy. This framework structures rather than determines political activity: the idea of a settlement-as-framework-guiding-political choices is a proverbial 'baby' that should not be thrown out with the consensus-as-willing-agreement-between-parties 'bathwater'. A consensual settlement reflects a framework of political ideas and values within which political activity takes place. It reinforces a set of attitudes which find expression in economic and social policy. This both underpins and reflects the prevailing paradigm within which political actors operate. A political consensus is therefore best defined as a shared adherence to a limited series of methods and objectives common to government rather than a commonly held direction of purpose. It is a form of conformity (if not outright compliance) with an established political agenda which defines what governing actors can do and what they should aspire to do. Political actors can come over time and through experience to internalise a set of political values that constrain and shape their behaviour rather then overtly determine their actions.

Of course a consensus may also be characterised by what it *excludes* rather than the political outlook it *embraces*. Because a consensus need not entail specific policy outcomes, the social democratic consensus can be adjudged by a range of policies incompatible with it and excluded from the governing political agenda subscribed to by political actors of all parties. Policies ruled out included: sacrificing full employment for the control of inflation; excluding the trade unions from the political system; establishing control of the Public Sector Borrowing Requirement as a central objective of government policy; considering the reduction of public expenditure to be a good thing in itself; reducing the level of public ownership to the absolute minimum; ruling out the possibility of increasing the income-tax take-up to maintain and/or expand public services. This negative aspect (what politicians rule out) of consensus politics reinforces the positive aspects (what politicians are prepared to consider) of the phenomenon.

A consensual settlement is almost a mock theory of governance, one which guides what governments (and, as importantly, what prospective governments) can and should do (and what they consider themselves able to do). Dramatic political change may be defined as the transition from one consensual settlement to another. Consensus, as a set of constraints which are deemed to limit what actors can and cannot do, therefore provides 'an exercise in containment', reflecting a political agenda derived from a variety of sources in which 'certain common principles' are enshrined in policy.[33] It reflects a series of contestable political beliefs that have over time become translated into a set of assumptions, and thus an implicit 'agreement' on the role of public administration, one existing as a 'framework', which reflects the preparedness of political actors to accept a prevailing political orthodoxy based upon a set of prescriptive and conceptual political ideas. This shapes a 'climate of opinion', not simply (or even significantly) the opinions and attitudes of the mass electorate but those of key opinion formers and other political players. This 'climate of opinion' is informed by the predominant values which set the boundaries of the acceptable for public policy. Certain policy approaches or political values may be deemed illegitimate because they conflict (or simply challenge) these core values: Here only 'safe' questions may be raised which do not threaten existing attitudes on the direction of policy and the ideological appeal that underpins it. A dominant set of prescriptive ideas come to inhibit political actors; they structure political activity and serve to define the limits of possibility. This is where the settlement between governing and would be governing political actors comes to pass.

Consensus as constraint: party convergence and a shifting middle ground

A consensus can therefore be described as an arrived-at unstated accommodation between parties on the various foundations of policy (what is government for; what can actors do; and, perhaps more important, what actors should expect to be able to do). It is this framework which constructs the set of 'parameters which bounded the set of policy options regarded by senior politicians and civil servants as administratively practicable, economically affordable and politically acceptable' to which Kavanagh and Morris refer in their definition of consensus.[34] It lies at the heart of consensus politics and determines the objectives and assumptions which structure policy choice. Adopting a spatial model of ideological competition stretching from left to right, consensus politics reflects a set of parameters enclosing a space on the political continuum within which political actors position themselves. From this perspective parties are divided (in addition to office seeking) by the technical question of which of them can successfully claim to better manage the status quo rather than change it. A consensus, characterised by what is considered to be feasible (not necessarily desirable), defines what is considered possible as illustrated by an essential bias in policy selection. It describes the conformity (if not outright compliance) with an established political agenda, an acceptance of common political values which define what governing actors can expect to do and what they should aspire to do. Over time and through experience parties come to internalise a set of political values that constrain and shape their behaviour and so influence their actions.

Political change is a reflection of the rise of new ideas and practices that political and economic elites come to accept as necessary, inevitable and, in certain cases, unchallengeable. Distinctive political ideas (should they demonstrate their economic, political and administrative viability) thus impact upon policy formation. They form part of a dominant political discourse, a series of micro-ideological propositions which, as a set of normative recommendations, shape a broadly informed belief system that has far reaching social implications when realised as public policy. Ideological prescriptions affect the political–economic–social context within which government operates. This structures what political actors and governmental institutions actually do and so impacts upon the outputs of the state. Of course, a pragmatic response to social and economic pressures may serve to modify the impact that a political ideology might have. Equally, the reception climate that greets an ideological project is an important factor. For one agenda to succeed, others have to fail; for change to prosper, the status quo has to be discredited. The failure of Keynesianism paved the way for the resurgence of market liberalism much as the limitations of individualism prepared the way for social democratic collectivism.

Party politics, as a response to wider political influences often structured by the form that party competition takes, comes to reflect a dominant micro-ideology such as social democracy or neo-liberalism, individualism or collectivism (as distinct from macro-ideology such as capitalism, socialism, communism and fascism). While major parties office seek in order to policy seek, their policy seeking in office (while influenced by their historical traditions as a party of the left or the right) will reflect 'prevailing wisdoms'. The abiding feature of the British party system (be it three-party politics in a two-party system) is that major protagonists broadly accept prevailing macro-ideological norms. While they can and do disagree on the micro-ideological alternatives by which existing society is managed and, if deemed necessary, reformed, parties do come to accept the primacy of a dominant micro-ideological alternative if it enhances their office-seeking role and can be linked to their historical ethos. Thus, the Conservative Party found itself able to live with the social democratic Britain fashioned after 1940 just as Labour has become accustomed to the neo-liberal agenda that characterises contemporary politics.

From this perspective consensus politics structures party attitudes as reflected in the political objectives they identify and the policy methods they choose. Given that parties do 'compete for votes by locating themselves on a optimal place on the ideological spectrum',[35] Sartori's model of party systems suggests that the ideological distance between parties is one factor determining the direction of party competition: where a short distance results in centripetal competition and a long distance centrifugal competition,[36] centripetal competition, convergence toward a centre, is part of a process where parties, competing against the background of a socio-economic and political environment, interact with one another. This centre (using the term as Sartori applies it) is of course defined politically; rather than being fixed it shifts (and is shifted) within the ideological continuum stretching from left to right. For example, the politics of Keynesianism came to symbolise the centre only because it reflected the statist, semi-collectivist ethos to characterise British politics in the post-war period; that particular centre ground is very different from the one that characterises contemporary politics. Hence, the nature of the ideological difference between parties is central to an understanding of political change (and to an acknowledgment of the light a theory of consensus politics can cast upon it).

Here, a political consensus as settlement embraces the notion of a centripetal accommodation between political parties, one which reflects a micro-ideological convergence between parties as part of a process of political change (and, in time, a form of political continuity once a convergence has taken place). This concept draws a clear distinction between the middle ground and the centre ground within an ideological continuum. The median ground is fixed, a hypothetical point on a spatial model between left and right. In contrast, the political middle ground is fluid, a movable point on the same space between these alternate poles. Therefore a shift in the location of the political middle ground serves to illustrate the prevailing 'ideological predilections' that characterise political activity at any one given time. What is commonly referred to as the median point is this political middle ground, a constantly shifting political construct.

For reasons explored in a previous chapter, a (changing) political middle ground must be distinguished from a (fixed) political median point equidistant between left and right. A shift to the right does not mean the end of the left (nor vice versa) but merely illustrates a shift in position on the part of parties or electors along the ideological axis: Fascism, as a demarcated point on the far right of the political spectrum, does not cease to exist because no political actor and few electors are prepared to endorse it. It is less significant than it might be, but it has not disappeared; it indicates ideological territory not occupied by major or significant actors. The 'end of ideology' thesis of the 1950s suggested the end of the ideological antithesis as the old left–right divide was variously challenged by new syntheses of 'the affluent liberal society', 'participatory democracy', 'environmentalism' and 'post-materialism'. Few post-war commentators foresaw saw that a neo-liberal variant of leviathan would one day rise up and sweep all before it. Hence, should an alteration of social structures necessitate party adaptation to maintain their electoral strength, a transformation of the ideological environment within which they are located will also exact the same reaction. In distinguishing left and right one must be therefore careful not to associate changing political appeals with an 'end of ideology' thesis. The distinction of left versus right remains the primary dimension of political competition between parties although the fulcrum of this axis is forever shifting. The centre of gravity within this left–right dimension along which parties are aligned can alter and move dramatically.

In explaining the shift from one micro-ideological agenda to another, consensus defines the changing political middle ground reflected in party location along the left–right axis of ideological engagement. While parties continue to compete (and compete fiercely) with one another in terms of office seeking, a dominant political discourse shapes the overall form that policy seeking takes. Ideological parameters (which define the ideological terrain they stake out) are clearly drawn within a process of centripetal party competition. That the parameters to characterise pre-1979 politics are very different from those of post-1999 is an illustration of political change as evidenced within party

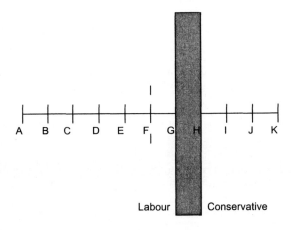

The new 'political middle' is the marked area between points G–H. This is the area of consensus characterised by party convergence on these two separate points. Here, points A–G and H–J are excluded from this consensus by the locations of the two parties. Of course, consensus on this 'middle ground' G–H (not 'centre ground' F – the median point between A–K) does not imply agreement: Labour is on point G while the Conservatives are located at H (G–H does however mark out the location of their agreement and therefore the extent of their disagreement). From point G Labour is closer to point F than are the Conservatives; similarly, the Conservatives are closer to point I than are Labour. Either party is closer to other points on the scale than their rival: hence, in ideological terms, Labour looks 'left' while the Conservatives look 'right'. None the less, the political attitudes and policy instruments consummate with location at political 'middle ground' G–H (as opposed to, say, political 'middle ground' E–F assuming both parties were located there) characterise the dominant political paradigm within which contemporary politics is conducted.

Figure 8.1   Party convergence around an altered political 'middle ground'

competition. 'Catch-up accommodation' (in addition to the process of preference shaping party competition) may therefore be an explanation of the process of change, adaptation and transformation; proof-positive of the existence of a series of consensus politics in which the shifting political middle ground is an illustration (see Figure 8.1).

This framework of analysis suggests that a dominant micro-ideological discourse can overshadow subordinate, less influential discourse and so influence elite (not necessarily popular) political opinion and determine the set of policies (the predisposition that informs policy choice). Consensus can be characterised as passive acquiescence rather than active endorsement. This idea lies at the heart of the idea of consensus as settlement: it involves a process of convergence around (not necessarily on) a new political middle ground, one illustrated by the micro-ideological agenda upon which parties come to settle. Parties continue to disagree not only because they are office seeking competitors but because they are located at the left and right of this political middle ground, political actors who can differ on specific objectives at the same time as they agree on the legitimacy of the general methods established by a dominant micro-ideology; Labour looks to the left of the political spectrum at the same time as the Conservatives look rightwards.

Consensuses are not arrived at but are constructed; they emerge as a result of the interaction of political actors through a process of synthesis involving both agreement and disagreement, where it is accepted that a set of constraints limit the horizons of the aspirations of political actors. Charles Webster suggests that the emergence and development of the National Health Service in 1945–55 was the product initially of conflict not consensus, its end form characterised by an uneasy compromise rather than a consensus.[37] The post-war consensus found expression in the concept 'Butskellism', a concept drawn from the now famous phrase coined by *The Economist* in 1954.[38] As is very well known, this drew attention to the similarity in approach between the Tory Chancellor of the Exchequer R. A. Butler and his Labour predecessor (and then opposition counterpart) Hugh Gaitskell and distinguished the moderate centrist positions of both individuals within their respective parties. Gaitskell was said to have liked the appellation, while Butler, fearful that it would damage him in the eyes of his parliamentary colleagues, hated it and rejected the assumption that his politics were similar to Gaitskell's: 'Both of us, it is true, spoke the language of Keynesianism. But we spoke it with different accents and with a different emphasis.'[39] Continuing differences and re-emphases thereby remain part of the scene of any period of consensus.

In 1963 Tony Crosland published *The Conservative Enemy* (not the sort of title associated with a harmonious association between parties or a cheerful, happy agreement), where he suggested 'deep differences exist between the two parties about the priority to be afforded social welfare. This is not because Conservatives are necessarily less humanitarian, but because they hold particular views as to the proper role of the state, the desirable level of taxation, and the importance of private as opposed to collective responsibility. Their willingness for social expenditure is circumscribed and the consequence is a quite different order of priorities.'[40] This illustrates how continuing differences can be perceived. Major British parties, of course, do not simply ape one another; even if they are not polarised at different ends of the ideological spectrum they remain to some extent both different and distinct.

The post-1945 welfare state and mixed economy were not reducible to Keynesianism (which was itself a tool utilised as part of a social democratic project). Keynesianism, a general way of looking at the economy rather than a specific doctrine, was not a rigid dogma but a tool of economic policy not in itself an ideological world view. As such, not merely at the rhetoric level but also in government, parties could (and did) interpret the policy tools and practices of the post-war consensus as simple mechanisms to be applied (or not applied) for differing objectives: where Labour stressed the 'egalitarian society', Conservatives spoke of the 'property-owning democracy'. Within the post-war consensus, '[T]he Labour and Conservative versions of Keynesianism were clearly distinct. Labour Keynesians like Hugh Gaitskell were ready to employ selective physical controls – such as import controls and controls over the export of capital. Conservative Keynesians like R. A. Butler preferred to rely on fiscal and monetary policy.'[41] Differences were, however, at the margin, one of emphasis rather than substance, simultaneously reflecting the shared micro-ideological perspective common to Labour and Conservatives and the fact that they respectively stood to the left and right of the political middle ground fashioned in the post-1940 period. This process of convergence results in parties coalescing around a middle ground; they do not converge on it. Given their pre-existing attitudes and background (political traditions and genetic code), each party will make of the new settlement what it will in terms of its appeal, ethos and, as significantly, the political platform it deploys to distinguish itself from political opponents in place on the same micro-ideological terrain. Here, this explains the juxtaposition of difference amid agreement.[42]

It is therefore important to emphasise that continuity as well as discontinuity is a feature of any political scene. The transition from a political discourse based upon a semi-collective social democratic ideology to one characterised by a fidelity to a revived market liberalism does not involve a total break from the politics of the earlier period. Elements of the former paradigm continue to exist, thus marking a process of continuity. This is characterised in the field of defence and foreign policy and, in the domestic field, by the state's perennial obligations to provide some form of welfare for its citizens such as education, housing, social insurance, and health care. Social democratic or neo-liberal, capitalism remains capitalism within a liberal democracy.

Thatcherism was constrained in policy terms by the public programmes it inherited from preceding administrations. The policy departures it could engineer were determined by the government's electoral and political freedom of manoeuvre and the administrative feasibility of the changes it hoped to make. As Rose suggests, 'Taken together, the Conservative and Labour parties are only part of the political system. While the fact of election gives the governing party a legitimacy denied many other groups, it does not ipso facto give it the power to do what it wishes.'[43] The political changes the Thatcher government brought about helped usher in a new dominant micro-ideology. Successive electoral outcomes can serve to structure elite discourse and to promote a consensual settlement embracing a new political 'middle ground'. A consensus is thus an 'arrived at' position, the result of the interaction of political forces over time, one of contesting positions (against the backdrop of economic and social structures and political events) in which there are winners and losers. In criticising the idea that parties make a difference, Rose does acknowledge the existence of what he terms a 'moving consensus'; one which arises from 'differences in the priorities of the parties and the disagreements thus generated'.[44] By 'taking an initiative' parties can break with 'the existing view that everything is all right in a given policy area'.[45]

From this perspective, where the status quo is dramatically challenged (what Kuhn refers to as 'revolutionary' versus 'normal' science), consensus is the outcome of a resolution of conflict realised by the triumph of one political agenda over others. The successful agenda forms a new paradigm, a backdrop against which politics is then conducted. Here, actors come to acknowledge this framework; they may criticise it, seek to alter it, or even work at its margin, but they are obliged (or, more particularly, feel themselves obliged) to choose to work within it. Politics as an art of the possible (buttressed by the dictates of office seeking) requires parties to choose this course of action. As such, dramatic political change is invariably followed by consolidation, as advocates of an unsuccessful position, having been seen to have been soundly trounced, withdraw from the political field hurt or else tailor their traditional appeal to the winning view. Certain political actors see themselves as going against the grain of current political realities. In so doing they thus capitulate to their opponents in recanting their earlier view or else bide their time in the hope of making some advance when a more propitious time permits. Agreement exists within limits; consensus is thus a form of settlement with parameters as discernible boundaries, not an agreement (in the dictionary sense of the word) freely entered into. Political change is thus characterised as an alteration in the ideological suppositions that govern the definition of policy options. It is a reflection of the impact that a paradigmatic shift can have on the 'belief systems' of political actors as evidenced in their intentions. A consensus reflects an altered policy universe, one provoked by an acknowledgment that a fundamental shift has been engineered in the form of political debate as parties come to accept a prevalent micro-ideology. Contra Downs, ideological convergence within a party system is not necessarily a reflection of median voter convergence but the result of a narrowing of the ideological distance between parties, one in which an electorally weakened party comes to accept the legitimacy of a micro-ideology for either instrumentalist or expressive reasons.

Consensus politics are therefore characterised by an imperfect transition in which one political tradition is influenced by another. In the contemporary world, Labour's social democratic appeal has been colonised by a neo-liberal politics. While social democratic ideals are not entirely replaced by a neo-liberal appeal the social democratic agenda becomes subsumed within a neo-liberal political agenda; Labour, the agency associated with social democratic ideas, becomes 'neo-liberalised' in much the same way as traditional Conservatism made its gradual historical compromise with liberal democracy post-1860 and the collectivist agenda after 1918, a shift typified by the post-war Tory embrace of 'Butskellist Keynesianism'. Of course, the ideology of the public sphere is not reducible to the dominant political mode; subordinate agendas continue to attract support at the same time as they are overshadowed by the dominant discourse.

Equally, the neo-liberal spectrum stretches from left to right, embracing both radical and moderate versions of the micro-ideology. Classical neo-liberalism was an ideal Thatcherism could not (indeed, would not) match up to in its entirety. While Thatcherites saw New Right politics as offering a perspective on social, economic and political reality that suggested a programme of political reform, they were would be reformists not revolutionaries. They found the world as it was and, where they could do so, they altered it. The neo-liberal political agenda they advanced did not sweep away all the social democratic world in its entirety, but only in part changed it (in certain policy areas more than others); in short, reformed it. Thatcher was a 'Thatcherite' and not a 'Hayekian'; her government's reforms began at the margins of the status quo and only moved toward the centre as far as it was possible to do so.

Root-and-branch transformation was not an option: 1979 was not a 'British Year Zero', and the identity of the state, economy and polity that characterised the pre-1979 social democratic world was only in part 'neo-liberalised'; it was not transformed utterly.

The process of paradigm-shift (as typified by the transition from a social democratic ideological discourse to one informed by neo-liberalism) is therefore one of gradual disengagement from the practices of the past combined with their partial retention in some form. Certain elements of the previous consensus prevail, however altered in form they may be. One aspect of the social democratic consensus to survive Thatcherism (thus far) is state welfarism (when compared to the reversal of the trade-off between inflation and full employment as the defining aspect of a dominant neo-liberal politics). Here, certain elements of the social democratic settlement can be seen to have been neo-liberalised; not all past policies have been abandoned, as the Beveridgean welfare state testifies. The past, from this perspective, can be more than prologue; refashioned by a newly dominant elite discourse, it may continue to exert an influence over what the state does and, as crucially, the expectations civil society has of it.

9
Thatcherism and the Reinvention of Labour

There is something of a vacuum at the heart of a theory of consensus when it is not related to political change. Malcolm Smith rightly suggests that of itself consensus as a concept may not demonstrate how it 'is arrived at, the mechanism by which general agreement [his definition] is reached, or how general agreement changes over time, how resistant or alternative stances are incorporated into a new, replacement general agreement'.[1] Writing of the efforts of Conservative ministers to block certain Labour initiatives in social policy reform after 1942, Paul Addison suggests that they were 'acting, nevertheless, in a field of force, created by Labour'.[2] Conservatives drew up plans for social reform that were 'closer to Labour ideals than they were to the ideals of Neville Chamberlain'.[3] The result of the return of the Conservatives to office after 1951 saw the collectivist advance of the 1940s stemmed but not reversed, and while the Churchill government may have gone some way to meeting the pledge to 'set the people free' by restoring some authority to market liberalism at the expense of collectivist planning, the Tory party stood on the right of the post-war political middle ground. Then, as now, political and ideological constraints determined what ministers as political actors could do. As with the post-war consensus, the contemporary consensual settlement is a reflection of a pre-set paradigm where the present-day Labour Party is, *pace* Addison and post-1945, acting, nevertheless, in a field of force, created by the Conservatives. That Labour now draws up plans for government that are closer to Thatcherite Conservative ideals than they are to the ideals of Hugh Gaitskell demonstrates the constraints imposed upon present-day actors by the free-market view of economic and political realities.[4]

For Blair's New Labour (and its Kinnock-led predecessor), nationalisation and public ownership was one more shibboleth to be laid to rest by modernisation, a distant echo of the outdated belief that the state should control industry. While it had traditionally supported public ownership on the grounds of efficiency, modernisation and productivity just as much as social justice and socialist politics, Labour now considers the very notion of public ownership and state enterprise hopelessly old-fashioned and irrelevant to contemporary needs. 'New' Labour's position on public ownership contrasts dramatically with that of 'Old' Labour (be it left or right). Although the retention of the existing public sector and an extension of public ownership had been a well-established mainstream feature of Labour politics, its abandonment is a reflection of Tony Blair's belief that the politics of 1997 were far removed from those of 1947 or 1967.[5]

In particular, Blair and others have suggested that Labour's support for nationalisation in the late 1970s and early 1980s was a central feature of the party's then extremism. Other than for electioneering purposes (specifically: distinguishing 'New' from 'Old' Labour), it is unclear why this period should be specifically singled out. In part, it is a received wisdom, contemporarily justifying 'New' Labour by a favourable comparison with the Labour Party of Michael Foot and Tony Benn. Yet, 'Old' Labour was of course also the party of , say, Harold Wilson, Denis Healey and Peter Shore. Labour's commitment to public ownership in the 1979 Parliament was never as extensive as prevailing wisdom would have it; indeed, the 1983 manifesto was explicitly cast from the same mould as earlier Labour policy statements, principally Labour's *Programme for Britain 1973*. Why should Blair ignore the Labour Party of the early 1970s? Or, for that matter, the Labour tradition of the 1940s, 1950s and 1960s?

Writing of Labour's principal revisionist, Tony Crosland (a leading Labour figure in the 1950s, 1960s and 1970s), David Reisman concludes that he was 'a selective nationaliser with a life-long commitment to a substantial public sector'.[6] The same can be said of the Labour Party of which Crosland was a member. Labour revisionism, while firmly based on the belief that state ownership of all industrial capital was no longer a condition of creating a socialist society, acknowledged it was a useful economic tool, one particular and specific means to an end where an unjust distribution of wealth could be 'cured in a pluralist as well as a wholly state owned economy'.[7] From the 1950s right through to the 1980s, Labour broadly accepted that a combination of existing public ownership (the public sector fashioned by the Attlee governments and its predecessors and successors), augmented in a variety of forms and when necessary extended, could (in concert with public expenditure, demand management and a system of planning) provide the means by which a progressive Labour government could bring about fundamental social, economic and political reform; while not an end in itself, a pluralist public sector granting the state the means to manage the market economy was an essential part of democratic socialist policy.[8] It is this tradition that New Labour has moved dramatically away from in recent years.

Gaitskellite schools of revisionism were decidedly 'old' Labour on the question of public ownership. While opposed to 'a massive nationalisation programme' (in Tony Crosland's words)[9] and the outright nationalisation of named successful firms, the Labour right and centre did re-emphasise a continuing support for an element of public ownership; they disagreed with any suggestion that nationalisation was an end in itself (revisionists had long favoured moving away from 'monolithic industry nationalisation toward nationalisation by company'[10]). Indeed, in 1974, while arguing that wide-ranging nationalisation was 'a wild fantasy'.[11] Crosland accepted that 'public ownership remains (along with taxation, legislation, government controls, trade union action and so on) one of a number of means to achieving our socialist ends'.[12] He also offered a number of specific candidates for 'aggressive public competition – for example, construction, machine tools, pharmaceuticals, the insurance companies and the building societies' (he was also to add the acquisition of development land).[13]

In similar vein (although more specific than Crosland would perhaps have wished), the February 1974 manifesto stated the objective of public ownership was to 'enable the government to control prices, stimulate investment, create employment, protect workers and consumers from the activities of irresponsible multi-national companies'.[14] By 1974, Labour accepted that nationalisation was not to be confined to loss-making firms but extended, where necessary, to profitable ones. Rather than being an end in itself, it still remained a means to a wider end; a mechanism to enable government to better manage the economy in the pursuit of political objectives such as equality and social justice.

While this stance was far more radical than moderate Labour MPs would perhaps have wished (and it was to be further radicalised in the 1976 and 1982 distillations of Labour's programme[15]), it nevertheless matched Labour's traditional support for the expansion of the role of the state in the management of the economy. In the 1979 Parliament, while not as much importance was given to public ownership as elements of the Labour left wanted, Labour policy was clear. While Militant-inspired demands for the nationalisation of the top 200 private monopolies, banks, finance houses and insurance companies were firmly rejected in successive Conference debates, it was widely accepted that public ownership was central to Labour's economic plans.[16] Drawing on *Labour's Programme 1976, Labour's Programme 1982*, a distillation of successive Conference resolutions and NEC statements was part of a rolling programme from which the 1983 manifesto would eventually be drawn. It explicitly stated that Labour's 'social and economic objectives can be achieved only through an expansion of common ownership substantial enough to give the community decisive power over the commanding heights of the economy'.[17]

The 1982 *Programme* committed Labour to a 'steady but decisive transformation in the economy – from one that is unregulated, unaccountable and dominated by the private sector , to one that is subject to planning, characterised by a wide range of socially owned industries and enterprises'.[18] Although the proposals were drawn up by a sub-committee chaired by Tony Benn, it was adopted by the NEC (on which a 'soft left'–right alliance led by Foot, Kinnock, and Healey could outvote the left) and overwhelmingly endorsed by the 1982 Labour Conference by the margin of 6,420,000 votes to 224,000. The 1982 *Programme* was not a 'Bennite' credo. It reflected a compromise hammered out between the Labour NEC, the Shadow Cabinet and (where they were consulted via the Labour/TUC Liaison Committee) the TUC General Council. It did however reflect the balance of forces at recent Party Conferences.[19] None the less, in hindsight, the 1982 Conference did mark the high tide of public ownership as a principal issue for the Labour Party.

The 1983 manifesto severely qualified the 1982 commitment to public ownership at the same time as it lent its support for it (specific candidates for public ownership were not spelled out). After 1983, the idea of extending public ownership became less fashionable in subsequent years. Here, 1983, as in so many other respects, was to prove a watershed. In contrast to 1970–4 and 1976–83, Labour opinion was to swing at first gradually and then dramatically away from the demand for a major extension of public ownership. Blair was eventually to follow where the Kinnock-led party had travelled; all commitments to the extension of public ownership were to be first diluted and then radically excised during the 1983 and 1987 Parliaments.

By the early 1990s, Labour's Clause Four had become the guiding principle that dare not speak its name. Blair's success in abandoning Clause Four in 1994–5 has often been compared to Hugh Gaitskell's abortive attempt to do likewise in 1959–60. While both saw electoral considerations as important, Gaitskell proposed to reform Clause 4 because he was fearful, firstly, that it would be interpreted as Labour favouring a massive extension of public ownership (the ubiquitous 'corner shop') and, secondly, because (with the exception of competitive public ownership) he wanted to endorse the then status quo, a mixed economy, while in no way ruling out extending the frontier of the public sector. In contrast, Blair's sponsored revision was essentially an endorsement of a privatised non-mixed economy; the post-Thatcher status quo. Gaitskell, the social democrat, and Blair, his politics a reflection of neoliberalism, clearly thought different things of the 'old' Clause Four.

In Blackpool in 1994, at the conclusion of his first set piece Conference speech as leader, Blair declared his intention to replace the famous (or infamous) Webb–Henderson Clause 4 drawn up in 1918. In its place was adopted the 'new' Clause 4, drawn up by Blair himself, agreed by the NEC in March 1995 and endorsed by a special Party Conference in April. In contrast to the former aspiration to 'secure for the workers by hand or by brain, the full fruits of their industry and ensured the most equitable distribution thereof on the basis of the common ownership of the means of production, distribution and exchange...', the Blair-sponsored Clause committed Labour to the 'enterprise of the market and the rigour of competition' in an economy where there is a 'thriving private sector and high quality public services' (not, one notes, a public sector). There was of course nothing new or dramatic in Blair's revision of a Clause he (and two-thirds of his Party Conference) no longer believed in.

In comparison with Gaitskell's failure to junk Clause Four, Blair's success owed much to the fact that circumstances were very much in his favour. It was yet another step in a long process of reform. Put simply, Blair had more power than had Gaitskell; he could command his party in ways that his predecessor could only dream of. He faced no alliance of 'fundamentalists', only an impotent, fractionalised and ghettoised minority Labour left, weakened trade unions with little political clout and no meaningful veto (what veto they retained they were unwilling to use). Repeated defeats (political as well as electoral) had demoralised those elements of the party who would have supported the retention of the old Clause at the same time as it strengthened the authority of a leadership eager to revise it. Moreover, Blair benefited by the enhanced power of the leadership and its ability to command (there are less veto players given the move away from a federal party democracy to one characterised by control of the agenda at the centre and plebicitory consultation at the periphery).

Indeed, the language employed by Blair and his supporters in urging the abandonment of the old Clause Four was akin to age-old

Conservative attacks on the supposed overweaning nationalising ambitions of the past. Blairite arguments centred on prevailing economic and political necessities and the need to highlight the fact of Labour's modernisation. Clause Four, very much associated with 'Old' Labour, had no place in Blair's vision of 'New' Labour. While a prevailing ideological wind hampered Gaitskell's very different attempts at reform in 1959–60, Blair's efforts were wind-assisted by the whirlwind assault of Thatcherite neo-liberalism on prevailing ideological wisdoms. The Blairite case for reform was simple: Why on earth should a doctrine be defended that could be so easily proven to be wholly out of date? Together with the 'old' Clause Four, Labour's commitment to public ownership, part of its ideological attachment to advancing statist solutions to the problems of the market economy, was to vanish into history. Rather than fashion something new, in abandoning Clause Four in 1994–5 Labour was acknowledging the extent to which it had changed. It formalised the fact that after 1989 (at least), the principal of extending public ownership had disappeared from the party's agenda, never, it would seem, to return: it had not featured in the 1992 Labour manifesto and unsurprisingly did not appear in that of 1997, nor in the 'business prospectus' Labour published to attract the support of corporate Britain.

Labour's altered position on the question of public ownership is a reflection of the ideological, political, economic, and, as significantly, electoral environment in which it has found itself. Here, as elsewhere, actually existing Thatcherism made the difference; it was to prove the agency of a fundamental and far-reaching policy departure that called into question the very premises upon which nationalisation was predicated. Privatisation was to prove this very significant policy departure. From small-scale beginnings, it was conceived, carefully tested and, once proved workable, gradually enacted over the lifetime of the Thatcher and Major administrations. The sale of large public utilities such as telecommunications, water, gas, electricity, coal, and rail, together with other asset sales such as steel production, car manufacture, ports, and airports, dramatically recast the public–private distinction in Britain. The 1984 sale of British Telecom was the key to all subsequent developments; where it led, other sales followed, as ministers demonstrated that the existing 'social democratic' state could be reformed and a new status quo established in its place.

Labour's changing response to privatisation was both dramatic and significant. In 1979–82, Labour (left, right and centre; Jim Callaghan as much as Tony Benn) strongly opposed all asset sales and pledged themselves to renationalise all such assets without compensation on its return to office. In 1983, Labour's policy had altered slightly; it now stood on a policy of re-nationalisation of all privatised assets but on the basis of no speculative gain, one where investors would receive only the monies they had originally paid. No compensation (adopted in the forlorn hope that it would deter would-be speculators from investing in privatised concerns) had been deemed a confiscatory method and abandoned at the 1982 Party Conference. After 1983, the privatisation floodgates opened with the extension of the programme into the heartlands of the public sector following the sale of British Telecom, gas, water and electricity. Although total opposition to privatisation was a feature of successive Labour Conferences in the 1983 Parliament, Labour was to dramatically review its attitude on this question. After 1986, it first accepted the principle of compensation on the basis of market worth before completely revising its overall commitment to re-nationalisation as part of its gradual abandonment of its opposition to privatisation.

While Labour continued to vehemently oppose each and every asset sale in the 1983 and 1987 Parliaments (leading a sustained parliamentary campaign against the sale of British Telecom in 1984 and British Gas in 1986), the leadership first accepted that the re-nationalisation of privatised assets such as, say, Sealink, Rolls-Royce, or British Airways operating in competitive markets was both infeasible and undesirable. Eventually, Labour came to terms with the privatisation bandwagon during the 1987 and 1992 Parliaments. While unhappy at the privatisation of utilities such as electricity, gas and water (and the sale of British Rail in 1993–5), Labour abandoned re-nationalisation by the 1992 general election on grounds (initially) of cost and priority and (eventually) necessity. The Policy Review, 1987–91, was the principal method by which the re-nationalisation commitment was unravelled.

By the 1997 general election, the Labour manifesto declared that the Blair government would 'leave intact the main changes of the 1980s in industrial relations and enterprise'.[20] Blair's many business supporters included two senior executives of privatised industries: Bob Ayling, Chairman of British Airways (who declined an offer to head up Blair's Policy Unit in Downing Street), and the Chief Executive of British Telecom, Iain Vallance, who let it be known he intended to vote Labour. While cautious not to cause offence to key sections of the Labour community in 1994–7, the party had shifted away from past commitments to undo privatisation, to the extent that it now appears willing to endorse it. Although he had previously likened the sale of British Telecom, British Airways and Rolls-Royce to 'political corruption',[21] Blair was privately said to consider privatisation a relative success story, a policy area where, despite short-term intentions, the Thatcher and Major governments had got it right.[22] Notwithstanding the considerable electoral capital resulting from an extensive 1994–5 media-based public relations campaign against 'privatised fat cats' targeting the excessive salaries and perks enjoyed by executives of former public enterprises, Blair drew the conclusion that asset sales had been desirable in themselves. In April 1997, he declared 'There is no overriding reason for preferring the public provision of goods and services, particularly where those services operate in a competitive market, then the presumption should be that economic activity is best left to the private sector with market forces being fully encouraged to operate.'[23]

In explaining Labour's accommodation to privatisation a great deal is made of the impact of so-called 'popular capitalism', the idea that privatisation converted Labour voters into Conservative voters and so dramatically eroded Labour's electoral base at the 1983 and (more particularly) the 1987 general elections.[24] This belief that 'the Labour Party has frightened off a substantial proportion of the relatively small number of its potential supporters who have bought shares in privatised companies targeted for some form of re-nationalisation'[25] led to a process of electoral myth-making. From a different perspective 'popular capitalism' may or may not have had a significant electoral effect but it did frighten Labour half to death; given the mass appeal of privatisation share issues it certainly made the advocacy of re-nationalisation far more difficult. Its long-term influence lies probably not in its impact on electoral behaviour but in the way key political actors interpreted electoral responses to its extension. Put simply, if the Labour Party were to be persuaded to believe (or come to accept) that privatisation and 'popular capitalism' was harming its electoral chances and weakening its opportunity to win office, Labour's perception of electoral trends would be as important (if not more so) than the electoral trends themselves, irrespective of the real influence the policy actually had (notwithstanding the actual influence the policy had over the electorate).

Between 1995–7 Labour seized on the concept of privatisation as a probable policy to be pursued in office. Pledged to defend Conservative spending figures in 1997–9 (including projected privatisation receipts of £1.5 billion in 1998–9), Blair and Gordon Brown countenanced privatisation as a way of filling possible 'black holes' in their finances, revenue raising if necessary through asset sales instead of upping taxes and increased borrowing. During the election campaign, Labour indicated it would be prepared to sell both the Tote and the Air Traffic Control network. This caused the party some embarrassment once journalists found proof of the extent of the party's U-turn on these issues. In place of re-nationalisation, Labour had announced the 'windfall tax', a one-off levy paid by targeted privatised monopolies, designed to cream off excess profits made under the Conservatives. It had the electoral utility of targeting utilities which were the subject of much criticism for rising prices, enormous profits, and 'fat cat' perks as well as the political usefulness of revenue raising and providing funding for a much advert-ised 'welfare to work' programme targeted at the young unemployed. As the centrepiece of the government's first budget in July, the windfall tax raised a £5.2 billion levy on a number of privatised utilities, among them British Telecom, British Gas, electricity companies, and regional water companies. Rather than seeing it as an attack on privatised indus-tries, advocates of the tax claimed it would only make up for the past absence of effective regulation. As a one-off scheme, the revenue it raised was intended to reduce welfare roles (and therefore shrink the welfare budget) as well as making employment provision.

In spite of the windfall levy, Labour's conversion by May 1997 was far more serious than simple electioneering. Privatisation was here to stay. Indeed, as one journalist noted: 'The decision to embrace privatisation is seen by Blair and Brown as crucial in their crusade to modernise Labour. "It's the final piece of the jigsaw" one insider said.'[26] It was clear that the Labour government would be willing to open the door to further priva-tisations, 'where', in Blair's words, 'they were in the public interest'.[27] Once in office, Labour strategists made it clear that further privatisations were both possible and desirable. Having shifted its position from op-position, through adaption, to likely adoption, Labour in government presided over state assets valued at some £15 billion which could be franchised, floated or otherwise sold to the private sector (among them the Post Office, Channel Four, Crown Estates, and London Under-ground). In late 1997, a root-and-branch review of government assets (and therefore privatisation options) had been carried out by the Treas-ury (as ever, the lead department in Whitehall privatisations).

The Labour government has made clear its support for a revamped version of the Conservative's Private Finance Initiative (PFI). It is hoped it will revenue-raise for the Treasury as well as finance much-needed investment in what are still referred to as the public services. In the case of the perilously underfunded London Underground, Labour ministers intend to attract private investment by selling the majority stake in London Underground Limited. This is exactly the policy the Thatcher government followed in 1984 with regard to British Telecom when 51 per cent of the industry was sold in the teeth of considerable opposition not least from the Labour Party. Labour's projected plan for the future of London Underground echoes the sale of British Telecom: it is, in short, privatisation by any other name, an illustration of how far Labour has travelled on this issue.

Throughout the 1980s and 1990s the Thatcher and Major-led Conservatives set a privatisation agenda Labour felt obliged to come to terms with; as spectator and not participant it has had to respond. A regular pattern emerged: having opposed each privatisation (first out of ideological conviction and later political concern), Labour spokespersons promised to renationalise all assets and then only principal utility assets. Subsequently, Labour acknowledged a variety of problems in pursuing re-nationalisation, be they unpalatable electoral consequences, financial restrictions, and, later, political expediency. As a result, Labour's policy of re-acquisition was deferred, first temporarily (in the form of a promise to renationalise 'as and when resources allow') and then permanently. This process can be evidenced with each sale after the privatisation of British Telecom and British Gas. By 1997, Labour had not only indicated its preparedness to live with privatisation but a willingness to embrace it when in government. This reappraisal of policy was prompted by major changes in Labour's economic policy.

Faced with the *fait accompli* of a privatised utility (particularly one presented as an economic success), a hamstrung Labour opposition found itself unable (and increasingly unwilling) to resist the relentless onslaught of the privatisation juggernaut: 'Opposition to privatisation per se (in contrast to its form) [has] proved ineffective, revealing just how successfully neo-liberalism has been able to define viable policy options.'[28] Each step of the way Labour's policy was gradually whittled away. This was less a response to circumstances as it was a reaction to events: it is an example of the way Labour came to terms with actually existing Thatcherism. In the case of public ownership and privatisation, it found its policy horizon bounded; the status quo ceaselessly redefined by the policy agenda of the Thatcher and Major governments.

In opposing privatisation, Labour initially defended what it latterly came to see as an untenable status quo. Forced to fall back on a so-called fail-safe justification encapsulated in the emotive appeal 'Private it's Theirs; Public it's Yours', the party despaired of attracting the support of a disgruntled public unaccustomed to considering nationalised utilities as their own property. Similar arguments employed against privatisation (defending Morrisonian, 'actually existing' nationalisation, public monopoly and cross-subsidisation) proved no match for the government's offensive. Defending the status quo was perhaps not the best terrain that advocates of social democratic principles of public enterprise could have chosen. As such they fought a rearguard action on the government's terrain, conducting a battle with weapons of the government's own choosing. Privatisation, symbolising a change in the political climate, made a significant contribution to the overall political changes ushered in by Thatcherism. Parties have always had to adapt to political change; such changes are often painful. After a decade of Thatcherism, the unfolding story of privatisation demonstrates most clearly that Labour felt obliged to adapt to the changes its advocates had engendered in the political agenda.

As with the post-war consensus, the contemporary consensual settlement, a conformity within limits, is a reflection of an emergent paradigm and not a purposeful agreement commonly accepted by political actors (as implied by the term 'consensus'). This example of political change both reflects and generates the political agenda which defines the dominant micro-ideology and its attendant set of political ideas, attitudes and values, one that has come to alter the perceptions of political actors regarding the possible role of government, its objectives and the methods available to it. Here, having been seen to 'win' the 1980s, the Conservative Party has led where Labour, having 'lost', has felt obliged to follow. David Held identifies a typology of compliance which can classify the various rationales behind political change, detailing the shift from opposition to (reluctant or enthusiastic) acceptance: (1) coercion; (2) tradition; (3) apathy; (4) pragmatic acquiescence; (5) instrumental acceptance; (6) normative agreement; (7) ideal normative agreement.[29] These stages, particularly (4) through (7), could all be taken to presage a process of consensus formation: where one party is deemed to have successfully led (for whatever reason), others will follow. 'Pragmatic acquiescence' and 'instrumental acceptance' imply a resigned acceptance of an unsatisfactory situation for instrumentalist reasons, accepting the need to accommodate to an altered status quo because it is deemed to be in the party's interest to accept something it may not be entirely at ease with.

The consolidation of a dominant agenda will involve the reconstitution of party antagonism around a new political axis, an altered political middle ground. Here party change takes the form of a relocation along the ideological spectrum – in the case of Labour post-1983, a shift rightward, or in the case of post-war Conservatism, a shift leftward. Thus, political changes initiated since 1979 can be related to Held's typology: persistent strains in the established social democratic consensus led to obvious crisis after 1973. This generated a polarisation in political opinion which saw the Labour Party shift leftward and the Conservatives rightward, both moving away from the established political 'middle ground' in a gradual process reflecting a centrifugal micro-ideological competition evidenced by the rise of Thatcherism on the one hand and 'Bennism' on the other, twin symbols of the crisis of social democracy and the post-war consensus it had engendered. Here, particularly after 1979, these alternative agendas (promoted in response to the perceived failings of the status quo) fought it out together with weak advocates of the pre-1979 status quo (the anti-Bennite Labour right and, initially, in 1981–3, the emergent SDP) in a 'war of position' eventually won by the Thatcherites, a process which saw the preferment of one agenda over another as evidenced in governmental decisions, policy initiatives, and, perhaps decisively, electoral outcomes in the form of the 1983 and 1987 general elections.

While Labour policy in 1970–87 was cast in a social democratic mould (albeit one cast in a radical form), the politics of 'catch-up' since 1987 indicates the nature of contemporary political change. Labour's accommodation to a new neo-liberal centre is a suitable illustration. It is a process which helps explain the emergence of the new neo-liberal paradigm and an instrumental feature of this (as any other) emergent 'post-Thatcher' political consensus. The course of the 1980s and 1990s witnessed the steady incremental encroachment of neo-liberalism as a dominant paradigm. From the beach-head established in 1979–85, Thatcherism has helped recast the form of British politics. Its ability to remake the political agenda was the outcome of a four-stage process:

1 A widespread discontent (at the level of the elite and the mass) with the post-war settlement provided.
2 The Thatcherite opportunity to offer an alternative politics.
3 This in turn activated the Thatcherite offensive as illustrated by its advocacy of a neo-liberal politics in practice (as tempered by the dictates of statecraft) post-1979.
4 This political approach, based upon 'actually existing Thatcherism', came over time to displace other alternatives, as opposed interests (most notably the Labour Party) recognised that an articulated alternative to the Thatcherite phenomenon would have to be worked out within the paradigm it had established.

Party strategy is defined by a party's reaction to a political agenda. This is an acknowledgement of a political transformation as a paradigmatic shift in the form that the dominant political project takes. The most potent appeal of Thatcherism was the belief that there was no alternative to its vision of society. David Marquand has rightly observed, 'The New Right still holds the ideological field ... On the all important plain of the political economy – the relationship between state and market, between collective provision and individual spending – New Labour has still not offered a comprehensive challenge to the New Right's world view.'[30] Given the influence that Thatcherism has had on the Labour Party this should have come as little surprise. A political agenda based upon neo-liberalism is the dominant micro-ideological paradigm which informs contemporary politics: As Marquand also makes clear, 'decisive political victories must follow ideological victories. The inner citadels of state power fall only to those who have already won the battle of ideas.'[31]

This is crucial to understanding the nature of contemporary political change in the UK; Thatcherism set the agenda. As Colin Leys argues: 'Thatcher could not have done what she has without the prior and continuing ideological offensive: she could not have won the elections and she could not have carried through the radical – in British terms, revolutionary – economic and political changes she has, without discrediting and displacing the ideological defences of the structures she set out to dismantle.'[32] He utilises a more refined notion of hegemony than similar writers: 'for an ideology to be hegemonic, it is not necessary that it be loved. It is merely necessary that it have no serious rival.'[33] The idea of the Thatcherisation of the traditional social democratic project indicates that Labour's transformation reflects its relocation from one political middle ground to another.[34]

Certain (and occasionally stark) differences naturally remain in evidence between Labour and the Conservatives. In economic terms Labour professes a belief in co-ordinated capitalism as distinct from the Tory commitment to minimal regulation of markets. It offers a partial vision of a 'developmental state' (encouraging industrial investment, training, re-equipment and development to strengthen the working of the market) at odds with current Tory policy, one that claims to modernise the capitalist economy to the benefit of all citizens. Constitutional reform is another issue that at present threatens to sharply divide the parties. Labour's professed belief in modernisation is thus one qualification which delineates 'New' Labour from 'Old' Conservatism, an appeal which distinguishes Labour from the Conservatives within the middle ground of contemporary politics. 'New' Labour often declares its commitment to improve society but, in contrast to past arguments (typified in their own way by Gaitskell and Bevan; Benn and Crosland), no longer

intends to use the state to reform capitalism in ways previously
envisaged. 'Co-ordinated capitalism' (while distinct from a belief in
the 'minimal regulation of the free market'[35]) was not the objective of
'Old' Labour, which saw the need to employ far reaching reformist
measures to reconstruct the market and harness capitalism for-definitive
social objectives.

None the less, Labour may not yet be a confirmed neo-liberal party. It
stands beyond the ranks of the conservative movement but it has been
profoundly influenced by that movement. Competing principles
remain and have to be taken into account; to some extent, Labour has
been neo-liberalised not become neo-liberal. Although far weaker than
previously, 'Old' Labour remains entrenched within the shell of 'New'
Labour. The record of the Blair government in office will perhaps provide definitive proof of the extent to which Labour's transformation has
truly taken root. Without engaging in any form of futurology, it is likely
that when forced to choose between the objectives of moving toward an
'inclusive society' or encouraging the enterprise economy Labour will
choose the second rather than the first. Only through the enterprise
economy, leading Labour ministers counsel, can you move toward the
more inclusive society (one invariably defined by less exclusivity rather
than more inclusivity).

While Labour modernisers contend that New Labour is not simply an
'accommodation of the right', Tony Blair, as did Kinnock before him,
has acknowledged that the New Right held the political initiative in the
1980s and 1990s. Their project, although, in Blair's words, it 'got certain
things right', was 'more successful at taking on and destroying some
outdated attitudes and prescriptions, than it was at building and creating'.[36] No doubt Keith Joseph's 1976 observation that Britain was 'over-
governed, over-spent, over-taxed and over-manned' would find
endorsement among the leading lights of Blair's administration: as
would the 'socialist anti-enterprise climate' of which he spoke, characterised by the 'indifference, ignorance and distaste on the part of politicians, civil servants and communicators for the process of wealth
creation and entrepreneurship',[37] an acknowledged feature of the era
of so-called 'Old' Labour. Claiming that the New Right successfully
tackled certain economic problems, Blair cites others – 'levels of investment in capacity and people, infrastructure, long-term unemployment,
the quality of education, crime and welfare' – that were neglected.[38] It is
these problems that New Labour claims it will address from the position
it has staked out on the left of the new neo-liberal consensus: party
differences remain within the established framework.

Yet, in terms of objectives as well as methods, 'New' Labour does not offer a distinctive political strategy dramatically at odds with the Thatcherite project. One selling point for an opposition party forced to accept the reforms of an entrenched government is to raise the standard of the 'better society'. This offers a rhetorical distinction to separate the pretender to the throne from its present occupant. Parties are invariably in favour of the 'better society' in much the same way that one is against sin, and such an appeal, a vision for the 'better tomorrow' in contrast to the 'inadequacies of today', can distinguish an opposition party from the government and so provoke a reason for the dissatisfied voter to support the call for a change of administration.

Labour may offer in opposition a vision of the 'good society' (in Blair's words: 'collective action for common good; wealth and opportunity in the hands of the many and not the few; rights matched by responsibilities; a just society based on solidarity and mutual respect'[39]). But this may be only a useful selling point for an opposition party, a legitimate sales pitch that distinguishes between competing parties. Thus, although critics of the 'catch-up' thesis are right to suggest that Labour and the Conservative parties have a very different understanding of the role of the state and market, the nature of the values that underpin society, and what constitutes the 'good society',[40] the fact that Labour's stated objectives differ from the Conservatives' does not weaken an accommodationist thesis: Labour has not aped the Conservative Party but recast itself in keeping with the contemporary agenda as set by the Conservative Party.

Bearing in mind the fact that dramatic ideological shifts in party identity are rare, a sea-change in the political attitudes that govern a party's policy selection reflects an altered ideological discourse (changed by the successful agenda-setting party). This becomes a feature of the public profile of the 'catching-up' party. Specifically, should party A be able to demonstrate that it has successfully marketed and sold product X (evidenced by electoral success), then party B may well choose to abandon its preferred product Y in favour of a variant of product X which has been the cause of such success for their competitor (when the product Y of party B has not produced the same result). Of course, parties are not free to directly copy their opponents; party B would not simply abandon product Y in favour of product X in light of the success of party A, but alter product Y in favour of a new product YX (product Y as altered by product X). To reiterate: party convergence is characterised not by agreement but by an association configured by a consensus around an altered political middle ground.

Thatcherism has had lasting consequences for British politics. Having tried to break with the old social democratic consensus more dramatically to the left as had the Thatcher Conservative Party to the right, Labour found itself hemmed in by a political opponent which had established a firm ideological bridgehead, one underpinned by proven electoral success. While Labour was severely weakened by defeat, Thatcherite Conservatism was strengthened by its success; the rejection of Labour's avowedly left-wing alternative taken as an effective endorsement of Thatcherite ideology. Having passed the acid test of electoral confirmation in 1983 and again in 1987 and 1992, Thatcherism, assessed in terms of its general impact and the consequences it had on British politics, took root. As a result, Labour modernisation offers a programme for acquiring office as well as for government. It is: (1) a reflection of political change as evidenced in party change where electoral politics reflect a political transformation; (2) a reaction to the Conservatives' ability to command the political scene; (3) a response to the Thatcher and Major governments' repeated political successes, the means by which they set the public agenda and so came to frame political debate. Where the Conservatives have led, Labour, modernised and new, has followed. A post-Thatcherite consensus (one reflecting the neo-liberal agenda fashioned between 1979 and 1999) now exists.

Rather than remake itself, Labour has been remade as a result of the impact of the 'external shocks' of the 1979, 1983, 1987 and 1992 general elections and the political changes wrought by those events. Labour's shift to the right is explained by the 'politics of catch-up', a process by which the party found itself persuaded of the need to 'modernise' itself in order to 'accommodate' to circumstances that had been changed. Labour's engagement with Thatcherism reflects the recasting of mainstream ideological politics. As an agency of change Thatcherism has helped construct the prevailing political agenda to which other office seeking (and policy seeking) political agents have had to accommodate. If parties do not always react by adjusting their appeals in line with electoral attitudes *à la* Downsian theory, they do respond to an altered set of parameters bounding the competitive ideological space as shaped by a successful (party) competitor. It therefore matters not just that Labour lost four consecutive general elections, but that the Conservative Party won them. As a result, Thatcherism is a continuing phenomenon, part of an ongoing process which still impacts upon public life and exerts a considerable influence upon contemporary politics. Describing this influence is important; understanding the form that Thatcherism took is more important; analysing this change and accounting for its impact even more so.

In adjusting its appeals in line with the dominant set of political ideas, Labour has responded to an altered set of parameters bounding the competitive ideological space shaped by a successful (party) competitor. While not simply a photocopy of Thatcherism nor is 'New' Labour a 'third way' between the New Right and the Old Left. Claims that it has a wholly distinct agenda in economic and social policy (constitutional reform being another entirely separate matter) are wrong; rather than actively challenge the Thatcherite legacy, Labour modernisation in fact first colludes with it before otherwise reforming it. In government it is clear that Labour's policy agenda involves a neo-liberal macroeconomic rectitude combined with the prospect of further liberalisation and retrenchment of the state's role in the economy: granting independence to the Bank of England in June 1997, the very first act of the incoming Blair government offers a case in point. Indications are that a dramatic cutting back of the welfare state and the introduction in some form of a workfare scheme will figure high on its list of priorities. Indeed, such is the continuing pull of liberalisation and the rolling back of the state in economic life, that the neo-liberal agenda underpinning the politics of Thatcherism may even be strengthened by Labour in office: a 'Nixon goes to China' syndrome, one which would mark the abnegation of the traditional social democratic project long associated with the Labour Party.

In discussing the political plight of the Major-led Conservatives in 1995, Andrew Gamble comments:

> The forces of the right are strong and confident, and are busy fashioning an agenda which borrows as freely from Newt Gingrich as from Mrs Thatcher, stressing the themes of economic prosperity, tax cuts, national sovereignty and public order. The policy agenda in Britain has already been shifted once in the last twenty years. The Thatcherite wing of the Conservative Party is confident it can be shifted again. They believe that this is the way to restore Conservative political hegemony in Britain; the great task still ahead is the dismantling of the welfare state.[41]

A political hegemony is one thing (electoral domination has never lasted indefinitely in Western liberal democracies), ideological hegemony another. The electoral beating suffered by the Conservatives in May 1997 may well place in context the contribution Thatcherism made to Tory politics. As a vehicle for Thatcherite neo-liberalism, the Conservative Party enjoyed considerable political success in 1975–92 but may have reaped an electoral whirlwind in 1997. The Conservative Party (the launch-pad for Thatcherism in the 1970s and 1980s) may have been fatally undermined by the gradual unravelling of a Tory One Nation tradition, and perhaps a 'kinder', 'gentler' Thatcherism, one unassociated with 1980s Toryism, is now in electoral vogue. Of course, it is too soon to comment on the future of any political party. Academic bookshelves are littered with such past titles as 'Must Labour Lose?', 'Can Labour Win?' and 'Is Labour Done For'. Such speculative predictions may prove as unfounded in the case of the post-Thatcherite Conservatives.

Whatever the current fortunes of the Conservative Party, Thatcherite policy initiatives were part of a coherent political and economic project rooted in the ideology of the New Right. Thatcherism did exhibit symptoms of crisis management and may well have been the product of an interplay of opportunity and circumstance, chance and fortune, but, given that over time it pursued an agenda based on a normative world view, it is best understood as a process enacted over time. At its very heart was an anti-statist commitment to roll back the frontiers not of the state *per se* but of the actually existing social democratic state. As a project simultaneously informed by an ideological doctrine and constrained by the dictates of statecraft, Thatcherism was an agent of political change, one eager to enact policy to reconfigurate both state and society at the same time as it was responsive to political realities and electoral pressures. Rather than spring from nothing, Thatcherism was constructed over time and through experience: it was an attempt to secure a series of goals by overcoming difficulties and renegotiating obstacles. Thus, while New Right ideology may not have been a blueprint, it was Thatcherism's guidebook; it informed rather than instructed, persuaded rather than determined. In short, it suggested policy options rather than pre-ordained them.

The new political middle ground marks out the changed micro-ideological space between Labour and Conservative. In programmatic terms Labour has followed where Thatcherism has led. In its pursuit of the 'politics of catch-up', a series of staging posts can be identified: among them, the 1983, 1987, 1987 and 1992 general elections; the shift in the Kinnock leadership in 1983–7; the Policy Review of 1987–91; and the Blair reforms post-1994. Together, these staging posts mark out the change from the party Labour was in 1980 to that it has become in 1997. While electoral outcomes may have promoted Labour's change *per se*, they did not specify the actual form these changes would in fact take. A gradual acknowledgement of an alteration in its electoral environment went hand in hand with the perception of a shift in the ideological climate of British politics, the one reinforcing the other. Its transformation was promoted through its engagement with Thatcherism and the new, altered status quo that Thatcherism constructed through eighteen years of policy-seeking.

Party change to the extent exhibited by the Labour Party reflects wider political change: it is not just a response to cumulative electoral defeats but a reaction to an altered political terrain. In contrast to the classical Downsian model (building upon that of Dunleavy), a model of party competition driven party change suggests that while electors do influence parties, parties influence electors but also separately influence other parties. The ultimate consequences of Thatcherism demonstrate that under certain circumstances successful parties shape the choices other less-successful parties make. Over time, party competition driven party change affects the location of the 'catching-up' party within the ideological continuum. Labour's transformation reflects the fact that party competition driven party change, the 'process of catch-up', results in the consequential interaction of parties where one party is obliged to follow where a competitor party leads. While electors can influence parties (the Downs model) and influence electors (the Dunleavy model) they also influence one another (while subject to the fact that the interaction of parties with electors facilitates the interaction of parties). Labour's 'catching-up' is an acknowledgement that the parameters which bound the ideological space within which parties locate themselves has changed and that accommodation to this form of political change (evidenced in party competition) is necessary.

The dominant paradigm that Thatcherism helped promote provides a compass by which successor governments navigate their procession though political and economic straits. Labour's transition is a reflection of the impact of Thatcherism and its direct influence on the pattern of mainstream ideological politics. Labour has moved ever rightward since 1994 whereas its programmatic stances in 1987 and 1992 were constructed under the same configuration of economic and social forces that apply in 1997. Neither Kinnock nor Blair have been working a blank canvas but a palimpsest already reworked by Thatcherism, one covered in markings Labour is unwilling (rather than just being unable) to erase.

As argued above: The methods of the Keynesian Welfare State may have been called into question but the objectives identified by revisionist socialism have also been questioned and also found wanting.

Labour's transformation indicates that parties are reactive as well as proactive institutions. As a response to an altered policy universe, one provoked by a fundamental ideological shift in the form of political debate, party change is reflected in the reshaping of a political appeal; an alteration of policy stance; or even a more general ideological reorientation. This is a process over time and an example of how parties adapt and transform themselves within party competition. As a reaction to (repeated) electoral defeat and a response to an altered policy universe, programmatic change is part of party change. It therefore matters not just that Labour lost four consecutive general elections, but that the Conservative Party won them. Modernisation is therefore a metaphor for the politics of 'catch-up', a reflection of a new political consensus, one informed not by post-war social democracy, but by Labour's accommodation to and adaption of Thatcherism's neo-liberal political agenda.

Notes

1 Exploring Political Change

1 Ruth Levine (ed.), *The Ideology of the New Right*, Cambridge: Cambridge University Press, 1986; Desmond King, *The New Right*, London: Macmillan, 1987; Kenneth Hoover and Raymond Plant, *Conservative Capitalism in Britain and the United States*, London: Routledge, 1989.
2 Hoover and Plant, *Conservative Capitalism in Britain and the United States*.
3 The Centre for Policy Studies, *Objectives and Style*, London: Centre for Policy Studies, 1975, pp. 3–4.
4 Maurice Duverger, *Political Parties*, London: Methuen, 1964, pp. 308–9.
5 W.H. Greenleaf, *The British Political Tradition: Volume 1. The Rise of Collectivism: Volume II. The Ideological Heritage*, London: Methuen, 1983: A.V. Dicey, *Lectures on the Relation Between Law and Opinion in England during the Nineteenth Century*, London: Macmillan, 1963.
6 Quoted in Andrew Gamble, 'Ideas and Interests in British Economic Policy', *Contemporary British History*, vol. 10. no. 2, 1996, p. 19.
7 Herbert Kitschelt, 'The Social Discourse and Party Strategy in West European Democracies', in C. Lemke and S. Marks (eds), *The Crisis of Socialism in Europe*, Durham: Duke University Press, 1992, 1994, p. 194.
8 Stephen Padgett and William E. Paterson, *A History of Social Democracy in Europe*, London: Longman, 1991, p. 1.
9 Ibid, p. 35.
10 David Miller, *Market, State and Community: Theoretical Foundations of Market Socialism*, Oxford: Oxford University Press, 1989, p. 8. Cf. Peter Clarke, *The Keynesian Revolution in the Making, 1924–36*, Oxford: Clarendon Press, 1988; Keith Middlemas, *Power, Competition and the State, Volume 1: Britain in Search of Balance, 1940–61*, London: Macmillan, 1986; Andrew Shonfield, *Modern Capitalism*, Oxford: Oxford University Press, 1965; Samuel Beer, *Modern British Politics*, London: Faber & Faber, 1965; Peter Jenkins, *Mrs Thatcher's Revolution: The Ending of the Socialist Age*, London: Jonathan Cape, 1987; Alec Cairncross, *The British Economy Since 1945*, Oxford: Basil Blackwell, 1992; David Marquand, *The Unprincipled Society*, London: Fontana, 1988; Andrew Gamble, *The Conservative Nation*, London: Macmillan, 1974.
11 Dennis Kavanagh, *Thatcherism and British Politics*, Oxford: Oxford University Press, 1990, p. 32.
12 For an overview of this debate, Anthony King, 'Overload: Problems of Governing in the 1970s', *Political Studies*, vol. 23, 1975, pp. 162–74; Richard Rose and Guy Peters, *Can Government Go Bankrupt?*, London: Macmillan, 1979; Robert Skidelsky (ed.), *The End of the Keynesian Era*, Oxford: Martin Robertson, 1977; Samuel Brittan, *Economic Consequences of Democracy*, London: Temple Smith, 1977; David Held, 'Power and Legitimacy in Contemporary Britain', in Gregor MacLennon, David Held and Stuart Hall (eds), *State and Society in Contemporary Britain*, Cambridge: Polity Press, 1984.

13   Anthony King, 'Political Change in Britain', in Dennis Kavanagh (ed.), *Electoral Politics*, Oxford: Oxford University Press, 1992, p. 47.
14   Ibid, p. 47.
15   Anthony Seldon, 'Ideas Are Not Enough', in David Marquand and Anthony Seldon (eds), *The Ideas That Shaped Post War Britain*, HarperCollins, 1996, pp. 263–6.
16   Colin Hay, *Restating Social and Political Change*, Buckingham: Open University Press, 1996, p. 45.
17   Peter A. Hall, 'The Politics of Keynesian Ideas', in Peter A. Hall (ed.), *The Political Power of Economic Ideas: Keynesianism across Nations*, Princeton, NJ: Princeton University Press, 1989.
18   Thomas Kuhn, *The Structure of Scientific Revolutions*, Chicago University Press, 1970.
19   Ibid.
20   In a phrase which has also become quite a cliché, Keynes suggested that '[T]he ideas of economists and political philosophers, both when they are right and when they are wrong, are more powerful than is commonly understood. Indeed the world is ruled by little else. Practical men who believe themselves to be quite exempt from any intellectual influences, are usually the slaves of some defunct economist.' J.M. Keynes, *The General Theory of Employment, Money and Interest*, London: Macmillan, 1936, p. 383.
21   David Knoke, Franz Urban Pappi, Jeffrey Broadbent and Yutaka Tsuinaka, *Comparing Policy Networks: Labor Politics in the US, Germany and Japan*, Cambridge: Cambridge University Press, 1996, p. 9.
22   Bob Jessop *et al.*, *Thatcherism: A Tale of Two Nations*, Cambridge: Polity Press, p. 13.
23   Peter Hall, 'The Politics of Keynesian Ideas', in Peter Hall (ed.), *The Political Power of Economic Ideas*, p. 30. Hall and his fellow authors argue that political parties (in concert with other factors) were instrumental in bringing about the advent of Keynesianism. For institutionalist explanations of political change, cf. Peter Hall, 'Policy Paradigms, Social Learning and the State', *Comparative Politics*, vol. 25, no. 3, 1993, pp. 275–96; Geoffrey Garrett, 'The Politics of Structural Change: Swedish Social Democracy and Thatcherism in Comparative Perspective', *Comparative Political Studies*, vol. 25, no. 4, 1993, pp. 521–47. Of course, while stressing the importance of electoral competition, other exogenous political circumstances can and do favour one reform programme over others.
24   David Marsh, 'Explaining Thatcherite Policies: Beyond Uni-Dimensional Explanations', *Political Studies*, vol. 43, no. 4, p. 609.
25   Where the task of entrepreneurs is to identify and exploit ways of challenging existing policies, Christopher Hood suggests that entrepreneurs play a catalytic role in that they straddle the distinction between ideas, interests and social context. Christopher Hood, *Explaining Economic Policy Reversals*, Buckingham: Open University Press, 1994. Thus opportunity and agency mesh when the political leader (collective rather than plural) acts as a catalyst; it can generate ideas when the status quo is discredited (or worse).
26   Cf. R.W. Cobb and C.D. Elder, *Participation in American Politics: The Dynamics of Agenda Building*, Baltimore, MD: Johns Hopkins University Press, 1972; John Kingdom, *Agendas, Alternatives and Public Policies*, 2nd edn, New York: Harper

College, 1995; John Kingdom, 'How Do Issues Get on Public Policy Agendas?', in W.J. Wilson (ed.), *Sociology and the Public Agenda*, London: Sage, 1993.

2 Beyond the Thatcher Decade: The Politics of 'New' Labour

1 Bernard Donoughue, *Prime Minister*, London: Jonathan Cape, 1987, p. 191.
2 As Dennis Kavanagh suggests: 'Few general elections or administrations map out a new agenda. Yet such a change can happen. A different set of policies, perhaps sustained over two or three elections, may force the defeated party to reconsider its strategy if it wants to remain electorally competitive. The adaptation of the Conservative Party to the post-war Labour Party initiatives is one example. The acceptance of the New Deal by many Republicans in the United States and the adoption of the social market approach and formal abandonment of Marxism by West Germany's Social Democrats are others. In the last two cases, decisive and successive election defeats convinced the party leaders that the centre of electoral opinion had moved away for them. Parties adopt or disavow policies not only to win forthcoming elections but also as a response to past electoral outcomes' (*Thatcherism and British Politics*, Oxford: Oxford University Press, 1990, p. 313).
3 Keith Middlemas, *Power, Competition and the State. Volume III: End of the Post-War Era*, London: Macmillan, 1991, p. 279.
4 Shirley Letwin, *The Anatomy of Thatcherism*, London: Fontana, 1992, p. 39.
5 Of course, in her first years as Prime Minister, Margaret Thatcher rarely called herself a Thatcherite. As the phrase stuck she came to adopt it as the 1980s drew to a close. Equally, she never referred to herself as a neo-liberal; in partisan terms she called herself a Conservative. Titles awarded to social phenomena can sometimes mislead: the phrase 'liberal' has very different meanings either side of the Atlantic, as is demonstrated by the fact that the US equivalent of social democracy is referred to as reform liberalism.
6 Tony Blair, 'Power for a Purpose', *Renewal*, vol. 3. no. 4, October 1995.
7 Tony Blair speech, Labour Party Press Release, April 1996.
8 Shirley Letwin, *Anatomy of Thatcherism*, pp. 350–1.
9 Richard Cockett, *Thinking the Unthinkable: Think Tanks and the Economic Counter Revolution*, London: HarperCollins, 1995, p. 322.
10 Will Hutton, *The State We're In*, London: Vintage, 1995, p. 16
11 Ibid.
12 An observation in a keynote speech to Murdoch's News Corporation Leadership Conference (itself an occasion that demonstrates the extent of Labour's political conversion). Tony Blair, transcript of speech to News Corporation Leadership Conference, 17 July 1995.
13 *The Times*, 5 January 1996.
14 The idea of 'New' Labour, an advertisers' campaign phrase that has well and truly stuck, was preceded by the phrase 'the New Model Labour Party', found throughout Colin Hughes and Patrick Wintour, *Labour Rebuilt: The New Model Party*, London: Fourth Estate, 1990. Its ancestry can be traced back to a former director of the Labour Party Campaign and Communication department. This one-time official, Peter Mandelson, is now a Labour MP and until 1998

was a minister in the Blair government. At the time of writing he remains a close confidant of the Prime Minister and a key figure within New Labour.

15 *Labour Party Annual Conference Report*, 1985.
16 Tony Blair Speech, Labour Party Press Release, May 1995.
17 Hutton was perceived by the Blair circle as a semi-private critic of Labour's contemporary stance. Following Labour's 1997 Conference he wrote 'Those of us who believe that Keynes, Beveridge, Tawney and Bevan have something to offer – albeit in a contemporary guise – are facing hard choices. The growing realisation is that we soon may not be able to look at the Labour party to represent what we believe' (*The Observer*, 5 October 1997). Hutton had previously expressed high hopes that Blair's election as leader would see Labour develop a traditional social democratic programme (*The State We're In*, p. 30).
18 Keith Joseph, House of Commons Debates, 18 May 1979, col. 709. See Dennis Kavanagh and Peter Morris, *Consensus Politics from Attlee to Major*, Oxford: Basil Blackwell, 1994.
19 Keith Joseph, ibid, col. 712.
20 At Blair's suggestion the Institute of Public Policy Research-sponsored Commission of Public Policy and British Business headed up by long-standing Labour supporter Clive Hollick brought together a number of senior representatives of corporate Britain with one trade unionist, John Monks, general secretary of the TUC. Leading business representatives who participated in the commission chaired by George Bain of the London Business School included Bob Bauman of British Aerospace, George Simpson of GEC, David Sainsbury, and Sir Christopher Harding of Legal and General.
21 Tony Blair, speech at launch of IPPR report of Commission of Public Policy and British Business, 21 January 1997.
22 *Daily Mail*, 26 March 1997.
23 Tony Blair, speech at launch of IPPR report of Commission of Public Policy and British Business, 21 January 1997.
24 *The Times*, 14 March 1997.
25 *The Sunday Times*, 28 May 1996. Other unlikely Labour supporters in 1997 included Rupert Murdoch and Andrew Neil, former editor of Murdoch's *Sunday Times*. After 1994, in Neil's words, both men 'came to see Tony Blair as a more credible heir to the Thatcher revolution than her Tory successor... Blair was saying many of the right neo-Thatcherite things on the economy, tax and welfare' (Andrew Neil, *Full Disclosure*, London: Pan Books, 1997, pp. xx and xxii).
26 Adam Przeworski, *Capitalism and Social Democracy*, Cambridge: Cambridge University Press, 1985. 'The very capacity of social democrats to regulate the economy depends upon the profitabity of the private sector and the willingness of capitalists to cooperate. This is the structural barrier which cannot be broken... investment and thus profits must be protected in the long run' (p. 42).
27 Costa Esping-Anderson, *Politics Against Markets*, Princeton, NJ: Princeton University Press, 1985.
28 Richard Rose, *Can Parties Make a Difference?*, London: Macmillan, 1984, p. 142.
29 Andrew Gamble, *The Free Economy and the Strong State: The Politics of Thatcherism*, London: Macmillan, 1988, p. 219.

30 Margaret Thatcher, *The Downing Street Years*, London; HarperCollins, 1993, p. 339. Thatcher made a similar claim in a speech to the Scottish Conservatives on the eve of the 1983 election: 'This is a historic election. For the choice facing the nation is between two totally different ways of life. And what a prize we have to fight for: no less than the chance to banish from our land the dark, divisive clouds of Marxist Socialism' (Hugo Young, *One of Us*, London: Pan Books, 1991, p. 323).

31 Christopher Hood, *Explaining Economic Policy Reversals*, Buckingham: Open University Press, 1994, p. 46.

32 James Douglas, 'The Changing Tide: Some Recent Studies of Thatcherism', *British Journal of Political Science*, vol. 19, no. 3, 1989, pp. 399–424, p. 423.

33 Martin J. Smith, 'Understanding the Politics of Catch-Up: The Modernisation of the Labour Party', *Political Studies*, vol. 42, 1994, pp. 708–15, p. 708. Cf. Smith, 'Neil Kinnock and the Modernisation of the Labour Party', *Contemporary Record*, vol. 8, 1994. While there are differences and nuances in the work of a number of commentators (essentially the debate around whether Labour's current stance is 'post-democratic', 'modernised social democratic', or 'non-social democratic'), Smith's distinction is artificial because 'modernisation' is in fact a form of 'accommodation' to an altered status quo, a reformed political environment.

34 Perry Anderson, 'The Light of Europe', *English Questions*, London: Verso, 1992; Gregory Elliott, *Labourism and the English Genius: The Strange Death of Labour England*, London: Verso, 1993; Colin Hay, 'Labour's Thatcherite Revisionism: Playing the "Politics of Catch-Up" ', *Political Studies*, vol. 42, 1994, pp. 700–7.

35 Richard Cockett, a historian of the New Right, argues: 'Much as it would have been difficult to find any substantive difference in economic policy between two such notorious political opponents as Messrs Gladstone and Disraeli in the 1870s, or between R.A. Butler and Hugh Gaitskell in the 1950s, so it is hard to discern any such differences between Messrs Major and Blair in the 1990s' (Richard Cockett, *Thinking the Unthinkable: Think Tanks and the Economic Counter-Revolution*, London: Harper Collins, 1995, p. 7). 'The new ideological axis around which each of the major parties revolve is that of the efficacy of the market economy – the only disputes arise as to the extent of "regulation" which might be desirable within that market economy' (p. 323).

3 The Politics of Thatcherism

1 Andrew Gamble, *The Free Economy and the Strong State*, 2nd edn, London: Macmillan, 1994, p. 7.

2 Ibid, p. 4.

3 Joel Wolfe, *Power and Privatisation*, London: Macmillan, 1996, p. 4.

4 As Shirley Letwin criticises this perspective: Shirley Letwin, *The Anatomy of Thatcherism*, London: Fontana, 1992, p. 25.

5 David Marsh and R.A.W. Rhodes, 'Implementing Thatcherism: A Policy Perspective', *Essex Papers in Politics and Government No. 62*, Colchester: University of Essex, 1989; David Marsh and R.A.W. Rhodes, 'Implementing Thatcherism: Policy Change in the 1980s', *Parliamentary Affairs*, vol. 45,

184   *Notes*

1990, pp. 33–51; David Marsh and R.A.W. Rhodes (eds), *Implementing Thatcherite Policies: Audit of an Era*, Buckingham: Open University Press, 1992.

6 David Marsh, 'Explaining Thatcherite Policies: Beyond Uni-Dimensional Explanations', *Political Studies*, vol. 43, no. 4, 1995, pp. 595–613.

7 Peter Taylor, 'Changing Political Relations', in Peter Clarke (ed.), *Policy and Change in Thatcher's Britain*, Oxford: Pergamon Press, 1992, p. 33.

8 Peter Riddell, *The Thatcher Era and its Legacy*, Oxford: Basil Blackwell, 1991, p. xx; Peter Riddell, *The Thatcher Decade*, Oxford: Basil Blackwell, 1989; Peter Riddell, *The Thatcher Government*, Oxford: Martin Robertson, 1983. Other commentators who broadly share Riddell's approach are Jim Bulpitt, 'The Discipline of the New Democracy: Mrs Thatcher's Domestic Statecraft', *Political Studies*, vol. 39, no. 1, 1985, pp. 19–39; Martin Holmes, *Thatcherism: Scope and Limits*, London: Macmillan, 1989; David Marsh and R.A.W. Rhodes, *passim*. For an overview of the literature on Thatcherism to 1989, cf. James Douglas, 'The Changing Tide: Some Recent Studies of Thatcherism', *British Journal of Political Science*, vol. 19, no. 3, 1989, pp. 399–442.

9 *The Times*, 4 April 1997.

10 David Marsh and R.A.W. Rhodes, 'Thatcherism: An Implementation Perspective', in Marsh and Rhodes (eds), *Implementing Thatcherite Policies: Audit of an Era*, p. 3. Cf. David Marsh and R.A.W. Rhodes, 'Evaluating Thatcherism: Over the Moon or Sick as a Parrot?', *Politics*, vol. 15, no. 1, 1995, pp. 49–54.

11 David Marsh, 'Explaining Thatcherite Policies: Beyond Uni-Dimensional Explanation', p. 603.

12 Ibid, p. 603.

13 Marsh and Rhodes (eds), *Implementing Thatcherite Policies: Audit of an Era*, p. 186.

14 Cf. Richard Heffernan, 'Exploring Political Change: Thatcherism and the Remaking of the Labour Party, 1979–1997', Unpublished PhD Thesis, London School of Economics, University of London, 1998.

15 David Marsh, David Dolowitz, Fiona O'Neill and David Richards, 'Thatcherism and the Three R's: Radicalism, Realism and Rhetoric in the Third Term of the Thatcherite Government', *Parliamentary Affairs*, vol. 49, no. 3, 1996, p. 447.

16 Ibid, p. 448.

17 Marsh and Rhodes (eds), *Implementing Thatcherite Policies: Audit of an Era*, p. 187.

18 Colin Hay, *Restating Social and Political Change*, Buckingham: Open University Press, 1996, p. 152. He rightly suggests that we should be 'extremely wary' of Marsh and Rhodes's conclusion that 'the Thatcherite revolution is more a product of rhetoric than of the reality of policy impact' p. 153.

19 Shirley Letwin, *The Anatomy of Thatcherism*, p. 30.

20 Peter Riddell falls into the first category. Commentators who fall into the second include Stuart Hall and Martin Jacques (eds), *The Politics of Thatcherism*, London: Lawrence & Wishart, 1983; Stuart Hall, 'Popular Democratic versus Authoritarian Populism', in Alan Hunt (ed.), *Marxism and Democracy*, London: Lawrence & Wishart, 1983: Stuart Hall, 'Authoritarian Populism: A Reply', *New Left Review*, no. 151, 1985; Stuart Hall, *The Hard Road to Renewal: Thatcherism and the Crisis of the Left*, London: Verso, 1988; Bob Jessop *et al.*, 'Authoritarian Populism: "Two Nations" and Thatcherism', *New Left Review*, no. 147, 1984; Bob Jessop *et al.*, *Thatcherism: A Tale of Two Nations*, Cam-

bridge: Polity Press, 1988; Colin Leys, 'Still A Question of Hegemony', *New Left Review*, no. 181, 1990; Joel Wolfe, 'State, Power and Ideology in Britain: Mrs Thatcher's Privatisation Programme', *Political Studies*, vol. 39, 1991, pp. 237–55; Joel Wolfe, *Power and Privatisation*, London: Macmillan, 1996; Jeremy Moon, *Political Leadership in Democracy: Policy Change Under Thatcher*, Aldershot: Dartmouth, 1993; Jeremy Moon, 'Innovative Leadership and Policy Change: Lessons From Thatcher', *Governance*, vol. 8, no. 1, 1995.

21 Desmond King, 'The New Right and Public Policy', *Political Studies*, vol. 42, 1994, pp. 490–1

22 Simon Auerbach, 'Mrs Thatcher's Labour Laws: Slouching Toward Utopia', *Political Quarterly*, vol. 64, no. 1, 1993, p. 45. Cf. Simon Auerbach, *Legislating for Conflict*, Oxford: Oxford University Press, 1991.

23 Auerbach, 'Mrs Thatcher's Labour Laws', p. 47.

24 Will Hutton, *The State We're In*, London: Vintage, 1996, p. 89.

25 Colin Hay, *Restating Social and Political Change*, p. 129.

26 David Marsh, 'Explaining Thatcherite Policies: Beyond Uni-Dimensional Explanation', p. 603.

27 A phrase Marsh uses to criticise commentators of this persuasion: ibid, p. 599.

28 Bob Jessop *et al.*, 'Authoritarian Populism: "Two Nations" and Thatcherism', p. 78.

29 Simon Auerbach, 'Mrs Thatcher's Labour Laws: Slouching Toward Utopia', p. 46.

30 Bob Jessop *et al.*, *Thatcherism: A Tale of Two Nations*, pp. 8–9.

31 Shirley Letwin, *The Anatomy of Thatcherism*, p. 29. This is a view Letwin ascribes to those who are invariably hostile to Thatcherism and set themselves up in opposition to it.

32 Simon Jenkins, *Accountable to None: The Tory Nationalisation of Britain*, Harmondsworth: Penguin, 1996, p. 1.

33 Ibid, p. 6.

34 Ibid, p. 9.

35 John Major was far more willing than Thatcher to countenance it: Thatcher thought '[Rail] Privatisation would be difficult and unpopular. As a result she shut her mind to it... When her last two ministers, Paul Channon and Cecil Parkinson, pressed to be allowed to go for privatisation she warned them off. Her sole interest was in selling the railways' "non core" assets to keep down the subsidy. She wanted to cut costs without frightening the natives' (ibid, p. 203). While Thatcher asked her last Transport Secretary, Cecil Parkinson, not to raise the issue at the 1990 Conservative Conference, John Major encouraged the initiative and it was his Cabinet which eventually brought forward the policy.

36 On think-tanks, cf. Richard Cockett, *Thinking the Unthinkable: Think Tanks and the Economic Counter Revolution, 1931–1983*, London: Harper Collins, 1995; Andrew Denham and Mark Garnett, 'The Nature and Impact of Think Tanks in Contemporary Britain', *Contemporary British History*, vol. 10, no. 1, 1996, pp. 43–61; Simon James, 'The Idea Brokers: The Impact of Think Tanks in British Government' *Public Administration*, vol. 71, 1993; Radhika Desai, 'Second Hand Dealers in Ideas: Think Tanks and Thatcherite Hegemony', *New Left Review*, 203, 1994; Tim Hames and Richard Feasey, 'Anglo American Think Tanks Under Reagan and Thatcher', in Andrew Adonis and

Tim Hames (eds), *A Conservative Revolution? The Thatcher–Reagan Decade in Retrospect*, Manchester: Manchester University Press, 1993; Diane Stone, *Capturing the Political Imagination: Think Tanks and The Policy Process*, London: Frank Cass, 1996. For a critical perspective arguing the limited (but useful) influence of think-tanks, cf. Richard Heffernan, 'Blueprint for a Revolution: The Politics of the Adam Smith Institute', *Contemporary British History*, vol. 10, no. 1, 1996, pp. 73–87.

37   Cf. Richard Rose and Philip Davies, *Inheritance in Public Policy*, New Haven: Yale University Press, 1995; Richard Rose, 'Inheritance Before Choice in Public Policy', *Journal of Theoretical Politics*, vol. 2, no. 1, 1990, pp. 263–91.

38   Nigel Lawson, *The View From No 11: Memoirs of a Tory Radical*, London: Bantam Press, 1992.

39   Hugo Young, *One of Us*, London: Pan Books, 1991, p. 552.

40   Ibid, pp. 300–1. Cf. Kenneth Hoover and Raymond Plant, *Conservative Capitalism in Britain and America*, London: Routledge, 1989, pp. 163–4; Geoffrey Howe, *A Question of Loyalties*, London: Macmillan, 1994.

41   Hoover and Plant, *Conservative Capitalism in Britain and America*, p. 165.

42   Andrew Gamble, *The Free Economy and the Strong State*, pp. 23–4. Although Gamble sees Thatcherism as a 'hegemonic project' (ibid, p. 141) he does not over-emphasise its ideological aspect: 'Thatcherism is better explained as statecraft rather than ideology' (ibid). For Gamble's recent work on Conservatism, cf. Andrew Gamble, 'The Crisis of Conservatism', *New Left Review*, 214, 1995, pp. 3–25. Here, Gamble argues that the Conservative Party is at a crossroads – its 'ideological tradition has become exhausted' (p. 24) even if '[t]he forces of the Right are strong and confident' (ibid). Although '[t]he foundations of Conservative political hegemony lay on the development of a statecraft … such was the radicalism of Thatcherism that it played an important part in weakening the pillars of Conservative political hegemony although, at the time of its ascendency, it appeared to be consolidating and extending them' (p. 38). None the less, Gamble argues that 'the strength of the Thatcherite legacy is that, although it is strongly criticised from every side, there are few coherent programmes for undoing it or going beyond it' (p. 24). In the wake of May 1997, Thatcherite Conservatism may be a temporarily busted flush politically; in ideological terms, the territory it has marked out prevails.

43   Jim Bulpitt, 'The Discipline of the New Statecraft: Mrs Thatcher's Domestic Statecraft', p. 21 'the art of winning elections and maintaining some kind of governing competence in office'.

44   Nicholas Ridley, *My Style of Government*, London: Hutchinson, 1991, pp. 84–5.

45   Ibid, p. 86.

46   Cf. Martin Burch and Ian Holliday, *The British Cabinet System*, London: Prentice Hall, 1995; Nigel Lawson, 'Cabinet Government in the Thatcher Years', *Contemporary Record*, vol. 8, no. 1, 1994; John Wakeham, 'A Lecture on Cabinet Government', *Contemporary Record*, vol. 8, no. 3, 1994.

47   Cf. Philip Norton, ' "The Lady's Not For Turning". But What About the Rest? Margaret Thatcher and the Conservative Party', *Parliamentary Affairs*, vol. 43, no. 1, 1990; Philip Cowley, 'How Did He Do That?', in David Denver *et al.* (eds), *British Elections and Parties Yearbook 1996*, London: Frank Cass, 1996; John Ranelagh, *Thatcher's People*, London; Fontana, 1992.

48 Thatcher could never make Cabinet appointments on the basis of the 'one of us' criteria. While able to dominate the government for long periods, she was never able to fashion the inner circles of government in her own image. After the routing of the Gilmour–Prior wets in 1981, for every true Thatcherite to enter Cabinet (Lawson, Tebbit, Parkinson, Ridley), others not entirely to Thatcher's thinking were also appointed (Hurd, Clarke, Rifkind, Patten). Following Lawson's resignation from the Treasury, she wanted to appoint Nicholas Ridley in his place but accepted it was impossible to do so. Thatcher was ultimately isolated within her own government at the time of her dismissal in November 1990 (in the wake of her ineffective first ballot lead in the contest with Michael Heseltine).

49 Peter Clarke, *A Question of Leadership*, London: Hamish Hamilton, 1991.

50 David Marsh, 'Explaining Thatcherite Policies: Beyond Uni-Dimensional Explanations'.

4 Explaining Thatcherism: Project and Process

1 Margaret Thatcher, *The Downing Street Years*, London: HarperCollins, 1993, p. 6.

2 Easily identified stepping-stones include: The translation of Von Mises into English in 1924; the publication of Hayek's *The Road to Serfdom* in 1944; the formation of the Mont Pelerin Society in 1947 and in its wake the Institute of Economic Affairs in 1957; the resignation of the Treasury Front Bench team in Macmillan's government in 1958; the crisis of confidence in Macmillan in 1961–3; 'Powellism' and the shift of the right by elements of the Conservative Front Bench in 1967–70 typified by the partial myth of 'Selsdon Man'; the failure of the Heath government and its defeat in the 'Who Governs' election of February 1974; the development and growth of the monetarist paradigm in the early and mid-1970s; the failure of Labour in office in 1974–9 typified by stagflation and rising unemployment; the implementation of a quasi-monetarist economic policy by that Labour government in the wake of the IMF crisis of 1976; the crisis of Corporatism symbolised by the Winter of Discontent of 1978–9.

3 Alastair B. Cooke, 'Introduction', to Margaret Thatcher, *The Revival of Britain: Speeches on Home and European Affairs 1975–1988*, London: Aurum Press, 1989, pp. vii and viii.

4 *The Guardian*, 25 March 1986.

5 'Thatcher found that the magnetism of power overwhelmed any disposition to repel it. She shared with Lord Hailsham a familiar syndrome among British politicians; an aversion to "elective dictatorship" when out of office and a sudden conversion to "its glorious subtleties" when in power. The libertine in office becomes the absolutist in office' (Simon Jenkins, *Accountable to None: The Tory Nationalisation of Britain*, Harmondsworth: Penguin, 1996, p. 262). Clearly, Thatcher was prepared to use the complete resources her office granted her, but the thing to note is that Thatcher wanted to go somewhere, not just anywhere. In certain policy areas the projected destination was reached; in others the government fell well, well short of its target.

6 Practical discontent on the political right in the early mid-1970s were the first stirrings of the coming neo-liberal assault on traditional politics. The crisis of Keynesian social democracy provided a window of opportunity for the Thatcher government in both electoral and political terms. As Andrew Gamble makes clear, government 'questioning of the post-war consensus, [and its] emphasis upon the failure of Keynesian economic policy and social democratic strategies created a space in which the ideas of the many variants of the right could flourish' (Andrew Gamble, *The Free Economy and the Strong State: The Politics of Thatcherism*, 2nd edn, London: Macmillan, 1988, p. 34). Urged on by the increasingly unshaken belief that the status quo was not working, the Conservative election victory in May 1979 granted the politics of the New Right its opportunity, it was not its crowning glory.

7 Paul Addison, *The Road to 1945*, London: Pimlico, 1994.

8 Bob Jessop *et al.*, *Thatcherism: A Tale of Two Nations*, Cambridge: Polity Press, 1988.

9 Colin Hay, *Restating Social and Political Change*, Buckingham: Open University Press, 1996, p. 148. He suggests that an emergent 'new Thatcherite state regime' was configurated by the emergence of a 'post-Thatcherite settlement' marked by 'Thatcherism after Thatcher; ideological deradicalisation; piecemeal reform; crisis management; attempted consolidation' (ibid).

10 Bob Jessop *et al.*, *Thatcherism: A Tale of Two Nations*, p. 67.

11 Joel Wolfe, 'State, Power and Ideology in Britain: Mrs Thatcher's Privatisation Programme', *Political Studies*, vol. 34, 1991, p. 175.

12 As Andrew Gamble notes: '[d]uring Thatcher's leadership of the Conservatives there was a substantial ideological shift within the Conservative Party, and that this shift has proved to be permanent under her successor. The party has abandoned the interventionist and collectivist social and economic programme it adopted in stages during the twentieth century, and shows no signs of returning to it. Economic liberalism now shapes the party's thinking about policy' (Andrew Gamble, 'An Ideological Party', in Steve Ludlam and Martin Smith, *Contemporary British Conservatism*, London: Macmillan, 1996, p. 35).

13 Again one must emphasis the role of the Thatcherites and not just that of Thatcher herself. In enforced retirement Thatcher commented: 'I had said at the beginning of the government "give me six strong men and true and I will get the job through". Very rarely did I have as many as six' (Margaret Thatcher, *The Downing Street Years*, p. 149). This is so obviously an overstatement, part of Thatcher's reaction to her effective dismissal in November 1990. Of this comment one arch Conservative critic of Mrs Thatcher, Ian Gilmour, a member of her Cabinet in 1979–81, waspishly commented it was remarkable that Mrs Thatcher needed only half the number of men to complete her work on earth that Jesus needed to establish his ministry (private information).

14 Margaret Thatcher, *The Downing Street Years*, p. 159.

15 Margaret Thatcher, Speech in New York, 15 September 1975, in Alastair B. Cooke (ed.), *Margaret Thatcher, The Revival of Britain: Speeches on Home and European Affairs 1975–1988*, London: Aurum Press, 1989, p. xxi.

16 Ibid, p. 16.

17 Margaret Thatcher, *The Downing Street Years*, p. 7.

18 Margaret Thatcher, *The Path to Power*, London; HarperCollins, 1994. For a more reasoned assessment of Conservatism immediately preceding 1975, cf. John Ramsden, *The Winds of Change: Macmillan to Heath 1957–1975*, London: Longman, 1996.

19 Leading Conservatives came to endorse the observation that 'there is at least a case for saying that the most impressive social democratic politician of the last thirty years was the author of *The Middle Way*, Harold Macmillan' (David Marquand, 'Has Social Democracy a Future?', *The Spectator*, 29 September 1979). Of course, 'impressive' would not have been the adjective employed.

20 Harold Macmillan, *The Middle Way*, London: Macmillan, 1938, quoted in Harold Macmillan, *The Winds of Change: Memoirs, 1914–1939*, London: Macmillan, 1966, pp. 223–4.

21 Keith Joseph, *Stranded on the Middle Ground*, London: Centre for Policy Studies, 1976, p. 20.

22 Ibid, p. 23. Note the famous *mea culpa* speech delivered in 1974: 'I first became a Conservative in 1974...'. Other significant Joseph texts include *Reversing the Trend*, London: Barry Rose, 1975; *Monetarism is Not Enough*, London: Centre for Policy Studies, 1975.

23 Joseph, *Stranded on the Middle Ground*.

24 Ibid, p. 26.

25 Ibid. As is so often noted, Keith Joseph was as significant a figure as Margaret Thatcher in the slow reorientation of the Conservative Party after 1974. In opposition between 1975 and 1979, he headed the Centre for Policy Studies, and as Director of Policy within the Shadow Cabinet he made a significant contribution to the return to first principles which lay behind the emergence of the distinctive Thatcherite agenda. For many Conservatives (not least Thatcher herself), Joseph's otherworldliness made him an unsuitable politician; although he had a significant public profile his contribution to the emergent Thatcherite agenda was not as considerable as is so often suggested. For many, Geoffrey Howe as Shadow Chancellor played as significant a part in the October 1974 Parliament (private information). Although a Thatcher insider, Joseph's star clearly waned in government. He had a reputation as a relatively ineffective minister and a propensity to abide by the mainstream view of his department, most notable in securing subsidies for so-called 'lame-duck' industries. Although still 'one of us' in government, he steadily moved from centre stage. As Secretary of State for Industry he was considered a grave disappointment by the more radical shock troops of the New Right, and at the Department of Education and Science after 1981 he was embroiled in teachers' disputes and an ineffective search for a workable voucher system before finally leaving government at his own request in 1986. A full biography of Joseph is much overdue. For a rudimentary introduction, cf. Morrison Halcrow, *Keith Joseph: A Single Mind*, London: Macmillan, 1989. For an introduction to the Centre for Policy Studies, see Michael Harris, 'The Centre for Policy Studies: The Paradoxes of Power', *Contemporary British History*, vol. 10, no. 2, 1996, pp. 51–64.

26 A phrase quoted in Peter Hennessy, *Whitehall*, London: Fontana, 1989, p. 629.

27 Simon Jenkins, *Accountable to None*, p. 181.

28 Ibid, p. 182.

29   Andrew Gamble, *The Free Economy and the Strong State*.
30   Ibid, p. 251.
31   David Marsh, 'Explaining Thatcherite Policies: Beyond Uni-Dimensional Explanations', *Political Studies*, vol. 43, no. 4, 1995.
32   Desmond King, *The New Right*, London: Macmillan, 1987.
33   Bob Jessop *et al.*, 'Farewell to Thatcherism: Neo-Liberalism and New Times', *New Left Review*, 179, 1990, p. 85.
34   John Gray, *After Social Democracy*, London: Demos, 1996, p. 10. Reprinted in John Gray, *Endgames*, Cambridge: Polity Press, 1997.
35   Ibid, p. 28.
36   Ibid.
37   Ibid, p. 11.
38   Bob Jessop *et al.*, 'Farewell to Thatcherism', *passim*.
39   Shirley Letwin, *The Anatomy of Thatcherism*, London: Fontana, 1992, p. 29.
40   Ibid.

5   Modernisation: The Transformation of the Labour Party

1   For different interpretations, see: Eric Shaw, *The Labour Party Since 1979: Crisis and Transformation*, London: Routledge, 1993; Eric Shaw, *The Labour Party Since 1945*, Oxford: Basil Blackwell, 1996; Richard Heffernan and Mike Marqusee, *Defeat From the Jaws of Victory: Inside Kinnock's Labour Party*, London: Verso, 1992; Stephen Fielding, *Labour: Crisis and Renewal*, Manchester: Baseline Books, 1995; Patrick Seyd, *The Rise and Fall of the Labour Left*, London: Macmillan, 1987; Maurice Kogan and David Kogan, *The Battle for the Labour Party*, London: Fontana, 1982; Paul Whiteley, *The Labour Party in Crisis*, London: Methuen, 1983; Lewis Minkin, *The Contentious Alliance: Trade Unions and the Labour Party*, Edinburgh: Edinburgh University Press, 1991; Leo Panitch and Colin Leys, *From New Left to New Labour: The End of Parliamentary Socialism*. London: Verso, 1997.
2   Cf. Tony Benn, *The End of an Era: Diaries, 1980–1990*, London: Hutchinson, 1992 (especially chapter 2, pp. 64–157); Jad Adams, *Tony Benn: A Biography*, London: Hutchinson, 1993; Richard Heffernan and Mike Marqusee, *Defeat From the Jaws of Victory*; Patrick Seyd, *The Fall and Rise of the Labour Left*; Maurice Kogan and David Kogan, *The Battle for the Labour Party*. The BBC television documentary, *Labour: The Wilderness Years*, produced by Fine Arts Productions and broadcast in 1995, provides a useful insight into this period.
3   Anthony King and Ivor Crewe, *SDP*, Oxford: Oxford University Press, 1996, p. 119.
4   Ibid. Crewe and King variously described the 1980 Labour Conference as 'not only unpleasant but positively insane' (p. 49); and criticised Tony Benn's 'demagoguery' and what they see as his 'self-sanctimoniousness' (p. 28).
5   Ibid. pp. 119–20.
6   This is a common theme of the Blair leadership, one captured in a number of the leader's speeches in 1994–7. Cf. Tony Blair, *New Britain: My Vision of a Young Country*, London: Fourth Estate, 1996.
7   Eric Shaw, *The Labour Party Since 1979: Crisis and Transformation*, London: Routledge, 1994, p. 13.

8   Cf. The Labour Party, *Labour's Programme 1976*, London: The Labour Party, 1976; The Labour Party, *Peace, Jobs, Freedom: Labour's Draft Manifesto*, London: The Labour Party, 1980; The Labour Party/TUC, *Economic Planning and Industrial Democracy*, London: The Labour Party, 1982; TUC, *Programme for Recovery*, London, TUC, 1982; The Labour Party; *The New Hope for Britain: The Labour Manifesto, 1983*, London: The Labour Party, 1983.

9   The Labour Party, *Because Britain Deserves Better: Labour's 1997 Manifesto*, London: Labour Party, 1997.

10 Martin J. Smith, 'A Return to Revisionism', in Martin Smith and Joanna Spear (eds), *The Changing Labour Party*, London: Routledge, 1992, p. 27.

11 Eric Shaw, *The Labour Party Since 1945*, Oxford: Basil Blackwell, 1996, p. 201.

12 Roy Hattersley, *Economic Priorities for a Labour Government*, London: Macmillan, 1987, p. 48.

13 Ibid, p. 6.

14 Ibid, p. 7. Hattersley also indicated his 'very strong' belief that 'a socialist economic policy is about the structure of the economic and the power within it. It is not about demand management of the economy'. Interview with Roy Hattersley, *Marxism Today*, October 1985.

15 Denis Healey, Campaign Statement for the Deputy Leadership of the Labour Party, May 1981. Cf. Heffernan and Marqusee, *Defeat From The Jaws of Victory*, chapter 2.

16 Noel Thompson, *Political Economy and the Labour Party*, London: UCL Press, p. 273.

17 *The Times*, 12 April 1996. *The Times* noted of one particular Blair speech (delivered in New York in April 1996) that 'Mr Blair is determined to allay the traditional suspicion among US businessmen of Labour governments in Britain. To most American bankers who have heard Mr Blair's message, he sounds like a solid Tory whose mission is not to undo the "Thatcher revolution" that was widely applauded in the US during the 1980s. One businessman said: "He says he's left of centre, but he could be right at the centre of the Tory party"' (ibid).

18 *Tribune*, 20 September 1985, 'Democratic Socialism: A Tribune Relaunch Statement'.

19 Ibid.

20 Ibid.

21 *Labour Weekly*, 14 March 1986.

22 *The Guardian*, 12 April 1997.

23 Ibid. In 1995, Blair told the CBI that penal rates of taxation do not make economic or political sense: 'They are gone for good. I want a tax regime where, through hard work, risk and success, people can become wealthy' (*Sunday Telegraph*, 6 April 1997).

24 Margaret Thatcher, *The Revival of Britain: Speeches, 1975–1988*, London: Aurum Press, 1989, p.16.

25 Neil Kinnock, 'Remaking the Labour Party', *Contemporary Record*, 1994, vol. 8, no. 4, p. 539.

26 Neil Kinnock, Personal Manifesto circulated to Constitutency Labour Parties in July 1983. Kinnock also claimed to have 'no quarrel with the policies of the last election' and stated that he would commit himself as leader 'to put those policies over to the electorate more persuasively' (ibid). While Kinnock

argued that immediate withdrawal from Europe was not an option he did associate himself with extended public ownership, increased public expenditure and strong trade unions. Cf. *Tribune*, 1 July 1983.

27 Kinnock has made much of his early commitment to revise Labour's then policy of withdrawal from the EEC. Indeed, he took steps to do so in 1983–4 but none the less made clear at the time his preparedness to retain the option of withdrawal if there was no fundamental reform of the Treaty of Rome which would liberate it from 'free market economy philosophy' (*New Socialist*, March 1984).

28 *The Financial Times*, 19 November 1986.

29 Tony Benn, *End of an Era: Diaries, 1980–1990*, 14 November 1986, p. 480.

30 Ibid.

31 Lewis Minkin, *The Contentious Alliance: Trade Unions and the Labour Party*, Edinburgh: Edinburgh University Press, 1991, p. 137.

32 Significant stepping-stones include: The Hayward–Hughes report of 1982; the introduction of the register of constitutional groups in 1982; the proscription of Militant in 1982; the expulsion of five members of the Militant editorial board in February 1983; the NEC investigation of the Liverpool District Labour Party in 1985–6 and the expulsions that followed; and the establishment of the National Constitutional Committee in 1986. Cf. Richard Heffernan and Mike Marqusee, *Defeat From the Jaws of Victory: Inside Kinnoch's Labour Party*, London: Verso; Michael Crick, *The March of Militant*, London: Faber & Faber, 1986; Eric Shaw, *Discipline and Discourse in the Labour Party*, Manchester: Manchester University Press, 1988. Note the significance of Militant ('a pestilential nuisance' according to Michael Foot) as a stick with which to beat the 'mainstream' Labour left.

33 Patrick Seyd, 'Bennism Without Benn', *New Socialist*, 27 May 1985; Richard Heffernan and Mike Marqusee, *Defeat From the Jaws of Victory*.

34 Eric Shaw, *The Labour Party Since 1979*, p. 52.

35 Neil Kinnock, *Making Our Way*, Oxford: Basil Blackwell, 1986, p. 192.

36 Neil Kinnock, *The Future of Socialism*, London: Fabian Society, 1985, p. 3.

37 Eric Shaw, *The Labour Party Since 1979*, p. 50.

38 For details of the Policy Review, see Martin Smith, 'A Return to Revisionism: The Labour Party Policy Review', and Andrew Gamble, 'The Labour Party and Economic Management', in Martin Smith and Joanna Spear (eds), *The Changing Labour Party*. See also Patrick Seyd, 'Labour: The Great Transformation', in Anthony King (ed.), *Britain at the Polls 1992*, London: Chatham House, 1993; Gerald Taylor, *Toward Renewal: The Policy Review and Beyond*, Basingstoke: Macmillan, 1997; Eric Shaw, 'Toward Renewal: The British Labour Party's Policy Review', in Richard Gillespie and William Paterson (eds), *Rethinking Social Democracy in Europe*, London: Frank Cass, 1989, pp. 112–32; Eric Shaw, *The Labour Party Since 1979*.

39 The Labour Party, *Meet the Challenge, Make the Change*, London: The Labour Party, 1989, p. 6.

40 The Labour Party, *Opportunity Britain*, London: The Labour Party, 1991, p. iii.

41 Tudor Jones, *Remaking the Labour Party: From Gaitskell to Blair*, London: Routledge, 1996, p. 126.

42 Tony Blair speech: Labour Party Press Release, 7 April 1997. Labour also published a separate 'Business Manifesto', a 20-page document launched

amid much fanfare at an event in the City. Claiming that Labour was now a party both of and for business, Blair went to great lengths during the election campaign to present himself as 'the entrepreneur's champion', winning the endorsement of a number of senior business executives. *The Guardian*, 12 April 1997.

43 *Sunday Telegraph*, 6 April 1997.
44 Quoted in Tudor Jones, *Remaking the Labour Party*, p. 125.
45 Neil Kinnock, *Making Our Way*, p. 97.
46 'Mandelson's true opinion of John Smith's leadership is glimpsed in an article he wrote for the *Fabian Review* just after the 1997 election: "We're doing so well now because we got our act together as a would-be government three years ago. We are enjoying the harvest of the hard work undertaken in opposition. There was a clarity of leadership and objectives, knowing what needed to be done to create a genuinely New Labour party, not simply a re-glossed, spray-on, re-shaped Labour Party." "Three years ago" was of course when Tony Blair became leader; everything that happened before belongs in the Mandelson view of history to Labour's "unelectable" era.' (Paul Anderson and Nyta Mann, *Safety First: The Making of New Labour*, London: Granta, 1997, p. 439).

6 How and Why Parties Change: Identifying Environmental Contexts

1 Ian Budge and Hans Keman, *Parties and Democracy: Coalition Formation and State Functioning in Twenty States*, Oxford: Oxford University Press, 1990, p. 132.
2 Otto Kirchheimer, 'The Transformation of the Western European Party Systems', in Joseph LaPalombara and Myron Weimer (eds), *Political Parties and Political Development*, Princeton, New Jersey: Princeton University Press, 1966.
3 Angelo Panebianco, *Political Parties: Organisation and Power*, Cambridge: Cambridge University Press, 1988.
4 Cf. Hans Daalder on party types, in Hans Daalder and Peter Mair (eds), *Western European Party Systems: Continuity and Change*, London: Sage, 1983, p. 23.
5 Pippa Norris and Ivor Crewe, 'In Defence of British Election Studies', in David Denver *et al.* (eds), *British Elections and Parties Yearbook 1991*, London: Frank Cass, 1991, pp. 19–20.
6 Giovanni Sartori, *Parties and Party Systems*, Cambridge: Cambridge University Press, 1976.
7 Peter Mair, 'Adaptation and Control: Toward an Understanding of Party and Party System Change', in Hans Daalder and Peter Mair (eds), *Western European Party Systems*, pp. 405–29; Peter Mair, 'The Problem of Party System Change', *Journal of Theoretical Politics*, 1, pp. 251–76. Cf. Peter Mair and Gordon Smith, *Understanding Party System Change in Western Europe*, London: Frank Cass, 1990.
8 Peter Mair, 'The Problem of Party System Change', p. 274. Cf. Peter Mair, 'Adaptation and Control: Toward an Understanding of Party and Party System Change'.

9   Mair, 'The Problem of Party System Change', p. 256.
10 The 'freeze hypothesis'. Cf. Seymour Martin Lipset and Stein Rokkan (eds), *Party Systems and Voter Alignments: Cross National Perspectives*, New York: Free Press, 1967. Cf Giovanni Sartori, 'The Sociology of Parties', in Otto Stammer (ed.), *Party Systems, Party Organisations and Politics of the New Masses*, Berlin: The Free University, 1969.
11 Mair, 'The Problem of Party System Change', p. 314.
12 Russell J. Dalton, Scott C. Flanagan and Paul Allen Beck, *Electoral Change in Advanced Industrial Democracies: Realignment or Dealignment?*, Princeton, NJ: Princeton University Press, 1984.
13 Moshe Maor, *Political Parties and Party Systems*, London: Routledge, 1997, p. 63.
14 Jan-Eric Lane and Svante Erison, *Politics and Society in Western Europe*, London: Sage, 1994, p. 40.
15 David Butler and Donald Stokes, *Political Change in Modern Britain*, London: Macmillan, 1974, p. 8.
16 Ibid.
17 Angelo Panebianco, *Political Parties*, p. 243.
18 That electoral instabilities are often exaggerated is illustrated by Bartolini and Mair: 'Mean volatility in Western Europe in the supposed era of change from 1966 to 1985 proved to be just 00.1% higher than in the period of steady state politics from 1945 to 1965' (Stefano Bartolini and Peter Mair (eds), 'Party Politics on Contemporary Western Europe', *West European Politics*, vol. 7, no. 4, 1984). Peter Mair and Stefano Bartolini, *Identity, Competition and Electoral Availability: The Stabilisation of European Electorates, 1885–1985*, Cambridge: Cambridge University Press, 1992, p. xvii. Cf. Peter Mair, 'Myths of Electoral Change and the Survival of Traditional Parties', *European Journal of Political Research*, vol. 24, pp. 121–33.
19 Cf. Ivor Crewe, Bo Saarlvik and James Alt, 'Partisan Dealignment in Britain, 1964–77', *British Journal of Political Science*, vol. 7, 1979, pp. 129–90; Ivor Crewe, 'Partisan Dealignment Ten Years On', *West European Politics*, vol. 6, 1983; Ivor Crewe and David Denver, *Electoral Change in Western Democracies: Patterns and Sources of Electoral Volatility*, London: Croom Helm, 1985.
20 Mark Franklin, *The Decline of Class Voting in Britain*, Oxford: Clarendon Press, 1985.
21 Hilde Himmelweit *et al.*, *How Voters Decide*, London: Academic Press, 1981.
22 Anthony Heath, Roger Jowell and John Curtice, *How Britain Votes*, Oxford: Pergamon Press, 1985; Anthony Heath *et al.*, *Understanding Political Change: The British Voter, 1964–1987*, Aldershot: Dartmouth, 1991.
23 Angelo Panebianco, *Political Parties*, p. 209. Richard Rose and Ian McAllister claim: 'The electorate today is wide open to change: three-quarters of voters are no longer anchored by a stable party loyalty determined by family and class... The question facing many voters today is not whether to maintain an established party loyalty. It is: which of the parties supported in the past should I vote for next time?' (Richard Rose and Ian McAllister, *Voters Begin to Choose*, London: Sage, 1986, p. 1). Cf. Richard Rose and Ian McAllister, *The Loyalties of Voters*, London: Sage, 1990.
24 Within what Panebianco describes as an electoral arena 'in which relations between parties and other organisations take place. They are like gaming

tables at which the party plays and obtains, in accordance with its performance, the resources it needs to function' (Angelo Panebianco, *Political Parties*,
p. 207). Foremost among these resources is electoral support. Of course,
parties are not static organisations but living organisms, the product of a
historical process, one in which the present is heavily constructed by the
past, conditioned as much by past events and previous electoral outcomes as
by the anticipation of future benefits and incentives such as office and, more
rarely, the opportunity to enact policy.

25 Peter Mair, 'The Problem of Party System Change', p. 255.
26 Ibid. This phenomenon can also be traced to shifts in the basis of partisan
    support due to alteration in party identification and social cleavages; cf.
    Russell J. Dalton *et al.*, *Electoral Change in Advanced Industrial Democracies*.
27 Of course, the Conservatives' electoral base often appeared somewhat shaky
    in between elections: 1980–2, 1984–6, 1989–90, and, crucially, 1992–7 when
    John Major's 'luck', as it were, ran out.
28 Kenneth Janda, Robert Harmel, Christine Edens and Patricia Goff, 'Changes
    in Party Identity: Evidence from Party Manifestos', *Party Politics*, vol. 2, no. 2,
    1995, pp. 171–96. Cf. Robert Harmel and Kenneth Janda, 'An Integrated
    Theory of Party Goals and Party Change', *Journal of Theoretical Politics*, vol.
    6, no. 3, 1994, pp. 259–87.
29 Robert Harmel, Kenneth Janda, Uk Heo and Alexander Tan, 'Performance,
    Leadership, Factions and Party Change', *West European Politics*, vol. 18, 1995,
    pp. 1–33, p. 11.
30 Ibid.
31 Dennis Kavanagh, *Thatcherism and British Politics*, Oxford: Oxford University
    Press, 1990, p. 313.
32 Robert Harmel, Kenneth Janda, Uk Heo and Alexander Tan, 'Performance,
    Leadership, Factions and Party Change', p. 2.
33 Panebianco has developed this notion of a 'dominant coalition' (*Political
    Parties*).
34 Robert Harmel and Kenneth Janda, 'An Integrated Theory of Party Goals and
    Party Change'.
35 Ian Budge and Hans Keman, *Parties and Democracy: Coalition Formation and
    Government Functioning in Twenty States*, Oxford: Oxford University Press,
    1990.
36 Cf. Kaare Strom, 'A Behavioural Theory of Competitive Political Parties',
    American Journal of Political Science, vol. 34, no. 2, 1990, pp. 565–98: 'Pure
    vote seekers, office seekers, or policy seekers are unlikely to exist. We can
    empirically identify party objectives, or mixes of objectives, through manifest
    party behaviour' (p. 570). Cf. Kaare Strom, 'Interparty Competition in
    Advanced Democracies', *Journal of Theoretical Politics'*, vol. 1, 1989, pp. 277–
    300.
37 Richard Katz and Peter Mair: 'The immediate source of change ... is to be
    found in the internal politics of the party. Often, however, the ultimate
    source is in the party's environment. ... This dynamic aggregates to the
    observation that parties adapt to changes in their environments' (Richard
    Katz and Peter Mair, *Party Organisation: A Data Handbook on Party Organisation
    in Western Democracies, 1960–1990*, London: Sage, 1992, p. 18).
38 Angelo Panebianco, *Political Parties*.

39 Giovanni Sartori, 'The Sociology of Parties', in Peter Mair (ed.), *The West European Party System*, Oxford: Oxford University Press, 1990, p. 179.
40 Giovanni Sartori, ibid; Giovanni Sartori, 'From the Sociology of Politics to Political Sociology', in Seymour Martin Lipset (ed.), *Politics and the Social Sciences*, Oxford: Oxford University Press, 1969; Giovanni Sartori, 'Parties and Party Systems'; cf. Steven Wolinitz, 'The Transformation of Western European Party Systems Revisited', *West European Politics*, vol. 2, no. 1, 1979, pp. 4–28.
41 Anthony Downs, *An Economic Theory of Democracy*, New York: Harper & Row, 1957.
42 Downs's preconception is that parties change within the existing electoral system by adjusting their appeal in line with voter preference. By contrast, party leaders can influence voters by making salient those issues that maximise the party's potential vote. Rather than simply giving electors what the majority want, parties also compete with one another by emphasising different issues rather then by taking different positions on the same issue. This selective emphasis of issues promotes electoral choice between selective policy agendas not specific alternative policies addressed to items on a universal agenda. Here: 'The idea that parties compete by emphasising the importance of different issues stands in sharp contrast to the traditional view of competition as parties offering different policies to the electorate on the same issue(s)' (Ian Budge and Dennis Farlie, 'Party Competition – Selective Emphasis or Direct Confrontation? An Alternative View with Data', in Hans Daalder and Peter Mair (eds), *Western European Party Systems: Continuity and Change*, London: Sage, 1983, p. 269). Parties invite (or entice) electors to choose between policy packages rather than giving them what they want. This indirect policy confrontation, where parties act as political actors arguing their own favoured issues, is one of selective emphasis where parties seek to set the agenda rather then just respond to a median voter.
43 Patrick Dunleavy, *Democracy, Bureaucracy and Public Choice*, Hemel Hempstead: Harvester Wheatcheaf, 1991; Patrick Dunleavy and Hugh Ward, 'Exogenous Voter Preferences and Parties with State Power: Some Internal Problems of Economic Models of Party Competition', *British Journal of Political Science*, vol. 11, no. 3, 1981, pp. 351–80.
44 G. Rabinowitz and S. E. MacDonald, 'A Directional Theory of Issue Voting'. *American Political Science Review*, vol. 33, no. 1, 1989, pp. 93–121.
45 Patrick Dunleavy and Christopher Husbands, *British Democracy at the Crossroads*, London: Allen & Unwin, 1985.
46 Patrick Dunleavy, *Democracy, Bureaucracy and Public Choice*. Dunleavy makes much of governing parties' ability to use the state to engineer a shift in the aggregate distribution of preferences and change individual voter preferences in their favour by (1) utilising partisan social engineering; (2) adjusting social relativities; (3) context management; or by (4) institutional manipulation. He suggests that opposition parties can respond by attempting to preference-shape by (1) capitalising on social tensions; (2) joint institutional management; (3) agenda setting; or (4) generating high expectations. Preference-shaping strategies deployed by the party of government granted access to the use of state power are more often than not successful.

47 Ibid, pp. 118–19. Dependent upon the degree to which 'preference shaping strategies...change the A[ggregate] D[istribution of] P[references curve] or surface, peoples' policy tastes and issue preferences are determined endogenously within the process of party competition itself' (p. 119).

48 Although Dunleavy does not pursue the point, negative preference-shaping is a significant issue in party competition. Here, rather than just cast themselves in as favourable a light as possible, parties campaign by casting their opponents in as unfavourable a light as possible. Certain electors voted Conservative because they were turned against Labour in 1983, 1987 and, as significantly, 1992. Parties can, through their own performance in either office or opposition, also 'negatively' preference-shape against themselves by alienating actual or potential supporters by their performance. An antipathy to Margaret Thatcher (the 'That Bloody Woman' factor) may have swung some voters into the Labour or Liberal camps. Equally, Labour's record in government under Wilson and Callaghan in 1974–9, in opposition under Michael Foot in 1980–3 or Neil Kinnock in 1992, may have been the factor in rallying some electors to the Conservative flag just as much as Tory efforts at preference-shaping. None the less, in either case parties can have power and as a result can exert some control over their situation.

49 Pippa Norris and Ivor Crewe, 'In Defence of British Election Studies', pp. 19–20.

50 Of course, they can respond to voter demands. Alternatively, they can give the appearance of doing so by adjusting their appeals in light of contemporary fads or other popular issues.

51 Patrick Dunleavy, *Bureaucracy, Democracy and Public Choice*, p. 5.

52 Principally, no doubt, by winning elections: Moshe Maor suggests that 'an increasing number of scholars recognize the intra-party arena as the key for understanding party behaviour. Party behaviour is shaped and probably dominated by intra-party considerations' (*Political Parties and Party Systems*, p. 236). While intra-party arenas are important in understanding party behaviour, inter-party relations may be more so.

53 Patrick Dunleavy, *Democracy, Bureaucracy and Public Choice*, p. 144.

54 Ibid, p. 253.

55 Ibid.

7 Party Competition Driven Party Change: The Politics of 'Catch-Up'

1 Andrew Gamble, *The Free Economy and the Strong State: The Politics of Thatcherism*, 2nd edn, London: Macmillan, 1994, p. 222.

2 *The Independent*, 9 May 1989.

3 Ivor Crewe, 'Values: The Crusade that Failed', in Dennis Kavanagh and Anthony Seldon (eds), *The Thatcher Effect*, Oxford: Oxford University Press, 1989, pp. 241–2. See also Ivor Crewe, 'Has the Electorate become Thatcherite?', in Robert Skidelsky (ed.), *Thatcherism*, London: Chatto & Windus, 1988. Cf. Ivor Crewe, 'Changing Votes and Unchanging Voters', *Electoral Studies*, vol. 11, no. 4, 1992.

4 Andrew Gamble, *The Free Economy and the Strong State*, p. 223.

5   Stuart Hall and Martin Jacques (eds), *The Politics of Thatcherism*, London: Lawrence & Wishart, 1983; Stuart Hall, 'Popular Democratic versus Authoritarian Populism', in Alan Hunt (ed.), *Marxism and Democracy*, London: Lawrence & Wishart, 1983; Stuart Hall, 'Authoritarian Populism: A Reply', *New Left Review*, no. 151, 1985; Stuart Hall, *The Hard Road to Renewal: Thatcherism and the Crisis of the Left*, London: Verso, 1988.

6   Cf. Christopher Hood, *Explaining Economic Policy Reversals*, Buckingham: Open University Press, 1994. For another thought-provoking analysis, cf. Tim Battin, *Abandoning Keynes*, London: Macmillan, 1997.

7   Arend Lijphart also identifies seven alternative dimensions of political difference in addition to the socio-economic dimension. Arend Lijphart, *Democracies: Patterns of Majoritarian and Consensus Democracy in 21 Countries*, New Haven, CT: Yale University Press, 1984, p. 129; and in Peter Mair (ed.), *West European Party Systems*, Oxford: Oxford University Press, 1984.

8   Giovanni Sartori also identifies four such dimensions, only one of which, again the left versus right dimension, is applicable. Giovanni Sartori, *Parties and Party Systems*, Cambridge: Cambridge University Press, 1976. Robert Harmel and Kenneth Janda also illustrate four left versus right party positions on economic policy: (1) government versus private ownership of the means of production; (2) a strong versus a weak governmental role in economic planning; (3) support of versus opposition to the redistribution of economic resources from the rich to the poor; (4) the expansion of versus the resistance to government social welfare programmes. Robert Harmel and Kenneth Janda, *Parties and Their Environments*, New York: Longman, 1982.

9   Peter Hall refers to a 'policy paradigm' which characterises 'normal politics' and are recognised as such. Institutional actors 'all operate within the terms of political discourse that are current within a nation at any particular time' ... [the parameters of discourse] define the context within which issues may be understood' (Peter Hall, 'Policy Paradigms, Social Learning and the State', *Comparative Politics*, vol. 25, no. 3, 1993, pp. 275–96, p. 290).

10 The classic work is Paul Addison, *The Road to 1945*, London: Pimlico Press, 2nd edn, 1994. See also Peter Hennessy, *Never Again*, London: Jonathan Cape, 1991.

11 Peter Hennessy and Anthony Seldon (eds), *Ruling Performance: British Government from Attlee to Thatcher*, Oxford: Basil Blackwell, 1987; Bill Schwarb, 'The Tide of History: The Reconstruction of Conservatism 1945–51', in Nick Tiratsoo, *The Attlee Years*, London: Pinter Press, 1991. An alternative view is given by John Ramsden, 'A Party for Owners or a Party for Earners?: How Far Did the British Conservative Party Really Change after 1945?', *Royal Historical Society Transactions*, 5th Series, 37, 1987.

12 R.A. Butler, *The Art of the Possible: Memoirs*, London: Hamish Hamilton, 1971. Cf. Anthony Howard, *Rab: The Life of R.A. Butler*, London: Jonathan Cape, 1987.

13 R.A. Butler, *The Art of the Possible*, p. 146.

14 Harold Macmillan, Conservative Prime Minister, 1957–63, commented that the Tories needed 'to convince a broad spectrum of the electorate, whose minds were scarred by inter-war memories and myths, that we had an alternative policy to socialism which was viable, efficient and humane, which would release and reward enterprise and initiative but without abandoning

social justice or reverting to mass unemployment'. In essence, the Conservatives had to show that they had 'accommodated themselves to a social revolution' (quoted in Nicholas Timmins, *The Five Giants: A Biography of the Welfare State*, London: HarperCollins, 1995, p. 164).

15   R.A. Butler, *The Art of the Possible*, p. 148.
16   Ibid.
17   Dick Morris, *Behind the Oval Office*, New York: Random House, 1997, pp. 317–18.
18   Thus, as Andrew Gamble suggests, 'the ideological polarisation which took place between the parties in the 1970s and 1980s is over, and that the new parameters of policy debate and the new estimate of what is politically possible substantially reflect the priorities which Thatcherism established' (Andrew Gamble, 'An Ideological Party', in Steve Ludlam and Martin J. Smith (eds), *Contemporary British Conservatism*, London: Macmillan, 1996, pp. 35–6).
19   In political historiography, election moments can evidence significant political change in so far as they mark a process of policy shift; part of a trend but for reasons explored earlier not in themselves a single event; the road to and from every so-called 'realigning election' is key to understanding how change takes place.
20   David Marquand, 'Joining the New Ship', *New Statesman and Society*, 6 October 1995.
21   Andrew Gamble, *Britain in Decline: Economic Policy, Political Strategy and the British State*, London: Macmillan, 3rd edn, 1990, p. 216.
22   David Marquand, 'Blair's Birthday: What is There to Celebrate?', *Prospect*, May 1998. In the same article Marquand suggests New Labour 'may have nothing in common with social democracy, but it is the nearest thing to Christian democracy that modern British Politics has known. And Christian democracy is light years away from Thatcherism.' It is, of course, equally as far removed from social democracy.
23   Eric Shaw questions the modernisers' desire to 'paint a portrait of their own Party in which accuracy was sacrificed not to enhance but to belittle the original'. He suggests that the past has been 'recreated to serve the present's strategic needs. To the modernisers the central problem was the inability of the Party – Old Labour – to obtain the trust and confidence of the public. The term New Labour was "deliberately designed to distance the party from its past" (*Independent* leader, 22 July 1995)' (Eric Shaw, *The Labour Party Since 1945*, Oxford: Basil Blackwell, 1996, p. 217.
24   Peter Mandelson and Roger Liddle, *The Blair Revolution*, London: Faber & Faber, 1996, pp. vii and 2. Writing of the 1979 Winter of Discontent, Mandleson and Liddle rail against the trade union power that threatened the Callaghan government: 'Some trade union and Labour activists gave the impression that every wage claim and every strike was justified – never mind the consequences for inflation, the economy, essential public services, and even the burial of the dead. In the eyes of the public the Labour government appeared a helpless bystander' (ibid, p. 25). This is a classic illustration of modern myth-making. The culpability of the Labour Cabinet in provoking trade union disputes in 1979 is unremarked (despite the fact that Denis Healey, architect of the 1978–9 pay policy, admits it was a mistake, a straw that broke the trade union back: Denis Healey, *The Time of My Life*, Har-

mondsworth: Penguin, 1989). Reference to 'even the burial of the dead' is an old chestnut, one aping a Conservative myth and a moral panic.

25 Perry Anderson, 'The Light of Europe', in *English Questions*, London: Verso, 1992, p. 346.

26 Quoted in the transcript of *Labour: The Wilderness Years*, BBC Television.

27 Peter Mandelson and Roger Liddle, *The Blair Revolution*, p. 20.

28 Dennis Kavanagh and Peter Morris, *Consensus Politics from Attlee to Major*, Basil Blackwell, 2nd edn, 1994, p. 34.

29 Anthony Crosland, *Socialism Now*, London: Jonathan Cape, 1974, p. 107.

30 Ibid, pp. 97–8.

31 Noel Thompson, *Political Economy and the Labour Party*, London: UCL Press, 1996, p. 273.

32 Political attitudes were of course occasionally tempered by cautious policy prescriptions offered in election manifestos; equally, as cautioned earlier, Labour in government frequently did not deliver what Labour in opposition promised.

33 One critic of Crosland, David Marquand, argues that Croslandite revisionism was predicated on economic growth: 'no growth, no redistribution – and no redistribution no revisionism. Growth was the solvent which made the Crosland compromise possible. The whole intellectual system rested on the assumption that rapid growth could occur, and that governments knew how to make it occur' (*The Progressive Dilemma*, London: Heinemann, 1991, p. 172).

34 *The Mail on Sunday*, 15 September 1996.

35 *The Guardian*, 27 February 1997. Contrary to Blair's approach, Roy Hattersley has consistently argued it is 'intellectually respectable and morally right' for the left to argue 'that the market had to be properly constrained and circumscribed'. 'Afterword', in Kenneth Hoover and Raymond Plant, *Conservative Capitalism in Britain and the United States*, London: Routledge, 1989, p. 321. In 1987, Hattersley criticised then Chancellor Lawson for his assertion that government can only provide the right framework for the market to prosper. This assertion is now a key Blairite assumption, in contrast to Hattersley's past claims that Labour's economic policy was about dealing with the very structure of the economy and the distribution of power within it: 'We are going to solve our economic problems by changing the structure of the economy' (Interview with Roy Hattersley, *Marxism Today*, October 1985).

36 Contrary to Blair, in opposition in the 1970s Tony Crosland and Roy Jenkins supported 'a significant increase in public ownership, a substantial redistribution of resources in favour of the poor at the expense, if necessary, of the majority of the population' (Noel Thompson, *Political Economy and the Labour Party*, p. 226).

37 Anthony Crosland, *The Future of Socialism*, London: Jonathan Cape, 1956, p. 30.

38 Ibid, p. 30.

39 David Owen, *A Future That Will Work*, Harmondsworth: Penguin, 1984.

40 The 'Owenite' SDP made much of this social market economy and it figured greatly in Owen's first speech as SDP leader at the Salford Conference in 1983. An article by Owen based on this (and earlier) speeches was published, somewhat tellingly, by the Institute of Economic Affairs under the title 'An

Agenda for Competition with Compassion', *Economic Journal*, vol. 4, no. 1, October 1984 (a phrase with a somewhat Blairite ring to it). Here, Owen recognised and welcomed the role of the market, giving a cautious exception to further 'denationalisation' (pre-British Telecom), 'de-monopolisation' and 'de-empowering organised labour' but none the less acknowledging a role for public sector enterprises as well as government intervention in the form of incomes policy and an industrial strategy. David Owen, *Time to Declare*, Michael Joseph: London, 1991. Cf. Duncan Brack, 'David Owen and the Social Market Economy', *Political Quarterly*, vol. 61, no. 4, Oct-Dec 1990, pp. 463–76.

41 Anthony King and Ivor Crewe, *SDP: The Birth, Life and Death of the Social Democratic Party*, Oxford: Oxford University Press, 1996, p. 364. Neither author is a great admirer of David Owen, to say the least.

42 Interview with David Owen, London, September 1997.

43 Not for nothing had Keith Joseph, the first UK politician to publicise the idea of a social market economy, been persuaded to drop the concept at the urging of Alfred Sherman and other colleagues at the Centre for Policy Studies. For the New Right the 'market' element of the social market economy was considered more important than its 'social' connotations.

44 Duncan Brack, 'David Owen and the Social Market Economy', p. 475.

45 In the mid-1980s Mrs Thatcher's private aside that Owen was the most likely next non-Conservative Prime Minister had been widely reported. Although many people thought the charge that Owen was a closet Thatcherite was damaging, the man himself was unconcerned, protesting only that he would never become a Conservative because he agreed with aspects of the Thatcherite agenda but not the project in its entirety. Interview with David Owen, September 1997.

46 Blair's rhetorical pitch for 'compassion with a hard edge' at the 1997 Labour Conference echoed Owen's call for 'tough but tender' policies and 'competition with compassion' some fourteen years earlier.

47 Anthony King and Ivor Crewe, *SDP*, p. 469.

48 Coates argues: 'What previous Labour governments did was work with the grain of market forces . . . to trigger privately generated economic growth, and that, of course, is precisely what New Labour is saying as well' (David Coates, 'Labour Governments: Old Constraints and New Parameters', *New Left Review*, 219, 1996, p. 67). Naturally, as a reformist rather than a revolutionary party this is what the Labour Party stands for. Yet Coates is mistaken to assume that 'New' Labour, and the policy stances associated with it, is fundamentally the same as past Labour practice.

49 Coates, ibid, p. 68.

50 Ibid.

51 Ibid, p. 72.

52 Tony Blair Speech, Labour Party Press Release, June 1996.

53 Bob Jessop, Kevin Bromley and Simon Bromley, 'Farewell to Thatcherism? Neo-Liberalism and New Times', *New Left Review*, no. 179, pp. 81–102, p. 98.

54 Brian Brivati, *Hugh Gaitskell*, London: Richard Cohen Books, 1997, pp. 298–9.

55 *Labour Party Annual Conference Report 1959*, p. 241.

56 Tony Blair Speech, Labour Party Press Release, October 1996.

57 *The Times*, 12 April 1986.
58 Stuart Hall, 'The Great Moving Right Show', in Stuart Hall and Martin Jacques (eds), *The Politics of Thatcherism*, London: Lawrence & Wishart, 1983.
59 Ralph Miliband, *Parliamentary Socialism*, London: Merlin Press, 1972, p. 344.
60 Ralph Miliband, *The State in Capitalist Society*, London: Quartet, 1969, p. 111.

8 A Theory of Consensus Politics

1 Dennis Kavanagh, 'Whatever Happened to Consensus Politics?', *Political Studies*, vol. 23, 1985, pp. 529–46.
2 Anthony Seldon, in Bill Jones, Andrew Grey, Dennis Kavanagh, Michael Moran, Philip Norton and Anthony Seldon, *Politics UK*, 2nd edn, Basingstoke: Harvester Wheatsheaf, p. 42.
3 David Marquand, *The Unprincipled Society: New Demands and Old Politics*, London: Fontana, 1988, pp. 2–3.
4 Ibid.
5 Nicholas Deakin, 'In Search of the Post War Consensus', *LSE Quarterly*, 1989, p. 78.
6 Ibid.
7 Paul Addison, *The Road to 1945*, 2nd edn, London: Pimlico, 1994.
8 Ibid, p. 283.
9 Ibid, p. 291. Cf. Daniel Bell, *The End of Ideology*, Chicago, IL: University of Chicago Press. 'There is today a rough consensus among intellectuals on political issues; the acceptance of the welfare state; the desirability of decentralised power; a system of mixed economy and of political pluralism. In that sense . . . the ideological age has ended' (p. 373).
10 Ben Pimlott, 'The Myth of Consensus', in *Frustrate Their Knavish Tricks*, London: Harper Collins, 1995, p. 237.
11 Paul Addison, 'Consensus Revisited', *Twentieth Century British History*, vol. 3, no. 1, 1993; Dennis Kavanagh, 'The Post War Consensus', *Twentieth Century British History*, vol. 1, no. 2, 1990, pp. 115–51.
12 Critics of the notion of consensus have tried to implode the whole idea: cf. Harriet Jones and Michael Kandiah (eds), *The Myth of Consensus? New Views of British History 1945–1964*, London: Macmillan, 1996; Anthony Butler, 'The End of Post-War Consensus', *Political Quarterly*, vol. 64, 1993. Also Neil Rollings, 'Poor Mr Butskell: A Short Life, Wrecked by Schzophrenia', *Twentieth Century British History*, vol. 5, no. 2, 1994; Kevin Jeffreys, *The Churchill Coalition and Wartime Politics, 1940–1945*, Manchester: Manchester University Press, 1991; Harriet Jones, 'The Post War Consensus in Britain: Synthesis, Antithesis, Synthesis', in Brian Brivati *et al.* (eds), *History Handbook*, Manchester: Manchester University Press, 1996, pp. 41–9. For an overview of the debate, see Paul Addison, 'Consensus Revisited'.
13 Kenneth O. Morgan, *Labour In Power, 1945–51*, Oxford: Oxford University Press, 1984, p. 329.
14 Anthony Butler, 'The End of Post-War Consensus', p. 435.
15 Anthony Seldon, 'Consensus: A Debate Too Long', *Parliamentary Affairs*, vol. 47, no. 4, 1994, pp. 501–14, p. 503. Seldon argues: 'Consensus might have

appeared to have existed, [revisionist historians] would argue, when looked at from a very broad perspective. But when viewed from close to the ground, or the documents, the reality was very different. To an extent, the difference typifies the different approach of historians, who tend to see the trees, and political scientists, who prefer to see the whole wood' (ibid).

16 J.D. Marlow, 'Questioning the Post-War Consensus: Toward an Alternative Account, A Different Understanding', unpublished PhD thesis, Department of Sociology, University of Essex, 1995, p. 7. Ben Pimlott also rightly suggests that 'the greatest problem with the consensus theory is in defining the essence of the consensus itself' ('The Myth of Consensus', p. 238).

17 Quoted in Bill Jones, Andrew Grey, Dennis Kavanagh, Michael Moran, Philip Norton and Anthony Seldon, *Politics UK*, Basingstoke: Harvester Wheatsheaf, 2nd edn, p. 42.

18 Paul Addison, *The Road to 1945*, p. 13.

19 The phrase 'commitments, assumptions and expectations' is from David Marquand, *The Unprincipled Society*, p. 18.

20 Ben Pimlott, 'The Myth of Consensus', p. 230.

21 Dennis Kavanagh and Peter Morris, *Consensus Politics From Attlee to Major*, Oxford: Basil Blackwell, 1994, pp. 13–14.

22 Interview with Tony Benn, London, August 1994.

23 Richard Rose, *Can Parties Make a Difference?*, London: Macmillan, 1984, p. 156.

24 Ibid, pp. 119–20.

25 Ben Pimlott, 'The Myth of Consensus', p. 235.

26 Ibid, p. 236.

27 That there is nothing new on this is typified by the age-old agreement on the rules which political actors accept as governing the constitutional game known as British government. There are sets of conventions which, as adhered to by political actors, may comprise a consensus of sort; expressed fidelity to established customs and conventions, for example the constitution; social mores; existing rules of behaviour; and patterns of authority; or the mode of production.

28 Colin Hay, *Restating Social and Political Change*, Buckingham: Open University Press, 1996, p. 44.

29 Ibid, p. 45.

30 Bob Jessop, 'The Transformation of the State in Post War Britain', in Richard Scase (ed.), *The State in Western Europe*, New York: St Martin's Press, 1980, p. 28. Cf. Colin Hay, *Re-Stating Social and Political Change*, p. 44.

31 Colin Hay, *Re-Stating Social and Political Change*, p. 44.

32 Ibid, p. 46.

33 Paul Addison, *The Road to 1945*, p. 238.

34 Dennis Kavanagh and Peter Morris, *Consensus Politics From Attlee to Major*, pp. 13–14.

35 Alan Ware, *Political Parties and Party Systems*, Oxford; Oxford University Press, 1996, p. 48.

36 Giovanni Sartori, *Parties and Party Systems*, Cambridge: Cambridge University Press, 1976.

37 Charles Webster, 'Conflict and Consensus: Explaining the British Health Service', *Twentieth Century British History*, vol. 1, no. 1, 1991, pp. 115–51;

Charles Webster, *The Health Service Since the War; Volume 1*, London: HMSO, 1990.

38   Attributed to then staff writer Norman McCrae.
39   Rab Butler, *The Art of the Possible*, London: Hamish Hamilton, 1973, pp. 162–3.
40   Anthony Crosland, *The Conservative Enemy*, London: Jonathan Cape, 1963, p. 123.
41   Paul Addison, *The Road to 1945*, p. 290.
42   Within a consensus characterised by party convergence upon a particular location within the socio-economic arena, parties distinguish themselves from their competitors by competition in sub-arenas where there policy appeal marks them out from others. Here, parties engage in both positive and negative campaigning, arguing their case and damning that of their opponent. Office-seeking can be dressed up as policy-seeking when parties attempt to distinguish themselves from one another in terms of the electoral campaigning profile they establish. Programmatic association as policy coincidence; the politics of catch up typifies this situation at the same time that aggressive office seeking continues. Policy disagreement is however less of an issue, one constructed through the prism of office rather than policy seeking where a ratio between these primary goals may be drawn. It is here that the combative inter party relationship may be defined. Fundamental policy disagreement is the exception rather than the rule.
43   Richard Rose, *Can Parties Make a Difference?*, p. 143.
44   Ibid, pp. 152–3.
45   Ibid, p. 153.

9   Thatcherism and the Reinvention of Labour

1   Malcolm Smith, 'The Changing Nature of the British State, 1929–1959: The Historiography of Consensus', in Brian Brivati and Harriet Jones (eds), *What Difference Did the War Make?*, Leicester: Leicester University Press, 1993, pp. 37–47, p. 42.
2   Paul Addison, *The Road to 1945*, 2nd edn, London: Pimlico, 1994, p. 282. Of course if the Tories were doing this in 1944 then their policy in 1954 (having accepted many of the changes initiated by the post-war Labour government) would be more constrained that had previously been the case.
3   Ibid.
4   Of course, as a counterfactual, this is not to argue that were Hugh Gaitskell to find himself alive and well in 1998 he would not be a Blairite moderniser. Given the man, it is very likely that he would be. A comparison between the Tony Blair of today and the Hugh Gaitskell of yesterday is illustrative of political change mapped out across time. Political actors are the product of their time. Their world views are fashioned by the prevailing environment within which they are located. Blair was a product of the 1980s just as much as Gaitskell was fashioned by the 1950s.
5   Labour Party, *Britain Will Win: The Labour Party Manifesto 1997*, London: The Labour Party, 1987.

6 David Reisman, *Anthony Crosland: The Mixed Economy*, Basingstoke: Macmillan, 1997, p. 153.

7 Anthony Crosland, *The Future of Socialism*, London: Jonathan Cape, 1956 edition, pp. 496–7.

8 In 1960, Hugh Gaitskell made clear the role that public ownership was intended to play in Labour's economic policy: 'Common Ownership takes varying forms, including state-owned industries and firms, producer and consumer co-operation, municipal ownership and public participation in private concerns. Recognising that both public and private enterprise have a place in the economy it believes that further extensions of public ownership should be decided from time to time in the light of these objectives and according to circumstances, with due regard to the views of the workers and consumers concerned' ('Amplification of Aims' (Gaitskell's addendum in lieu of revising Clause 4 in 1959–60), *Labour Party Annual Conference Report 1960*, p. 59).

9 Ibid, p. 91.

10 Anthony Crosland, *Socialism Now*, London: Jonathan Cape, 1974.

11 Mark Wickham-Jones, *Economic Strategy and the Labour Party: Politics and Policy Making, 1970–1983*, Basingstoke: Macmillan, 1997, p. 97.

12 Anthony Crosland, *Socialism Now*, p. 38.

13 Ibid, p. 43. Crosland also favoured 'an active policy of competitive public enterprise, that is the establishment (either from scratch or by take over) of state companies or joint ventures to compete with private enterprises – to act as highly competitive price-leaders and pace setters, provide a yard stick for efficiency, support the government's investment plans, and above all produce a better product or service' (ibid, p. 38).

14 The Labour Party, *Britain Will Win With Labour: February 1974 Manifesto*, London: The Labour Party, 1974; The Labour Party, *Labour's Programme for Britain*, London: The Labour Party, 1973.

15 The Labour Party, *Labour's Programme 1976*, London: The Labour Party, 1976; The Labour Party, *Labour's Programme 1982*, London: The Labour Party, 1982.

16 Labour Party NEC/TUC Liaison Committee Statement, *Economic Issues Facing the Next Labour Government*, London: The Labour Party, 1981.

17 Labour Party, *Labour's Programme 1982*, p. 9.

18 Ibid, p. 17.

19 Richard Heffernan and Mike Marqusee, *Defeat From the Jaws of Victory: Inside Kinnock's Labour Party*, London: Verso, 1992, p. 26. At the same Conference a constituency resolution proposing the nationalisation of 25 of the 100 largest private sector manufacturing companies was endorsed by the NEC and carried by 3,735,000 votes to 2,873,000. Most notable was that this resolution was commended to Conference on behalf of the NEC by Roy Evans of the ISTC (who claimed that the extension of public ownership would be at the core of Labour's 'new national plan'). Evans was a right-wing anti-'Bennite' trade unionist elected courtesy of trade union votes marshalled by the AEUW–APEX caucus which denied the left an NEC majority in both 1981 and 1982.

20 The Labour Party, *Because Britain Deserves Better: The Labour Manifesto 1997*.

21 *News on Sunday*, 1 November 1987.

22 Private information.

23 Tony Blair speech to a business seminar: Labour Party Press Release, 8 April 1997.

24 A number of commentators singled out privatisation and popular capitalism as the key weapon in the Conservatives' electoral armoury. Writing in *Marxism Today*, Andrew Gamble observed, 'There can be no doubt that this policy has been a masterstroke for the government. It has made significant inroads into the Labour vote.' Similar views were widely expressed within and without the Labour movement throughout and beyond the summer of 1987. Writing in *The Independent*, Peter Jenkins was in no doubt that the spread of share ownership was playing a significant part in eroding Labour's traditional support base. Cf. Andrew Gamble, 'Crawling from the Wreckage', *Marxism Today*, July 1987, quoted in Anthony Heath, Roger Jowell, John Curtice and Geoff Evans, 'The Extension of Popular Capitalism', *Strathclyde Papers on Government and Politics*, no. 60, 1989; and Peter Jenkins, *The Independent*, 17 June 1987, quoted in Saunders and Harris, *Privatisation and Popular Capitalism*, Buckingham: Open University Press, 1994. p. 120. For the directors of the 1983 and 1987 British Election Studies, Anthony Heath, Roger Jowell and John Curtice, privatisation had little direct effect on voting behaviour. Cf. Anthony Heath, Roger Jowell and John Curtice, *How Britain Votes*, Oxford: Pergamon Press, 1985; Heath *et al.*, 'The Extension of Popular Capitalism': 'There is no change at all in [new owners'] relative propensity to vote Conservative, Labour or Alliance' (p. 7). See also Pippa Norris, 'Thatcher's Enterprise Society and Electoral Change', *West European Politics*, vol. 13, no. 1, January 1990; Ian McAllister and Donley T. Studlar, 'Popular versus Elite Views of Privatisation: The Case of Britain', *Journal of Public Policy*, vol. 9, no. 2, 1989, pp. 157–8.

25 As suggested by Peter Saunders and Colin Harris, *Privatisation and Popular Capitalism*, p. 136.

26 *Sunday Times*, 6 April 1997.

27 *The Guardian*, 8 April 1997.

28 Joel Wolfe, 'State Power and Ideology in Britain: Mrs Thatcher's Privatisation Programme', *Political Studies*, vol. 39, 1991, 239–52, p. 250.

29 David Held, 'Power and Legitimacy in Contemporary Britain', in Gregor MacLennan, David Held and Stuart Hall (eds), *State and Society in Contemporary Britain*, Cambridge: Polity Press, 1984; David Held, *Models of Democracy*, Cambridge: Polity Press, 1986.

30 *The Observer*, 7 April 1996.

31 Ibid. As Marquand claims of post-war politics: 'Though [the parties'] differences of interest and belief were real and important, what stands out in retrospect is the extent to which their policies overlapped in practice. Social democracy may be defined as the philosophy of the overlap... However strongly its adherents disagreed on other matters, they agreed in repudiating the dichotomies of market versus state; Capital versus Labour; private enterprise versus public ownership; personal freedom versus social justice' (David Marquand, *The Unprincipled Society: New Demands and Old Politics*, London: Fontana, 1988, pp. 18–19).

32 Colin Leys, 'Still A Question of Hegemony', *New Left Review*, no. 181, 1990, pp. 119–28, p. 126.

33 Ibid, p. 127.

34 In exploring Labour's transformation, changing attitudes to the Party should also be noted. Mention should be made of the rapprochement between Labour and a great many Thatcher-supporting newspapers. Because Thatcher had no firmer champion than Rupert Murdoch's News International, relations between Murdoch newspapers and Labour were rock-bottom for most of the 1980s and early 1990s. This changed dramatically following Blair's accession to the leadership in 1994. After a series of private meetings the Labour leader accepted Murdoch's invitation to address a NewsCorp Conference in Australia in July 1995. Although strong denials were made that any private deal was struck, Labour did move closer to Murdoch by heavily qualifying its past support for media regulation and cross-media ownership while abandoning plans to investigate the Murdoch empire. For its part, News International swung heavily behind Blair-led Labour. Amazingly, given their unrelenting opposition (and outright hostility) to Labour in past elections, both *The Sun* and the *News of the World* strongly supported Labour in the 1997 general election. Blair also won a number of friends among executives and journalists of Associated Newspapers and the Express Group which publish the Tory-supporting *Daily Mail* and *The Express*. *The Express* halfheartedly supported the Conservatives while the *Daily Star* supported Labour; although the *Daily Mail* still called for a Conservative vote (as did the *Express*, even in 1997 its readership was heavily stacked in favour of diehard Conservative voters) it did not attack Labour in the fashion it had done previously. Indeed, after the election Lord Rothermere, the owner of Associated Newspapers, indicated his strong support for Blair and his decision to 'associate' with the Labour whip in the House of Lords. It is interesting to note that News International titles always couched their support in terms of 'for Blair', the personality, rather than 'Labour', the Party.

35 Mark Wickham-Jones, 'Recasting Social Democracy', *Political Studies*, vol. 43, no. 5, December 1995, p. 699.

36 Tony Blair Speech, Labour Party Press Release, 17 July 1995.

37 Keith Joseph, 'Monetarism is Not Enough', in *Stranded on the Middle Ground*, London: Centre for Policy Studies, 1975, p. 8.

38 Tony Blair Speech, Labour Party Press Release, 17 July 1995.

39 Ibid.

40 Martin J. Smith, 'Understanding the Politics of Catch-Up: The Modernisation of the Labour Party', *Political Studies*, vol. 42, no. 4, 1994, p. 710.

41 Andrew Gamble, 'The Crisis of Conservatism', *New Left Review*, 214, 1995, p. 25.

Bibliography

Jad Adams (1993), *Tony Benn: A Biography*, London: Hutchinson.

Paul Addison (1993), 'Consensus Revisited', *Twentieth Century British History*, vol. 4, no. 1.

Paul Addison (1994), *The Road to 1945*, 2nd edition, London: Pimlico.

Paul Anderson and Nyta Mann (1997), *Safety First: The Making of New Labour*, London: Granta.

Perry Anderson (1992), 'The Light of Europe', in Perry Anderson, *English Questions*, London: Verso.

Simon Auerbach (1990), *Legislating for Conflict*, Oxford: Oxford University Press.

Simon Auerbach (1993), 'Mrs Thatcher's Labour Laws: Slouching Toward Utopia', *Political Quarterly*, vol. 64, no. 1, pp. 37–48.

Kenneth Baker (1993), *The Turbulent Years: My Life in Politics*, London: Faber & Faber.

Stefano Bartolini and Peter Mair (eds) (1984), 'Party Politics in Contemporary Western Europe', *West European Politics*, vol. 7, no. 4.

Tim Battin (1997), *Abandoning Keynes*, London: Macmillan.

Samuel Beer (1965), *Modern British Politics*, London: Faber & Faber.

Samuel Beer (1982), *Britain Against Itself*, London: Faber & Faber.

Tony Benn (1993), *End of An Era: Diaries, 1980–1990*, London: Hutchinson.

Matthew Bishop and John Kay (1988), *Does Privatisation Work?*, London: London Business School.

Tony Blair (1994), *Let Us Face The Future: The 1945 Anniversary Lecture*, London: The Fabian Society.

Tony Blair (1995), 'Power for a Purpose', *Renewal*, vol. 3, no. 4.

Tony Blair (1996), *New Britain: My Vision of a Young Country*, London: Fourth Estate.

Duncan Brack (1990), 'David Owen and the Social Market Economy', *Political Quarterly*, vol. 61, no. 4, pp. 463–76.

Samuel Brittan (1975), 'The Economic Contradictions of Democracy', *British Journal of Political Science*, vol. 5, no. 2, pp. 129–59.

Samuel Brittan (1984), 'The Politics and Economics of Privatisation', *Political Quarterly*, vol. 55, no. 2, pp. 109–27.

Brian Brivati (1997), *Hugh Gaitskell*, London: Richard Cohen Books.

Ian Budge and Hans Keman (1990), *Parties and Democracy: Coalition Formation and Government Functioning in Twenty States*, Oxford: Oxford University Press.

Jim Bulpitt (1986), 'The Discipline of the New Democracy: Mrs Thatcher's Domestic Statecraft', *Political Studies*, vol. 34, pp. 19–39.

Martin Burch and Ian Holliday (1995), *The British Cabinet System*, London: Prentice Hall.

Anthony Butler (1993), 'The End of Post-War Consensus: Reflections on the Scholarly Uses of Political Rhetoric', *Political Quarterly*, vol. 64, no. 4, pp. 435–46.

David Butler and Donald Stokes (1974), *Political Change in Modern Britain*, London: Macmillan.

David Butler, Andrew Adonis and Tony Travers (1994), *Failure in British Government: The Politics of the Poll Tax*, Oxford: Oxford University Press.

Rab Butler (1973), *The Art of the Possible*, London: Hamish Hamilton.

Alec Cairncross (1992), *The British Economy Since 1945*, Oxford: Basil Blackwell.

John Campbell (1993), *Edward Heath*, London: Jonathan Cape.

Peter Clarke (1990), *A Question of Leadership*, Harmondsworth; Penguin.

Peter Clarke (1997), *Hope and Glory*, Harmondsworth: Penguin.

David Coates (1980), *Labour in Power*, London: Longman.

David Coates (1989), *The Crisis of Labour: Industrial Relations and the State in Contemporary Britain*, London: Philip Allan.

David Coates (1996), 'Labour Governments: Old Constraints and New Parameters', *New Left Review*, 219, pp. 62–77.

R. W. Cobb and C. D. Elder (1972), *Participation in American Politics: The Dynamics of Agenda Building*, Baltimore, MD: Johns Hopkins University Press.

Richard Cockett (1995), *Thinking the Unthinkable: Think Tanks and the Economic Counter Revolution*, London: HarperCollins.

The Conservative Party (1976), *The Right Approach*, London: Conservative Central Office.

The Conservative Party (1977), *The Right Approach to the Economy*, London: Conservative Central Office.

Philip Cowley (1996), 'How Did He Do That?', in David Denver *et al.* (eds), *British Elections and Parties Yearbook 1996*, London: Frank Cass.

Ivor Crewe (1988), 'Has the Electorate become Thatcherite', in Robert Skidelsky (ed.), *Thatcherism*, London: Chatto & Windus.

Ivor Crewe (1989), 'Values: The Crusade that Failed', in Dennis Kavanagh and Anthony Seldon (eds), *The Thatcher Effect*, Oxford: Oxford University Press.

Ivor Crewe (1992), 'Changing Votes and Unchanging Voters', *Electoral Studies*, vol. 11, no. 4, pp. 335–46.

Ivor Crewe, Bo Saarlvik and James Alt (1979), 'Partisan Dealignment in Britain, 1964-77', *British Journal of Political Science*, vol. 7, pp. 129–90.

Ivor Crewe and Donald Searing (1988), 'Ideological Change in the British Conservative Party', *American Political Science Review*, vol. 82, no. 2, pp. 361–61.

Anthony Crosland (1956), *The Future of Socialism*, London: Jonathan Cape.

Anthony Crosland (1963), *The Conservative Enemy*, London: Jonathan Cape.

Anthony Crosland (1974), *Socialism Now*, London: Jonathan Cape.

Anthony Crosland (1975) *Social Democracy in Europe*, Fabian Tract 483, London: Fabian Society.

Hans Daalder and Peter Mair (eds) (1983), *Western European Party Systems: Continuity and Change*, London: Sage.

Russell J. Dalton, Scott C. Flanagan and Paul Allen Beck (1984), *Electoral Change in Advanced Industrial Democracies: Realignment or Dealignment?*, Princeton, NJ: Princeton University Press.

Nicholas Deakin (1989), 'In Search of Consensus', *LSE Quarterly*, Summer.

Andrew Denham and Mark Garnett (1996), 'The Nature and Impact of Think Tanks in Contemporary Britain', *Contemporary British History*, vol. 10, no. 1, pp. 43–61.

David Denver and Gordon Hands (eds) (1992), *Issues and Controversies in British Electoral Behavior*, Hemel Hempstead: Harvester Wheatsheaf.

Radhika Desai (1994a), *Intellectuals and Social Democrats*, London: Lawrence & Wishart.

Radhika Desai (1994b), 'Second Hand Dealers in Ideas: Think Tanks and Thatcherite Hegemony', *New Left Review*, 203, pp. 15–41.

Mariusz Dobeck (1993), 'Privatisation as a Political Priority: The British Experience', *Political Studies*, vol. 41, no. 1, pp. 24–40.

Bernard Donoughue (1987), *Prime Minister*, London; Jonathan Cape.

James Douglas (1989), 'The Changing Tide: Some Recent Studies of Thatcherism', *British Journal of Political Science*, vol. 19, no. 3, pp. 399–442.

Anthony Downs (1957), *An Economic Theory of Democracy*, New York: Harper & Row.

Patrick Dunleavy (1986), 'Explaining the Privatisation Boom', *Public Administration*, vol. 64, pp. 13–34.

Patrick Dunleavy (1991), *Democracy, Bureaucracy and Public Choice*, Hemel Hempstead: Harvester Wheatsheaf.

Patrick Dunleavy and Christopher Hood (1994), 'From Old Public Administration to New Public Management', *Public Money and Management*, vol. 14, no. 3, pp. 9–16.

Patrick Dunleavy and Christopher Husbands (1985), *British Democracy at the Crossroads*, London: Allen & Unwin.

Patrick Dunleavy and Hugh Ward (1981), 'Exogenous Voter Preferences and Parties with State Power: Some Internal Problems of Economic Models of Party Competition', *British Journal of Political Science*, vol. 11, no. 3, pp. 351–80.

Maurice Duverger (1964), *Political Parties*, London: Methuen.

John Eatwell (1992), 'The Development of Labour Policy, 1979–1992', in J. Michie (ed.), *The Economic Legacy*, London: Academic Press.

Stephen Edgell and Vic Duke (1991), *A Measure of Thatcherism: A Sociology of Britain*, London: HarperCollins.

Gregory Elliott (1993), *Labourism and the English Genius: The Strange Death of Labour England*, London: Verso.

Costa Esping-Anderson (1985), *Politics Against Markets*, Princeton, NJ: Princeton University Press.

Stephen Fielding (1995), *Labour: Crisis and Renewal*, Manchester: Baseline Books.

Mark Franklin (1985), *The Decline of Class Voting in Britain*, Oxford: Clarendon Press.

Andrew Gamble (1996) 'Ideas and Interests in British Economic Policy', *Contemporary British History*, vol. 10, no. 2, pp. 1–17.

Andrew Gamble (1974), *The Conservative Nation*, London: Macmillan.

Andrew Gamble (1988), *The Free Economy and the Strong State: The Politics of Thatcherism*, London: Macmillan.

Andrew Gamble (1989), 'Privatisation, Thatcherism and the British State', *Journal of Law and Society*, vol. 16, no. 1, pp. 1–20.

Andrew Gamble (1992), 'The Labour Party and Economic Management', in Martin Smith and Joanna Spear (eds), *The Changing Labour Party*, London: Routledge.

Andrew Gamble (1994a), *Britain in Decline: Economic Policy, Political Strategy and the British State*, 4th edition, London: Macmillan.

Andrew Gamble (1994b), *The Free Economy and the Strong State: The Politics of Thatcherism*, 2nd edition, London: Macmillan.

Andrew Gamble (1995), 'The Crisis of Conservatism', *New Left Review*, 214, pp. 3–25.

Andrew Gamble (1996), 'An Ideological Party?', in Steve Ludlam and Martin J. Smith (eds), *Contemporary British Conservatism*, London: Macmillan.

Geoffrey Garrett (1993), 'The Politics of Structural Change: Swedish Social Democracy and Thatcherism in Comparative Perspective', *Comparative Political Studies*, vol. 25, no. 4, pp. 521–47.

Ian Gilmour (1992), *Dancing With Dogma: Britain Under Thatcherism*, London: Simon & Schuster.

W. H. Greenleaf (1983a), *The British Political Tradition volume I: The Rise of Collectivism*, London: Methuen.

W. H. Greenleaf (1983b), *The British Political Tradition volume II: The Ideological Heritage*, London: Methuen.

Peter A. Hall (1989a), 'The Politics of Keynesian Ideas', in Peter A. Hall (ed.), *The Political Power of Economic Ideas: Keynesianism Across Nations*, Princeton, NJ: Princeton University Press.

Peter A. Hall (ed.) (1989b), *The Political Power of Economic Ideas: Keynesianism Across Nations*, Princeton, NJ: Princeton University Press.

Peter A. Hall (1993), 'Policy Paradigms, Social Learning and the State', *Comparative Politics*, vol. 25, no. 3, pp. 275–66.

Stuart Hall (1983), 'Popular Democratic Versus Authoritarian Populism: Two Ways of "Taking Democracy Seriously"', in Alan Hunt (ed.), *Marxism and Democracy*, London: Lawrence & Wishart.

Stuart Hall (1985), 'Authoritarian Populism: A Reply', *New Left Review*, 151.

Stuart Hall (1988), *The Hard Road to Renewal*, London: Verso.

Stuart Hall and Martin Jacques (eds) (1983), *The Politics of Thatcherism*, London: Lawrence & Wishart.

Tim Hames and Richard Feasey (1993), 'Anglo American Think Tanks Under Reagan and Thatcher', in Andrew Adonis and Tim Hames (eds), *A Conservative Revolution? The Thatcher Reagan Decade in Retrospect*, Manchester: Manchester University Press.

Robert Harmel and Kenneth Janda (1982), *Parties and Their Environments*, New York: Longman.

Robert Harmel and Kenneth Janda (1994), 'An Integrated Theory of Party Goals and Party Change', *Journal of Theoretical Politics*, vol. 6, no. 3, pp. 259–87.

Robert Harmel, Kenneth Janda, Uk Heo and Alexander Tan (1995), 'Performance, Leadership, Factions and Party Change', *West European Politics*, vol. 18, pp. 1–33.

Roy Hattersley (1987), *Economic Priorities for a Labour Government*, London: Macmillan.

Roy Hattersley (1996), *Who Goes Home*, London: Little, Brown.

Colin Hay (1994), 'Labour's Thatcherite Revisionism: Playing the "Politics of Catch-Up"', *Political Studies*, vol. 42, pp. 700–7.

Colin Hay (1995), 'Structure and Agency', in David Marsh and Gerry Stoker (eds), *Theories and Methods in Political Science*, London: Macmillan.

Colin Hay (1996), *Restating Social and Political Change*, Buckingham: Open University Press.

Colin Hay (1997), 'Anticipating Accommodations, Accommodating Anticipations: The Appeasement of Capital in the "Modernisation" of the British Labour Party', *Politics and Society*, vol. 25, no. 2, pp. 234–56.

Anthony Heath, Roger Jowell and John Curtice (1985), *How Britain Votes*, Oxford: Pergamon Press.

Richard Heffernan (1996), 'Blueprint for a Revolution? The Politics of the Adam Smith Institute', *Contemporary British History*, vol. 10, no. 4, pp. 73–87.

Richard Heffernan (1997), 'Ideology, Practical Politics and Political Consensus: Some Thoughts on the Process of Political Change in the United Kingdom', in Gerry Stoker and Jeffrey Stanyer (eds), *Contemporary Political Studies 1997*, Oxford: Basil Blackwell.

Richard Heffernan and Mike Marqusee (1992), *Defeat From the Jaws of Victory: Inside Kinnock's Labour Party*, London: Verso.

David Held (1984), 'Power and Legitimacy in Contemporary Britain', in Gregor MacLennan *et al.* (eds), *State and Society in Contemporary Britain*, Cambridge: Polity Press.

David Held (1996), *Models of Democracy*, 2nd edition, Cambridge: Polity Press.

Hilde Himmelweit *et al.* (1981), *How Voters Decide*, London: Academic Press.

Brian Hogwood (1992), *Trends in British Public Policy: Do Governments Make a Difference?*, Buckingham: Open University Press.

Martin Holmes (1989), *Thatcherism: Scope and Limits*, London: Macmillan.

Christopher Hood (1994), *Explaining Economic Policy Reversals*, Buckingham: Open University Press.

Kenneth Hoover and Raymond Plant (1988), *Conservative Capitalism in Britain and the United States*, London: Routledge.

Geoffrey Howe (1994), *Conflict of Loyalties*, London: Macmillan.

Colin Hughes and Patrick Wintour (1990), *Labour Rebuilt: The Making of the New Model Party*, London: Fourth Estate.

Will Hutton (1996), *The State We're In*, London: Vintage.

Simon James (1993), 'The Idea Brokers: The Impact of Think Tanks in British Government' *Public Administration*, Vol. 71.

Kenneth Janda, Robert Harmel, Christine Edens and Patricia Goff (1995), 'Changes in Party Identity: Evidence from Party Manifestos', *Party Politics*, vol. 2, no. 2, pp. 171–96.

Kevin Jeffreys (1987), 'British Politics and Social Policy During the Second World War', *Historical Journal*, vol. 30, no. 1, pp. 123–44.

Kevin Jeffreys (1991), *The Churchill Coalition and Wartime Politics, 1940–1945*, Manchester: Manchester University Press.

Peter Jenkins (1989), *Mrs Thatcher's Revolution: The Ending of the Socialist Age*, London: Pan Books.

Simon Jenkins (1996), *Accountable to None: The Tory Nationalisation of Britain*, Harmondsworth: Penguin.

Bob Jessop (1989) 'Thatcherism: The British Road to Post Fordism', *Essex Papers in Politics and Government*, no. 68.

Bob Jessop (1990), *State Theory: Putting the Capitalist State in its Place*, Cambridge: Polity Press.

Bob Jessop (1992), 'From Social Democracy to Thatcherism: Twenty Five Years of British Politics', in Nick Abercrombie and Alan Warde (eds), *Social Change in Contemporary Britain*, Cambridge: Polity Press.

Bob Jessop, Kevin Bonnett and Simon Bromley (1990), 'Farewell to Thatcherism? Neo-Liberalism and New Times', *New Left Review*, 179, pp. 81–102.

Bob Jessop, Kevin Bonnett, Simon Bromley and Tom Ling (1988), *Thatcherism: A Tale of Two Nations*, Cambridge: Polity Press.

Harriet Jones (1996), 'The Post War Consensus in Britain: Synthesis, Antithesis, Synthesis', in Brian Brivati *et al.* (ed.), *The Contemporary History Handbook*, Manchester: Manchester University Press.

Harriet Jones and Michael Kandiah (eds) (1996), *The Myth of Consensus? New Views of British History 1945–1964*, London: Macmillan.

Tudor Jones (1996), *Remaking the Labour Party: From Gaitskell to Blair*, London: Routledge.

Keith Joseph (1975), *Reversing the Trend*, London: Barry Rose.

Keith Joseph (1976), *Stranded on the Middle Ground*, London: Centre for Policy Studies.

Richard Katz and Peter Mair (1992), *Party Organisation: A Data Handbook on Party Organisation in Western Democracies, 1960–1990*, London: Sage.

Dennis Kavanagh (1985) 'Whatever Happened to Consensus Politics?', *Political Studies*, vol. 23, no. 4, pp. 529–47.

Dennis Kavanagh (1990), *Thatcherism and British Politics*, Oxford: Oxford University Press.

Dennis Kavanagh (1992), 'The Postwar Consensus', *Twentieth Century British History*, vol. 3, no. 2, pp. 175–90.

Dennis Kavanagh (1997), *The Reordering of British Politics*, Oxford: Oxford University Press.

Dennis Kavanagh and Peter Morris (1994), *Consensus Politics From Attlee to Major*, Oxford: Basil Blackwell .

Dennis Kavanagh and Anthony Seldon (eds) (1989), *The Thatcher Effect: A Decade of Change*, London: Macmillan.

Dennis Kavanagh and Anthony Seldon (eds) (1994), *The Major Effect*, London: Macmillan.

William Keegan (1984), *Mrs Thatcher's Economic Experiment*, Harmondsworth: Penguin.

Anthony King (1975), 'Overload: Problems of Governing in the 1970s', *Political Studies*, vol. 23, no. 2, pp. 284–96.

Anthony King (1992a), 'The Implications of One-Party Government', in Anthony King (ed.), *Britain at the Polls*, Chatham, NJ: Chatham House.

Anthony King (1992b) 'Political Change in Britain', in Dennis Kavanagh (ed.), *Electoral Politics*, Oxford: Oxford University Press.

Anthony King and Ivor Crewe (1996), *SDP: The Birth, Life and Death of the Social Democratic Party*, Oxford: Oxford University Press.

Desmond King (1987), *The New Right: Politics, Markets and Citizenship*, London: Macmillan.

Desmond King (1994), 'The New Right and Public Policy', *Political Studies*, vol. 42, pp. 486–91.

Desmond King (1995), *Actively Seeking Work: The Politics of Unemployment and Welfare Policy in the United States and Great Britain*, Chicago: Chicago University Press.

John Kingdom (1993), 'How Do Issues Get on Public Policy Agendas?', in W. J. Wilson (ed.), *Sociology and the Public Agenda*, London: Sage.

John Kingdom (1995), *Agendas, Alternatives and Public Policies*, 2nd edition, New York: HarperCollins.

Neil Kinnock (1986), *Making Our Way*, Oxford: Basil Blackwell.

Neil Kinnock (1994), 'Remaking the Labour Party', *Contemporary Record*, vol. 8, no. 3, pp. 535–54.

Otto Kirchheimer (1966), 'The Transformation of the Western European Party Systems', in Joseph LaPalombara and Myron Weimer (eds), *Political Parties and Political Development*, Princeton, NJ: Princeton University Press.

Herbert Kitschelt (1992), 'The Social Discourse and Party Strategy in West European Democracies', in C. Lemke and S. Marks (eds), *The Crisis of Socialism in Europe*, Durham: Duke University Press.

Herbert Kitschelt (1993), 'Class Structure and Social Democratic Party Strategy', *British Journal of Political Science*, vol. 23, pp. 299–337.

David Knoke, Franz Urban Pappi, Jeffrey Broadbent and Yutaka Tsuinaka (1996), *Comparing Policy Networks: Labor Politics in the US, Germany and Japan*, Cambridge: Cambridge University Press.

Maurice Kogan and David Kogan (1982), *The Battle for the Labour Party*, London: Fontana.

Joel Krieger (1986), *Reagan, Thatcher and the Politics of Decline*, Cambridge: Polity Press.

Thomas Kuhn (1970), *The Structure of Scientific Revolutions*, Chicago: Chicago University Press.

The Labour Party (1957), *Industry and Society*, London: The Labour Party.

The Labour Party (1973), *Labour's Programme for Britain*, London: The Labour Party.

The Labour Party (1976), *Labour's Programme 1976*, London: The Labour Party.

The Labour Party (1980), *Peace, Jobs, Freedom: Labour's Draft Manifesto*, London: The Labour Party.

The Labour Party (1982), *Labour's Programme 1982*, London: The Labour Party.

The Labour Party (1983) *The New Hope for Britain: The Labour Manifesto*, London: The Labour Party.

The Labour Party (1986), *Social Ownership*, London: Labour Party.

The Labour Party (1987), *Britain Will Win: The Labour Manifesto*, London: The Labour Party.

The Labour Party (1989), *Meet the Challenge, Make the Change*, London: The Labour Party.

The Labour Party (1991), *Opportunity Britain*, London: The Labour Party.

The Labour Party (1992), *Let's Get Britain Working Again: The Labour Manifesto*, London: The Labour Party.

The Labour Party (1997), *Because Britain Deserves Better: Labour's Manifesto*, London: Labour Party.

The Labour Party/TUC Liaison Committee (1981), *Economic Issues Facing the Next Labour Government*, London: The Labour Party.

The Labour Party/TUC Liaison Committee (1982), *Economic Planning and Industrial Democracy*, London: The Labour Party.

Jan-Eric Lane (1996), *The Public Sector*, London: Sage.

Jan-Eric Lane and Svante Erison (1994), *Politics and Society in Western Europe*, London: Sage.

Michael Laver (1989), 'Party Competition and Party System Change', *Journal of Theoretical Politics*, vol. 1, no. 3, pp. 301–24.

Nigel Lawson (1992), *The View From Number 11*, London: Bantam Press.

Nigel Lawson (1994), 'Cabinet Government in the Thatcher Years', *Contemporary Record*, vol. 8, no. 3, pp. 440–52.

Adam Lent (1997), 'Labour's Transformation: Searching for the Point of Origin', *Politics*, vol. 17.

Shirley Letwin (1992), *The Anatomy of Thatcherism*, London: Fontana.

Ruth Levine (ed.) (1986), *The Ideology of the New Right*, Cambridge: Polity Press.

Colin Leys (1989), *Politics in Britain*, 2nd edition, London: Verso.

Colin Leys (1990), 'Still a Question of Hegemony', *New Left Review*, 181, pp. 119–28.

Colin Leys (1996), 'The Labour Party's Transition from Socialism to Capitalism', in Leo Panitch (ed.), *The Socialist Register 1996*, London: Merlin Press.

Arend Lijphart (1984), *Democracies: Patterns of Majoritarian and Consensus Democracy in 21 Countries*, New Haven, CT: Yale University Press.

Arend Lijphart (1990) in Peter Mair (ed.), *West European Party Systems*, Oxford: Oxford University Press.

Rodney Lowe (1989), 'The Second World War: Consensus and the Foundations of the Welfare State', *Twentieth Century British History*, vol. 1, no. 2.

Andy McSmith (1996), *Faces of Labour: The Inside Story*, London: Verso.

Peter Mair (1983), 'Adaptation and Control: Toward an Understanding of Party and Party System Change', in Daalder and Mair (eds), *Western European Party Systems*, pp. 405–29.

Peter Mair (1989), 'The Problem of Party System Change', *Journal of Theoretical Politics*, vol. 1, pp. 251–76.

Peter Mair (1993), 'Myths of Electoral Change and the Survival of Traditional Parties', *European Journal of Political Research*, vol. 24, pp. 121–33.

Peter Mair and Stefano Bartolini (1992), *Identity, Competition and Electoral Availability: The Stabilisation of European Electorates, 1885–1985*, Cambridge: Cambridge University Press.

Peter Mair and Gordon Smith (1990), *Understanding Party System Change in Western Europe*, London: Frank Cass.

Peter Mandelson and Roger Liddle (1996), *The Blair Revolution*, London: Faber & Faber.

Moshe Maor (1997), *Political Parties and Party Systems*, London: Routledge.

David Marquand (1988), *The Unprincipled Society: New Demands and Old Politics*, London: Fontana.

David Marquand (1992), *The Progressive Dilemma*, London: William Heinemann.

David Marquand (1997), *The New Reckoning: Capitalism, States and Markets*, Cambridge: Polity Press.

David Marquand and Anthony Seldon (eds) (1996), *The Ideas That Shaped Post-War Britain*, London: HarperCollins.

David Marsh (1991), 'Privatisation Under Mrs Thatcher', *Public Administration*, vol. 69, pp. 459–80.

David Marsh (1992), *The New Politics of British Trade Unionism: Union Power and the Thatcher Decade*, London: Macmillan.

David Marsh (1995), 'Explaining Thatcherite Policies: Beyond Uni-Dimensional Explanations', *Political Studies*, vol. 43, no. 4, pp. 595–613.

David Marsh and R.A.W. Rhodes (1989), 'Implementing Thatcherism: A Policy Perspective', *Essex Papers in Politics and Government no. 62*, Colchester: University of Essex.

David Marsh and R.A.W. Rhodes (1990), 'Implementing Thatcherism: Policy Change in the 1980s', *Parliamentary Affairs*, vol. 45, pp. 33–51.

David Marsh and R.A.W. Rhodes (eds) (1992), *Implementing Thatcherite Policies: Audit of an Era*, Buckingham: Open University Press.

David Marsh and R.A.W. Rhodes (1995), 'Evaluating Thatcherism: Over the Moon or Sick as a Parrot?', *Politics*, vol. 15, no. 1, pp. 49–54.

David Marsh, David Dolowitz, Fiona O'Neill and David Richards (1996), 'Thatcherism and the Three R's: Radicalism, Realism and Rhetoric in the Third Term of the Thatcherite Government', *Parliamentary Affairs*, vol. 49, no. 3, pp. 455–70.

Keith Middlemas (1979), *Politics in Industrial Society*, London: Andre Deutsch.

Keith Middlemas (1986), *Power, Competition and the State, Volume I: Britain in Search of Balance, 1940–61*, London: Macmillan.

Keith Middlemas (1990), *Power, Competition and the State, Volume II: Threats to the Post War Settlement, 1961–74*, London: Macmillan.

Keith Middlemas (1991), *Power, Competition and the State, Volume III: The End of the Post War Era*, London: Macmillan.

Ralph Miliband (1974), *Parliamentary Socialism*, London: Merlin Press.

Ralph Miliband (1982), *Capitalist Democracy in Britain*, Oxford: Oxford University Press.

David Miller (1989), *Market, State and Community; Theoretical Foundations of Market Socialism*, Oxford: Oxford University Press.

Lewis Minkin (1991), *The Contentious Alliance: Trade Unions and the Labour Party*, Edinburgh: Edinburgh University Press.

Dick Morris (1997), *Behind the Oval Office*, New York: Random House.

Pippa Norris (1990), 'Thatcher's Enterprise Society and Electoral Change', *West European Politics*, vol. 13, no. 1, pp. 63–78.

Pippa Norris and Ivor Crewe (1991), 'In Defence of British Election Studies', in David Denver *et al.* (eds), *British Elections and Parties Yearbook 1991*, London: Frank Cass.

Philip Norton (1990), ' "The Lady's Not For Turning". But What About the Rest? Margaret Thatcher and the Conservative Party', *Parliamentary Affairs*, vol. 43, no. 1, pp. 41–58.

David Owen (1984), *A Future That Will Work*, Harmondsworth: Penguin.

Stephen Padgett and William E. Paterson (1991), *A History of Social Democracy in Europe*, London: Longman.

Angelo Panebianco (1988), *Political Parties: Organisation and Power*, Cambridge: Cambridge University Press.

Leo Panitch (1976), *Social Democracy and Industrial Militancy*, Cambridge: Cambridge University Press.

Leo Panitch and Colin Leys (1997), *The End of Parliamentary Socialism: From New Left to New Labour*, London: Verso.

Ben Pimlott (1988), 'The Myth of Consensus', in Ben Pimlott, *Frustrate Their Knavish Tricks*, London: HarperCollins.

Adam Przeworski (1985), *Capitalism and Social Democracy*, Cambridge: Cambridge University Press.

G. Rabinowitz and S.E. MacDonald (1989), 'A Directional Theory of Issue Voting', *American Political Science Review*, vol. 33, no. 1, pp. 93–121.

John Ranelagh (1992), *Thatcher's People*, London: Fontana.

Peter Riddell (1983), *The Thatcher Government*, Oxford: Martin Robertson.

Peter Riddell (1989), *The Thatcher Decade*, Oxford: Basil Blackwell.

Peter Riddell (1991), *The Thatcher Era and its Legacy*, Oxford: Basil Blackwell.

Nicholas Ridley (1991), *My Style of Government*, London: Hutchinson.

Neil Rollings (1994), 'Poor Mr Butskell: A Short Life, Wrecked by Schizophrenia', *Twentieth Century British History*, vol. 5, no. 2, pp. 183–205.

Richard Rose (1984), *Can Parties Make a Difference?*, London: Macmillan.

Richard Rose (1990), 'Inheritance Before Choice in Public Policy', *Journal of Theoretical Politics*, vol. 2, no. 1, pp. 263–91.

Richard Rose and B. Guy Peters (1978), *Can Government Go Bankrupt?*, London: Macmillan.

Richard Rose and Ian McAllister (1986), *Voters Begin to Choose*, London: Sage.

Richard Rose and Ian McAllister (1990) *The Loyalty of Voters*, London: Sage.

Richard Rose and Philip Davies (1995), *Inheritance in Public Policy*, New Haven: Yale University Press.

David Sanders (1993), 'Why the Conservatives Won – Again', in Anthony King (ed.), *Britain at the Polls 1992*, Chatham, NJ: Chatham House.

Giovanni Sartori (1969), 'From the Sociology of Politics to Political Sociology', in Seymour Martin Lipset (ed.), *Politics and the Social Sciences*, Oxford: Oxford University Press.

Giovanni Sartori (1976), *Parties and Party Systems*, Cambridge: Cambridge University Press.

Giovanni Sartori (1990), 'The Sociology of Parties', in Peter Mair (ed.), *The West European Party System*, Oxford: Oxford University Press.

Peter Saunders and (Affairs (1994), *Privatisation and Popular Capitalism* Buckingham: Open University Press.

Bill Schwartz (1991), 'The Tide of History: The Reconstruction of Conservatism, 1945–51', in Nick Tiratsoo (ed.), *The Attlee Years*, London: Pinter Press.

Anthony Seldon (1993) 'What Was the Post War Consensus?', in Bill Jones *et al.* (eds), *Politics UK*, Hemel Hempstead: Harvester Wheatsheaf.

Anthony Seldon (1994), 'Consensus: A Debate too Long', *Parliamentary Affairs*, vol. 47, no. 4, pp. 501–14.

Anthony Seldon (1996), 'Ideas are not Enough', in David Marquand and Anthony Seldon (eds), *The Ideas That Shaped Post-War Britain*, London: Harper-Collins.

Patrick Seyd (1987), *The Rise and Fall of the Labour Left*, London: Macmillan.

Patrick Seyd (1993), 'Labour: The Great Transformation', in Anthony King (ed.), *Britain at the Polls 1992*, Chatham, NJ: Chatham House.

Patrick Seyd and Paul Whiteley (1992), *Labour's Grassroots: The Politics of Party Membership*, Oxford: Clarendon Press.

Eric Shaw (1993), 'Toward Renewal: The British Labour Party's Policy Review', in Richard Gillespie and William Paterson (eds), *Rethinking Social Democracy in Europe*, London: Frank Cass.

Eric Shaw (1994), *The Labour Party Since 1979: Crisis and Transformation*, London: Routledge.

Eric Shaw (1996), *The Labour Party Since 1945*, Oxford: Basil Blackwell.

Malcolm Smith (1993), 'The Changing Nature of the British State, 1929–1959: The Historiography of Consensus', in Brian Brivati and Harriet Jones (eds), *What Difference Did the War Make?*, Leicester: Leicester University Press.

Martin J. Smith (1992), 'A Return to Revisionism', in Martin Smith and Joanna Spear (eds), *The Changing Labour Party*, London: Routledge.

Martin J. Smith (1994), 'Understanding the Politics of Catch-Up: The Modernisation of the Labour Party', *Political Studies*, vol. 42, no. 4, pp. 700–7.

Martin J. Smith and Michael Kenny (1996), 'Reforming Clause IV: Tony Blair and the Modernisation of the Labour Party', Paper presented to the Political Studies Association Conference, University of Glasgow.

Martin J. Smith and Michael Kenny (1997), 'Misunderstanding Blair', *Political Quarterly*, vol. 68, no. 3, pp. 220–30.

Martin J. Smith and Joanna Spear (eds) (1992), *The Changing Labour Party*, London: Routledge.

Kaare Strom (1989), 'Interparty Competition in Advanced Democracies', *Journal of Theoretical Politics*, vol. 1, pp. 277–300.

Kaare Strom (1990), 'A Behavioural Theory of Competitive Political Parties', *American Journal of Political Science*, vol. 34, no. 2, pp. 565–98.

Gerald Taylor (1997), *Toward Renewal: The Policy Review and Beyond*, Basingstoke: Macmillan.

Peter Taylor (1992), 'Changing Political Relations', in Peter Cloake (ed.), *Policy and Change in Thatcher's Britain*, Oxford: Pergamon Press, p. 33.

Margaret Thatcher (1989), *The Revival of Britain: Speeches, 1975–1988*, London: Aurum Press.

Margaret Thatcher (1993), *The Downing Street Years*, London: HarperCollins.

Noel Thompson (1996a), 'Supply Side Socialism: The Political Economy of New Labour', *New Left Review*, 216, pp. 37–54.

Noel Thompson (1996b), *Political Economy and the Labour Party*, London: UCL Press.

Alan Ware (1996), *Political Parties and Party Systems*, Oxford: Oxford University Press.

Charles Webster (1990), 'Conflict and Consensus: Explaining the British Health Service', *Twentieth Century British History*, vol. 1, no. 2.

Paul Whiteley (1983), *The Labour Party in Crisis*, London: Methuen.

Paul Whiteley, Patrick Seyd and Jeremy Richardson (1994), *True Blues: The Politics of Conservative Party Membership*, Oxford: Clarendon Press.

Mark Wickham-Jones (1995), 'Recasting Social Democracy', *Political Studies*, vol. 43, no. 5, pp. 698– 702.

Mark Wickham-Jones (1997a), *Economic Strategy and the Labour Party: Politics and Policy Making, 1970–1983*, Basingstoke: Macmillan.

Mark Wickham-Jones (1997b), 'Anticipating Social Democracy, Preempting Anticipations: Economic Policy Making in the British Labour Party, 1987–1992', *Politics and Society*, vol. 23, no. 4, pp. 465–94.

Joel Wolfe (1991), 'State Power and Ideology in Britain: Mrs Thatcher's Privatisation Programme', *Political Studies*, vol. 34, pp. 237–52.

Joel Wolfe (1996), *Power and Privatisation*, London: Macmillan.

Steven Wolinetz (1979), 'The Transformation of Western European Party Systems Revisited', *West European Politics*, vol. 2, no. 1, pp. 4–28.

Stephen Wolinetz (ed.) (1988), *Parties and Party Systems in Liberal Democracies*, London: Routledge.

Hugo Young (1991), *One of Us*, London: Pan Books.

Hugo Young and Anne Sloman (1986), *The Thatcher Phenomenon*, London: BBC Books.

Stephen Young (1986), 'The Nature of Privatisation in Britain, 1979–1985', *West European Politics*, vol. 9, pp. 235–52.

Index

Note: page numbers in **bold** type refer to illustrative figures or tables.

219

222   *Index*

  as constraint on reform agenda   14
  impact on office-seeking
    capacity   89–90
  see also politics
electricity, privatisation of   32
Elliott, Gregory   183
employment, full
  in 1950s   140
  abandoned to fight inflation   6
  called into question   xii
  lack of commitment to   20
  see also unemployment
Employment Act (1980)   34
'enterprise society'   20
entrepreneurial spirit, wealth created
  by   55
Erison, Svante   194
ERM *see* Exchange Rate Mechanism
Esping-Anderson, Costa   24, 182
Europe
  leadership of, in New Labour agenda
    23
  similarity of economic problems in
    48
  Thatcher government errors of
    judgement in   39
European Economic Community
  (EEC), Labour commitment to
    withdraw from   77
Evans, Geoff   206
Exchange Rate Mechanism (ERM),
  divisions over   41
exchange rate policy   41

Falklands War   49
Fatchett, Derek   74
Feasey, Richard   185
Fielding, Stephen   190
Financial Times, The   75, 192
Finer, S.E.   145
Finklestein, Danny   133–4
fiscal constraints on reform agenda   14
fiscal policy, influence of Thatcherite
  3
fiscal prudence as priority of Labour in
  government   viii, 24
fiscal stability as priority of Labour in
  government   21, 65

Fisher, Mark   74
Flanagan, Scott C.   194
Foot, Michael   26, 66, 68, 70, 75, 76,
  95, 160, 162, 192, 197
foreign affairs
  continuity in   155
  maintaining social-democratic
    stance post-1979   6
Franklin, Mark   91, 194
freedom
  enhanced by privatisation   62–3
  restricted by collectivism and state
    provision   1
free market capitalism
  determining New Labour
    strategy   128
  as objective of Thatcherism   29
  providing redistribution and
    efficiency   131
  victory of   20
free trade, rise of, in nineteenth
  century   13
Friedman, Milton, historical
  classification of   4

Gaitskell, Hugh   22, 134–5, 136, 137,
  140, 155, 159, 162–4, 171, 183, 205
Gamble, Andrew   25, 29, 41, 57, 128,
  175, 179, 182, 183, 186, 188, 190,
  192, 197, 199, 206, 207
'gang of three', defection of   68–9
Garrett, Geoffrey   180
gas
  compromise over sale (1985–6)   41
  privatisation of   32, 165
General Theory (Keynes)   11
Gillespie, Richard   192
Gilmour, Ian   4
Gladstone, William   183
globalised economy
  as constraint on reform agenda   14
  perceived decline of UK within   63
Goff, Patricia   195
'good society', competing definitions
  of   27, 173
Gould, Bryan   82, 129
governance, ineffective, Thatcherism
  addressing crisis of   3